RIGHT HERE, RIGHT NOW

EXPLORING LIFE-SPACE INTERVENTIONS
FOR CHILDREN AND YOUTH

KIARAS GHARABAGHI
Ryerson University

CAROL STUART
Vancouver Island University

Toronto

Vice-President, Editorial Director: Gary Bennett
Editor-in-Chief: Michelle Sartor
Editor, Humanities and Social Sciences: Joel Gladstone
Marketing Manager: Lisa Gillis
Supervising Developmental Editor: Madhu Ranadive
Project Manager: Lesley Deugo
Manufacturing Coordinator: Susan Johnson
Production Editor: Misbah
(MPS Limited, a Macmillan Company)

Copy Editor: Linda Jenkins
Proofreader: Lisa LaFramboise
Compositor: MPS Limited, a Macmillan Company
Art Director: Julia Hall
Cover Designer: Miguel Acevedo
Cover Image: Laine Robertson

Credits and acknowledgments borrowed from other sources and reproduced, with permission, in this textbook appear on the appropriate page within text.

Statistics Canada information is used with the permission of Statistics Canada. Users are forbidden to copy the data and redisseminate them, in an original or modified form, for commercial purposes, without permission from Statistics Canada. Information on the availability of the wide range of data from Statistics Canada can be obtained from Statistics Canada's Regional Offices, its World Wide Web site at **www.statcan.gc.ca**, and its toll-free access number 1-800-263-1136.

If you purchased this book outside the United States or Canada, you should be aware that it has been imported without the approval of the publisher or the author.

Library and Archives Canada Cataloguing in Publication
Gharabaghi, Kiaras, 1967–
   Right Here, Right Now: Exploring Life-Space Interventions for Children and Youth / Kiaras Gharabaghi, Carol Stuart.
Includes index.
ISBN 978-0-13-215512-0

   1. Social work with children. 2. Social work with youth.
3. Family social work. I. Stuart, Carol, 1957– II. Title.

HV713.G43 2011   362.7   C2011-903391-7

ISBN 978-0-13-215512-0

Contents

Chapter 3   Caring: The Foundation of Life-Space   53

Chapter 4   Engagement Strategies for Life-Space Interventions   75

Preface

In the winter of 2009, a 15-year-old boy in central Ontario left his family home in pro-test because his parents had imposed on him restrictions related to playing video games. Parent–teen conflicts of this nature take place in many family households across North America and beyond. Most of the time, parents and teens find themselves stuck in a power struggle, but with time and lots of venting, some yelling, and typically a calming down phase, everything returns to normal and the power struggle is resolved. Certainly this was the expectation when the 15-year-old boy left his home on that fateful winter afternoon.

But things worked out differently. The boy did not return home by nightfall, and the concerned parents called police. Inquiries with neighbours and family acquaintances yielded no results, and even calls to the boy's friends provided no answers to his where-abouts. Hours of anxiety turned into days, and the local community conducted searches of the forests and the fields in the area, but to no avail. After two weeks, the mystery was solved, albeit in a tragic manner. Hunters found the body of the boy at the foot of a tree in the forest. It was later learned that he had climbed a tree to spend the night, somehow fell down and was rendered immobile. In time, he froze to death.

The boy in this story was not an exceptional teenager. He attended school, he lived in a nice home with both his parents, he had friends, and he was not known to suffer from any particular mental health concerns or disabilities. He did, however, really enjoy playing video games. In fact, he increasingly neglected his other involvements and activities, and focused solely on the virtual world in which he had found his place. His parents had tried many ways of limiting his involvement in gaming, and on the fateful afternoon they did what most parents surely would have done: They demanded that he relinquish his gaming unit altogether.

This is a story about life-space. Most stories about life-space don't end so tragically, but many have the potential to end this way, and far more than we publicly acknowledge actually do end this way. This is why we decided to write a book about life-space inter-vention. To fully appreciate the nature of life-space, you'll need to read the whole book. But just to set the scene a bit, this is what we mean when we use the term *life-space*: It is the complex entanglement of physical, mental, virtual and relational spaces where our lives unfold.

When we think about the boy who left his home after having his video game console confiscated, we can hypothesize about the significance of this experience from the per-spective of the boy. The virtual world of gaming *was* where his life unfolded every day, perhaps more intensely and in a more real way than in his experience of the physical world. Home, school, the mall, the peer group and other spaces in his life had become less important than the virtual world of gaming. Confiscating the console, well-intended as it was, turned out to be a much bigger consequence than his parents anticipated. From the perspective of the boy, his access to where he felt his life unfolded had been removed. Rendering himself homeless by running away was secondary to the real disaster of that day – an imposition on his life-space that destroyed his sense of Self and belonging.

Life-space has been a theme in child and youth care practice, and indeed in other human service disciplines, for decades. We recognize that the term *life-space* has undergone various historical, cultural and disciplinary transformations. For example, it was used by the Nazis during the 1930s and early 1940s to rationalize aggression against other countries in order to expand the life-space (*Lebensraum*) of Germans. The writings of Kurt Lewin (1948) characterized the life-space as a complex socio-cultural environment composed of activity, physical space, goals, social interaction, and multi-group membership, as well as boundaries and limits created by Self, Other, and cultural expectations and norms. During the late 1950s, Redl and his colleagues talked about the life-space interview, which reflected their emphasis on institutional treatment intervention, where the institution served as the temporary life-space (place of residence) for troubled young people. From the late 1970s onward, *life-space* has become closely associated with Bronfenbrenner's ecological perspective, in which multiple levels of systems affect and interact with the individual young person. Additionally, the concept of life-space crisis intervention (Long, Wood, & Fecser, 2001) emerged from Redl's work and has been developed to mean a counselling intervention in the milieu in response to aggressive or other anti-social behaviours that helps young people understand and proactively change their responses to adult demands.

We wrote this book because we believe that the idea of life-space remains an important one in child and youth care practice, and indeed in any scenario in which we engage with young people on a day-to-day basis. However, we also believe that it is time to update the concept in order to reflect the changes in social conventions, in technology, and in the evolving cultural diversity across many jurisdictions in North America and in Europe. As a result, we draw on the work of child and youth care scholars who have advanced our understanding of relationship, engagement, therapeutic activities, boundaries, and the Self, and we integrate what we have learned over the years into a framework for life-space intervention. Within our framework, we emphasize four dimensions of life-space: The physical, the virtual, the mental and the relational, and we argue that life-space intervention is fundamentally about promoting the process of learning for young people. In other words, there is something profoundly pedagogic about life-space intervention, and much of the book is really about exploring the pedagogic character of being with young people where their lives unfold.

We have written this book in such a way that it can be read at different levels of complexity. On the one hand, we want the ideas presented to be accessible and meaningful to those just starting out in the field of child and youth care practice, who are perhaps currently involved in post-secondary training and education in the field. On the other hand, we also want to make a contribution to scholarship and advanced critical reflection on the field and its core assumptions. We think that a graduate student, an established scholar, or an experienced practitioner will be challenged by the ideas and arguments as well, given that person's ability to read the text in its nuances and to extrapolate the implications of what we are suggesting.

The book is structured along two design elements, one very traditional and the other perhaps more creative and forward-looking. The traditional design element is the sequence from theory to practice and a return to theory. Newcomers to the field might find the first two chapters a little boring and abstract, but more experienced individuals will have much to ponder with respect to our approach to framing life-space intervention in the structure-agency dilemma (see Chapter 2). Chapters 3 through 6, however, ought to be highly engaging for those wondering how to bring life-space intervention to life in the field and its many different service settings. These chapters also ought to provide much to reflect on and critically evaluate for experienced readers who can contemplate their own stories and experiences in the field. Chapter 7 ties the theoretical and practical elements of the book into a unified argument centred on the idea of learning. In that final chapter, we use the language of social pedagogy, which will be new to North American readers and most readers from the U.K., Australia and New Zealand, but very familiar to those in Europe. We think that much can be learned from the disciplinary integration of social pedagogy and child and youth care practice.

Discussion questions and exercises are provided at the end of Chapters 1 through 6. These exercises are built around the concept of learning style and pedagogy, and they use a variation of the experiential learning cycle. Readers can choose a form of reflection that resonates with their own learning style, or they can complete all four exercises to challenge themselves to learn through the full experience of the learning cycle. Reflection *in* practice exercises ask the reader to do something and focus in the moment on their awareness of the action or the mental processes that are unfolding. These are the action/experience moments of learning, and instructors may find them useful for concrete illustrations of the concepts. Reflection *on* practice exercises help the reader review and explore an event that has happened in light of the new concepts presented in the chapter. Sometimes new practitioners lack experience to do this, and the stories in the chapter can be used as part of this reflection. Reflection *for* practice sections ask the reader to consider how to apply the concepts to practice scenarios, and are intended to prepare readers for their own practice. Theory in action questions reinforce the theoretical and conceptual ideas by asking readers to look for theory explicitly in practice. We believe that using the exercises and designing new ones in the same structure will help readers fully understand how theory and practice relate and how we can use one to understand the other.

The more creative and forward-looking design element of the book is the integration of stories into each of the chapters. For the newcomer to the field, these stories serve as examples of how the ideas and concepts discussed in the chapters might come to life in a practice setting. They also provide a model for thinking about and preparing for life-space intervention as new practitioners embark on a career in child and youth care practice. The more experienced reader will quickly recognize these stories as being much more than examples of the conceptual and more abstract work in the book. Indeed, these stories, individually and even more so collectively, are themselves a life-space that we have created to demonstrate the entanglements of the dimensions of life-space. The stories have characters and settings, plots and tension, culture and identity, drama and humour. In Chapter 7, these stories come together into one shared experience for all of the characters. In fact, in Chapter 7 the story takes precedence over the theory and the practice, and therefore we have designed the text of that chapter to be the story while the theoretical elements of the final chapter are boxed in the same way that the stories were in the previous chapters.

We must acknowledge some limitations in how we have designed this book, specifically the stories. The characters we created are all quite different individuals facing different circumstances. Both the practitioners and the youth represent different cultures and identities, and they bring these differences to their everyday engagement with others. We did, however, maintain some degree of uniformity among the stories. All of the youth featured in the stories are teenagers, and none are facing notable developmental challenges or physical disabilities. Life-space intervention is not limited to a particular profile of young people, and we do not want to suggest that child and youth care practice with pre-teens or young people facing developmental challenges or managing physical disability should be informed by something other than life-space intervention. We believe that the concepts and ideas presented in this book have relevance to any young person we might encounter in child and youth care practice. However, we also believe that our approach to practice must always be personalized to be congruent with the circumstances of the young person, the setting, the employment context, and so on. In fact, we realize that child and youth care practice extends beyond the young person to include family and community. Although this has not been the focus of this book, perhaps our next book could apply the ideas we present in this book to those contexts as well.

Finally, we want to acknowledge that the ideas of this book and our capacity to articulate them have been furthered by other people. We have both benefited from support and encouragement, as well as critiques and expressions of bewilderment, from colleagues, friends and family. In thanking those that have influenced and assisted us in proceeding, we want to first (in the spirit of the physical dimension of life-space) give credit to place. The idea of this book was conceived in the natural beauty of Muskoka, hiking on the billion-year-old Canadian Shield and overlooking the glacial remnants now known as Lake Muskoka. The idea of social pedagogy entered our thinking in a more active and influential way after spending two weeks together driving a BMW on the German autobahn, visiting residential institutions in southern Germany and attending a wonderful conference in beautiful Groningen in the Netherlands.

The novelty of life-space and its multiple dimensions is that some parts are shared in the physical dimension, and yet we bring to it the uniqueness of our own relational dimension of life-space. Within this uniqueness, we want to thank the following:

Kiaras Gharabaghi: I want to thank those who have for many years influenced my thinking and challenged my core assumptions, including friends and colleagues such as Thom Garfat, Bill Carty, Pat Gaughan, Mark Krueger, Gerry Fewster and Jack Phelan. A number of South African friends and colleagues re-ignited my passion for the life-space, especially Jacqui Michael, Merle Allsopp, Zeni Thumbadoo and Brian Gannon. And nothing much happens in my life-space without the love and support of my family: Patricia, Alex, Jett and Siena. In this collaborative project of co-authoring a book, I have learned this lesson: Find yourself a brilliant, creative, wonderful and amazing co-author, and all will be well. That's what I did.

Carol Stuart: Kiaras and I began this work when we were both at Ryerson University and have finished it from opposite sides of the country when the physical dimensions of my life-space changed radically. We have been able to manage this change because of the way we think about our life-space(s) and the dimensions available to us, and like the influence of Muskoka and the German autobahn, driving across North America and living on Vancouver Island continues to shape how I think about life-space. I want to acknowledge that while I share and acknowledge many of the same colleagues mentioned by Kiaras, and they have influenced my thinking over time, I must also thank others, such as Frances Ricks, Melanie Panitch and Jennifer Martin, who have pushed me to think in different ways about the virtual and relational dimensions of life-space, and about the boundaries of what we do physically and in relationship to our lives and involvement with others. I must also thank my family, Iain, Kirstin, Megan and Shirol, who patiently listened while I talked about the work of writing or the ideas of the life-space dimensions and who have continued to adapt to and manage the changes in all our lives. In addition, Laine, Kyle and Talia enthusiastically contributed art work to the project, illustrating the stories that were inspired by the experiences of other young people encountered over the years.

We feel it is important to highlight the work and contributions of the artists, Laine, Kyle and Talia, not only as a way of saying thank you to them, but also as a point of principle when thinking and writing about young people. Much has been said and written in recent years about youth engagement and providing opportunities for young people to have a voice. We invited these three young people to provide the drawings and photographs for much of the book in order to ensure that our representation of young people in their life-space was juxtaposed to theirs. We used different media for our respective representations. As authors, we focused on prose. As illustrators and artists, Laine, Kyle and Talia translated our words into visuals.

We want to acknowledge here also the support of Joel Gladstone from Pearson Canada for agreeing from the outset that the involvement of young people in this capacity was not only fine, but warranted an investment on the part of the publisher. Finally, we are grateful to Madhu Ranadive for managing all aspects of this project, and for remaining patient with our various attempts to navigate through the process.

Thank you also to the professors who provided feedback on this manuscript at various stages of development: Dr. Sibylle Artz, University of Victoria; Rick Kelly, George Brown College; Karen Marr, St. Clair College; Richard Teskey, Lambton College; Donna Jamieson, Grant MacEwan University; Donna Serafini, Algonquin College Community Studies; and Karen Marr, St. Clair College.

We hope that in reading the ideas that are presented, in contemplating how the ideas are illustrated in the stories that weave through the book, and in further contemplating the meaning of the art that accompanies each chapter, readers will develop their understanding of life-space beyond what we have been able to articulate, and will therefore further advance the concepts and the interventions that are described here for the benefit of all young people that you encounter in your own life-space.

Kiaras Gharabaghi & Carol Stuart
January 2012

Artist Biographies

Cover

The cover image was created by Laine Robertson. The photo captures the dynamic, risky, beautiful and sometimes lonely nature of youth.

Talia Jackson-King

Talia Jackson-King lives in Canada, where winter is cold and dreary. She is a high school student with interests in things like art. She is pretty sure she wants to be an artist. Her current goal in life is to do something interesting. Talia's paintings are mostly abstract, representing the thoughts and emotions that swirl throughout life but are not present in the concrete world.

Laine Robertson

Hey, my name's Laine, I'm 17 years old, I live in Newmarket, Ontario, and I'm finishing Grade 12. I first found interest in photography when I first started high school, around Grade 10. During high school I've acquired a Nikon D300S, along with multiple film cameras and expired film. Experimenting a lot with expired film sparked a growing amusement in the art of surrealism. When I started to get into the history of photography, I found artists like Gregory Scott and Jerry Uelsmann. Gregory's photos push for the unbelievable, incorporating paintings into photographs or playing with the differing notions of dimensionality and illusion. Jerry Uelsmann combines the realism of photography and the fluidity of our dreams by keeping the photography fairly simple, but creating an image only you could imagine. Overall, I'm trying to explore photography that goes beyond communication as we know it. So much of what we know involves being able to state something in words. There's another level in which we understand things in a visual way, that we can't really respond to. I'm taking the simplicity of an object and putting it together with the unrealism of a strange concept. I'm exploring more than the meaning of the object; I'm considering how I could change the viewer's perspective to see something that not only I am seeing.

Kyle Stewart

I was born and raised in Keswick, Ontario, Canada. Art has always been a major part of my life, from the written word, to the musical arts, to photography and, most importantly, the visual arts. I hope to one day become a high school art teacher, and have the time to do the arts I love, day in and day out. The stories in this book inspired me to create images of the people that I saw in them.

Supplements

CourseSmart for Instructors (978-0-13-707444-0)

CourseSmart goes beyond traditional expectations, providing instant, online access to the textbooks and course materials you need at a lower cost for students. And even as students save money, you can save time and hassle with a digital eTextbook that allows you to search for the most relevant content at the very moment you need it. Whether it's evaluating textbooks or creating lecture notes to help students with difficult concepts, CourseSmart can make life a little easier. See how when you visit www.coursesmart.com/instructors.

CourseSmart for Students (978-0-13-707444-0)

CourseSmart goes beyond traditional expectations, providing instant, online access to the textbooks and course materials you need at an average savings of 60 percent. With instant access from any computer and the ability to search your text, you'll find the content you need quickly, no matter where you are. And with online tools like highlighting and note-taking, you can save time and study efficiently. See all the benefits at www.coursesmart.com/students.

Technology Specialists

Pearson's Technology Specialists work with faculty and campus course designers to ensure that Pearson technology products, assessment tools, and online course materials are tailored to meet your specific needs. This highly qualified team is dedicated to helping schools take full advantage of a wide range of educational resources by assisting in the integration of a variety of instructional materials and media formats. Your local Pearson Education sales representative can provide you with more details on this service program.

MySearchLab

MySearchLab offers extensive help to students with their writing and research project and provides round-the-clock access to credible and reliable source material.

Research

Content on MySearchLab includes immediate access to thousands of full-text articles from leading Canadian and international academic journals, and daily news feeds from The Associated Press. Articles contain the full downloadable text—including abstract and citation information—and can be cut, pasted, emailed, or saved for later use.

Writing

MySearchLab also includes a step-by-step tutorial on writing a research paper. Included are sections on planning a research assignment, finding a topic, creating effective notes, and finding source material. Our exclusive online handbook provides grammar and usage support. Pearson SourceCheck™ offers an easy way to detect accidental plagiarism issues, and our exclusive tutorials teach how to avoid them in the future. And MySearchLab also contains AutoCite, which helps to correctly cite sources using MLA, APA, CMS, and CBE documentation styles for both endnotes and bibliographies.

To order this book with MySearchLab access at no extra charge, use ISBN 978-0-13-28640-2.

Take a tour at **www.mysearchlab.com**.

Pearson Custom Library

For enrolments of at least 25 students, you can create your own textbook by choosing the chapters that best suit your own course needs. To begin building your custom text, visit www.pearsoncustomlibrary.com. You may also work with a dedicated Pearson Custom editor to create your ideal text – publishing your own original content or mixing and matching Pearson content. Contact your local Pearson Representative to get started.

CHAPTER 1

What Is Life-Space?

Andre

Source: Kyle Stewart

Child and youth care practitioners have long recognized that **intervention** in the life-space is a foundational method of working with children, youth and families. Practitioners from many disciplines are increasingly recognizing that the success of therapeutic interventions is enhanced when intervention is undertaken in environments that are most similar to the daily lives of "clients." In this book, we will explore the fundamentals of life-space intervention in today's global context.

In this chapter, we will articulate what we mean by life-space theoretically and experientially. We will start by exploring the idea of living space, in contrast to life-space, and we will consider how physical location, social context, and social conventions create expectations about the nature of living spaces and the relationships that we have in them. We will then introduce readers to new ways of thinking about the concept of life-space, suggest that people live in a single life-space, and argue that intervention is about how children, youth and families manage and engage with their construction of that life-space.

Where Do You Live?

This is a simple question that most people have asked and answered many times. Whether we are asking the question or responding to it, there is likely some consensus that the question is related to a place, a physical location. Typical responses might include broad indicators of place, such as "in Canada" or "in the United States." Or they might be more specific indicators of place, such as a particular neighbourhood or community in the city, "Campbell's Corners" in the country, a street address, or a description of a building. As simple as the question appears, it nevertheless takes on different meanings based on social context and the intention of the person asking. A school principal might ask a student this question as a way of determining not a physical location, but rather the type of home environment. The conventional response might include "I live at home," or perhaps "I live in a group home" or "at the shelter." The same question could probe more deeply to ascertain the social context of someone's living environment. Responses might include "I live with my mom and dad," "I live with foster parents," or "I live on my own."

Living Space

The question "Where do you live?" provides the foundation for the concept of "living spaces." While the spaces themselves might be articulated as social contexts rather than physical places (as in "I live with my parents"), living spaces are physically premised inasmuch as they describe the physical proximity of the person to his or her primary indicators of everyday living. All of the examples of possible responses above have in common the description of place. In some cases the description is limited to the location of a specific place, while in other cases it includes a description of the place itself (house, apartment building, gated community), who else lives there (parents, siblings, peers) or what the social context is (group home, shelter, public housing unit).

Living spaces are subject to social conventions. These conventions appear reasonable and meaningful, but they can sometimes mislead us about the life experiences of another person, and they are often culturally determined and associated with family relationships. One such social convention is that when we inquire about where someone lives, we typically expect the response to reflect something quantifiable – you live where you spend most of your time. This is why we sometimes lightheartedly refer to someone who works many hours as living in his or her office or living at work. You "own" where you live, having paid a price for that ownership. Young people may be characterized as living on the street when they don't live at home and yet don't pay rent anywhere else. We also typically expect the response to have a residential component – you live where you sleep most of the time, and yet youth who sleep in a shelter are considered homeless.

Story: The Places Where Life Unfolds

Andre lives with his dad and his older brother. At 15 he is busy with karate, attending school, and hanging out with his friends. He lives in a house that was built in the late 1940s, after the war. His father's work takes him away for several days at a time. Andre doesn't know his mother or where she lives; it's just always been that way. The house is a small, drafty, square box still decorated in the orange and brown colour scheme of the 1970 renovation, completed just before Andre's grandfather bought the house. His high school is across town, because Acadian New Brunswick only has one high school. He doesn't have much use for academic subjects and is repeating Grade 10 English and taking the Applied Math. Andre has ridden the school bus for years, but recently his friend, who's a year older, got his final driver's licence, so now Andre catches a ride nearly every day. He dreams about getting his own licence and his own car. Karate gives Andre a physical outlet, and he hangs out with a collection of young people around his age. So far he's dated one of the girls and he really hopes to date another. He admires the sensei, who runs his own business, and Andre hopes to do something similar one day. He has a really good memory for the *kata* that they practise, and he fights well. He's doing well in competition.

The physical spaces where Andre lives his life, including school, the dojo, his friend's car, and his father's house, are quite different from the space where life unfolds for him. Subtle creases and not so subtle tears in the carefully constructed landscape of his day-to-day interactions are revealed when Andre goes to the youth centre on Friday nights. He's been going since he was 12. At first it was practical – his father needed some down-time or had a date, and he would drop Andre and his brother off at "the Youth." Andre first met the sensei during a demonstration at the centre, and was so fascinated that he decided to join. Denis, the youth worker, always checks in with him. "How are you?" A few minutes after the ordinary answer, "I'm fine," is done, Denis asks again. Andre has discovered over the years that he's not "fine." Maybe someone at school has pissed him off, or he's confused about careers, or he misses his mom and is angry at her for vanishing. It's not every Friday that life unfolds for him in this way, but Denis has a good understanding of the spaces and places in Andre's life. Without needing to offer a lot of detail, Andre can explore those spaces and feel accepted, cared about, and engaged in understanding them a little differently.

We also draw on additional social conventions, such as associating living spaces with family or other important social relationships, so that where you "live" is your "home," though not necessarily where you spend the most time. We might encounter someone who travels a great deal and spends the majority of nights in hotels. We would expect an articulation of the living space to be based on where that person's family lives, or perhaps where his or her furniture is placed. A young prostitute may also spend the majority of nights sleeping in hotels and the majority of days on the road, but we would not apply the same social conventions to our expectations of his or her "living space." We can easily recognize the limitations of the concept of living space when it is mediated by social conventions and cultural assumptions. Expanding the concept to a more global perspective, refugees, war orphans, child soldiers, and those who have nomadic lifestyles – culturally or by choice – do not fit these conventions and assumptions.

Fundamentally, we associate where we live with something different from where we work, where we play, or where we hang out. The place where we live has primacy over other spaces. While the specific context of any given individual may vary, all people are assumed to have one space that is primary and considered to be their living space. Yet the person asking the question "Where do you live?" may have a very different set of social conventions to the person receiving the question. The social construction of living space leads us to the concept of life-space.

Life-Space

In contrast to living spaces, the concept of **life-space** is not meant to correspond to the social conventions associated with concepts such as family or home, where we may have "ownership" of a physical place. If we want to know about someone's life-space, we do not ask, "Where do you live?" Instead, we might ask, "Where do you live your life?" or "Where does your life unfold?" While *where* still prioritizes place as the primary focus for a response, by asking where life unfolds, we expand the nature of possible places. Such places could include a physical location, but may be static or transient; they could be real space or virtual space; and they could be real or imagined. Asking about the act of living life as opposed to the location of living expands the conversation from information gathering to **relational** engagement. We might expect the response to include an articulation (at whatever level of depth) of the person's experiences, day-to-day interpretation of those experiences, and relationships to a multitude of places, spaces, and social identities. In short, we begin to understand their social and psychological construction of life. When we ask where life unfolds, we begin the process of being present with another person where they are, right here, right now.

The Changing Landscape of Life-Space: Rethinking Structure and Agency

Life-space intervention, as a fundamental concept in child and youth care practice, was founded on the creation and manipulation of a therapeutic milieu. This milieu included planned physical environments, routine daily activities, and practitioners who were physically present in the lives of young people and supported therapeutic change in their living spaces. This approach to life-space intervention focuses on the **structures** – including physical structures, activities, and routines – that are built into residential and institutional living spaces.

The initial thinking about life-space intervention focused on constructing structure within the child's life by using routines, activities, and stable relationships with child and youth care practitioners. Living spaces were designed to meet the developmental needs of the children, and caretakers developed goals for children and youth, primarily in residential settings. Redl and Wineman (1951, 1952) suggested that the goal of life-space intervention was re-education for life in a way that allowed young people to transfer new basic life-skills to other living spaces (family, school, community). Developmental phase, pathology, and familial context were all accounted for in the construction of goals by the caregivers. In essence, the physical aspects of a single living space (the residence) and the relationships that caretakers developed with young people in that living space were considered to be the tools of life-space intervention. They created the structure for therapeutic change and the learning of new behaviours and ways of social interaction. There was little thought given to the young people's capacity for autonomous thought and action, or **agency**, and while adaptations in response to the unique needs of particular young people were encouraged theoretically, such adaptation often didn't occur in practice (Lawson, 1998). In well-functioning residential programs, staff were found to be responsive and respectful, and to share power and decision-making (Anglin, 2002). However, even in current research and theory, the thinking continues to equate the 24/7 environment of a residential setting with the "life-space."

From the perspective of the practitioner, the concept of "being present" within this conceptualization of life-space was literal. Being present meant being physically in the residential unit or the institution, and being available to impose the program structure and routines on the children and youth living there. The life-space interventions of the practitioner were primarily created through structure. Therefore, the practitioner was the means by which the therapeutic content of the program was transferred from the program structure to the young person. Within this construction of being present, neither the practitioner nor the young person was explicitly imbued with agency. That is, neither had the capacity to take action, either physically or emotionally, in order to affect either each other or the structure of therapeutic intervention itself. To the extent that young people did take action, their actions were seen as symptomatic of the identified problem, and the practitioner's responsibility was to "re-educate" the young person and negate any impact of those actions. Protecting the purity of the therapeutic intervention – "being consistent" and therefore prioritizing structure over agency – was one of the core components of "being present."

A significant shift in thinking about life-space intervention occurred with the recognition that young people often learn best "in the moment," and the concept of *moment* included not only time (its literal meaning) but also space. Increasingly, it was recognized that the transfer of learning from an institutional context to the living spaces of young people who left the institution was limited and difficult to sustain. By the 1990s, a renewed effort to find more relationship-based approaches to therapeutic intervention was emerging (Fewster, 1990a; Fox, 1985; Garfat, 1998; Krueger, 1991; VanderVen, 1995). As relationships were affirmed as the core of therapeutic approaches to child and youth care practice, a renewed focus on the development of practitioners themselves ensued, manifested by an increasing interest in the concept of Self (Fewster, 1990b).

With the renewed focus on the practitioner, the primacy of structure over agency was shaken up. The field recognized that practitioners did in fact exercise agency in their approach to being present, as long as they accepted the idea of being present in the moment. Such presence was no longer articulated as a mere tool for the imposition of structure. Instead, it became the core element of relationship-based work. Through the presence of the practitioner, the engagement with the young person is affected by the individual practitioner. Practitioner values, ethics and biases are tools of agency and components of therapeutic intervention. The use of Self as a tool for therapeutic intervention requires a major shift in the responsibilities of the practitioner, away from imposing structure and routines and toward moderating structure and routine so that they correspond to the unique circumstances of that young person's life.

As the field recognized the importance of practitioners' agency with respect to being present in the life of a child or youth, new opportunities for engaging young people have evolved that include a more complex spatial understanding of life-space intervention. Rather than limiting the notion of life-space to the institution or residential care facility, service providers have deployed child and youth care practitioners in a range of spaces where young people live their lives, including the community, the family home and the school. Service providers recognized that opportunities for learning "in the moment" occur in many different spaces and are often the result of a perceived crisis in the lives of young people as they struggle to cope with an event that seems beyond their control. When these struggles created a conflict with the caregiver or with a peer, that struggle could be used as a learning opportunity. If practitioners were focused on the structure of the life-space and/or unaware of their own agency in the interaction, then the conflict could be perpetuated and therapeutic effect would be minimal. Life-space crisis intervention and life-space as therapeutic milieu are two examples of approaches that reflect this expanded understanding of the life-space.

Life-space crisis intervention [LSCI] (Wood & Long, 1991; Long, Wood, & Fecser, 2001) introduced an intervention process that included exploring the young person's construction or understanding of the crisis/conflict, introducing new ways of understanding that conflict, and therefore introducing new ways of behaving in the future. LSCI techniques required practitioners to understand their role or agency in the discussion, which includes control of the young person's escalating and out-of-control behaviour, awareness of their own thoughts, feelings, and actions in the moment, and their values, beliefs and ethics. The conceptualization of life-space in LSCI focuses on the relational aspects of the life-space and the learning opportunities available in the typical living spaces where young people in conflict travel, such as schools, family, courts, and community centres.

Life-space as a therapeutic milieu is conceptualized by Burns (2006) as having a number of structural elements that the practitioner can manipulate, thereby exerting agency. According to Burns, life-space and life-space intervention include elements of the physical environment, the emotional environment of the participants, the social context within that setting (still a singular life-space defined by where the practitioner works), and elements of the other social and cultural contexts in which the young person participates. Burns also recognizes the ideologies of systemic and organizational structures, and the potential they have to be manipulated in order to influence the nature of the young person's learning and therapeutic change.

While life-space intervention has been developed and articulated in increasingly sophisticated ways, it has continued to focus on defining life-space to include the structure of a single living space and the agency of the practitioner as central components. We propose that the concept of the life-space needs to be re-examined to include the constructions of the young people we work with and their understanding of a unified space in which they exist. The addition of the practitioner's agency to the articulation of life-space interventions and the concept of being present have added considerably to the value of therapeutic interventions. The next logical step is to incorporate the agency of the young people with the agency of the practitioners themselves. New technologies and virtual spaces mean that young people understand their life-space differently, construct it differently, and think about it in a more unified manner. Practitioners need to understand young people's role in constructing their life-space as well as the relational aspects of that space – not just the practitioner/youth relationship, but other relationships as well. As children develop into adolescents and young adults, their ability to understand the abstract and virtual spaces around them increases. This implies that the construction of life-space has a developmental component, and that how a young person understands life-space changes with the passage of time.

In many respects, our rationale for re-examining the concept of life-space intervention right here, right now is based on developments in the past and developments we anticipate for the future. As institutional residential care declines and child and youth care practitioners are more often found in non-institutional and community-based locations, structure is no longer the primary focus over agency. Being present simply through physical presence in a specific place has limited applicability when practitioners are engaged with young people in multiple spaces that are mediated through a wide range of social and psychological constructions of identity and related cultures, ethnicities, gender, sexual orientations, and abilities. In addition, we do not think that we have to look too far into the future to recognize that new technologies have altered our presence in the lives of young people. Social networking, texting and other virtual ways of engaging in relationships are clearly present now, and are likely to develop further into significant and potentially dominant spaces of social interaction and relational engagement. What separates such spaces from previous adjustments in our engagements with young people is the degree of agency that the young people exercise in these spaces. In addition to having virtually unlimited access to a network of external relationships (that is, external to the practitioner/youth relationship), young people are shaping the structure of these relationships based on how they have constructed their identity and sometimes multiple identities. The agency of young people in their life-spaces requires the practitioner to re-evaluate the core elements of a child and youth care approach to life-space intervention. Thus, we explore in this chapter a new model of life-space that leads to new ways of applying life-space intervention.

Discreet Places and Connected Spaces

If we begin with the question "Where do you live your life?" it surely will not take long to identify a multitude of places where we experience our day-to-day lives. These spaces and places may be thought of by the young person and/or the practitioner as discreet, unified, or a blend of both. For young people, there are some places that simply reflect the experience of childhood and adolescence. Thus, life unfolds at home, at school, with peers in the community and possibly in other places such as the sports club, in the homes of extended family members, and in the homes of individuals with whom they have other significant relationships. When we consider these places, we recognize that the social dynamics associated with each place are quite different. The rules, routines, expectations and activities at school are not the same as those for interacting with peers in the community. In other words, there are differences in the structure of these places, giving each place the appearance that it is discreet and separate from the others.

This discreetness was, for many years, taken for granted in programs and services for young people. Not surprisingly, therefore, child and youth care practitioners worked almost exclusively in the living space where problems had been identified (usually by parents, but sometimes by other professionals such as teachers or police officers). While there was recognition at the time that the isolation of residential care often did not produce learning or developmental growth that easily transferred to the other locations of young people, the deployment of child and youth care practitioners to the home environment, or even into schools, did not significantly influence the nature of intervention within a life-space perspective. This lack of influence may have been mitigated by the practitioner's ability to use his or her agency in the engagement with the young person, but ultimately the practitioner was still deployed in selected and singular life-spaces, restricted by physical location.

There were some exceptions to this limited view of life-space intervention, such as the introduction of Multiple Systemic Therapy (MST). MST, originally developed in South Carolina (Henggeler, 1993), is premised on the idea that young people experience their lives in a multitude of places, and that any effective life-space intervention must therefore target all of these places rather than selecting only a few. Even within MST, however, these places were not explicitly articulated as being connected in any way. The focus was on impacting all of the places where young people might be influenced to *prevent* them from entering that dreaded of all spaces – the residential youth custody institution – where life-space was so strictly associated with a single physical living space.

It becomes apparent that the concept of life-space intervention takes on an entirely different meaning if we re-examine the discreetness of the multitude of places where young people spend time. One way of challenging the discreet nature of "place" is to consider the connections between places, and to focus on how unified such connections are, both from the perspective of how young people understand them and the perspective of the practitioner.

The idea of life-space as a unified concept is perhaps our most radical departure from previous thinking about life-space. In today's global world, the notion that there are multiple separated life-spaces has vanished, as evidenced by the way in which people, including young people, position themselves in this new world. They log into social networking sites and interact with friends across the country and around the world, sharing information and learning about and meeting people who are friends of their friends. They join groups with common interests and develop relationships with people they have never met, sharing ideas, values and beliefs. People telecommute to work, thereby interacting through email, video conferencing and teleconferencing in order to develop projects with others who are located at great distances. Even sophisticated health and mental health services are delivered at a distance through telehealth and telepsychiatry programs available throughout much of North America. The time and space for "work" has shifted to accommodate different time zones. Internet delivery of educational courses creates asynchronous interaction and the ability to learn at the time that best suits the learner. People meet and develop relationships online. Business and even vacation travel may be a time for talking with friends or family, reading, or turning on the computer or smart-phone in order to work or socialize. In other words, travel is no longer about getting away – it now includes relational interaction with people in other locations. More and more, we carry our life-space with us in imagination, in emotional connection, and in relationship to others, as well as in activities and relationships with people and things that blend into a singular understanding of the space in which we live our life.

We recognize that a typology of life-spaces would fail to capture the nuances of connectivity and continuity of different places. We argue, therefore, that it is possible to identify several dimensions of a singular notion of life-space without negating the possibility that a person experiences different places as a fully integrated and unified space. There are four dimensions of life-space in particular that we will highlight:

- the physical dimension
- the mental dimension
- the relational dimension
- the virtual dimension

We will provide a brief description of each of these dimensions, and then use some of the core concepts of child and youth care practice (caring, engagement, relationship, boundaries) to develop these dimensions and their implications for life-space interventions further. In addition, we believe that the concept of agency in the life-space – specifically the importance of the young person's agency – implies that the core activity of therapeutic change is learning. Therefore, a brief discussion of learning as a function of the life-space and therapeutic change follows our discussion of the four dimensions of the life-space.

Physical Dimension

The physical dimension of life-space is best understood by considering the five senses: Sight, hearing, taste, touch and smell. If life-space is a singular concept for a young person, there is no difference between the meta-environment (Burns, 2006) or the mesosystem (Bronfenbrenner, 1979) and the therapeutic environment where the child and youth care practitioner is. The relational continuity between different locations negates the distance between such locations, thus creating one unified life-space. A young person may, for example, have different meanings for identifiable spaces within his or her home, such as the kitchen versus the bedroom, but all of these spaces are still manifestations of a unified place called "home." Similarly, friendships that extend from the schoolyard to the community playground negate the distance between these locations even if the physical contexts of these locations are discreet. Within the physical dimension of the life-space, then, movement and transition are undoubtedly present, but time blends the physical locations into one environment. Therefore, the changing sensations and experiences of the different physical locations become important aspects of describing life-space.

The physical aspects of life-space involve what we see, hear, taste, touch and smell, and how those sensations change and influence the unfolding of our lives. For example,

- the impinging sights and busy noise of a crowded street or the relative silence of a lake in the wilderness
- the smell of a mother's perfume or the taste of a favourite food after smelling it cooking for the last three hours
- the soft touch of a kiss good night or the pain of an alcohol-impaired slap as it connects with a young person's head

The most dominant aspects of life-space for many people are likely the visual and auditory components of the physical dimension of life-space. With the exception of those with visual or auditory impairments, the evidence for the importance of these aspects is reflected in how people and places are captured on film or video. The sensory inputs of the physical life-space affect who we are and how we cope with the problems presented to us.

Story: Physicality and Life-Space

Andre thinks of the whole town as his playground. When he heads to Main Street, he encounters his uncle's hardware store right next to the dojo where he works out and the youth centre where he hangs out. He's recently taken up parkour for fun and to enhance his aerobic fitness for karate. The challenge of moving efficiently from home to school to the dojo and then to the youth centre has given him an even stronger sense of wholeness in the various places that he feels a part of.

Andre is going to the youth centre tonight and has decided to try a new route. He pulls on his running shoes, a special pair that he was able to afford after the summer working as a deck-hand on a fishing boat. The rest of his summer money went to his dad. He enjoys the weightless feel of the light mesh runners with the thin soles. They let him feel the ground and understand intuitively where his body needs to go when he lands lightly on the balls of his feet after a *lache* (swing) or a *passe muraille* (wall hop).

He heads out the door and turns south directly toward the youth centre, whereas normally he would head east before cutting south. His current route requires that he navigate the railroad tracks and the top of a water control dam, dropping down about 3 metres into an abandoned lot before sprinting to hop a 1.5-metre fence that protects the area from Main Street. He sprints along the railroad tracks, running on the rails to improve his balance. He notices the fall colours along the tracks – the sumacs are brilliant crimson, and the poplars have turned yellow. Mixed in is the occasional oak and maple along with the scrub evergreens.

He is distracted by a memory of his mother and starts to recite the colours in French; somehow they seem more brilliant when he uses the French words. A slight vibration in the rail draws his attention back to the task at hand, and he leaps off the tracks onto the edge of the dam. The concrete is cold and the water is loud but smells refreshing. He slips a little as he pushes forward off the end of the dam, but he lands safely, bouncing up to sprint across the lot and swing over the fence just behind the coffee shop on Main Street. He can smell the roast beans from the open back door, and he waves at his uncle, who is putting out the garbage next door at the hardware store. Then he sprints up the narrow alley between the two buildings to the front, where he can hear the mix of his mother's Acadian French and the Scottish/English dialect of the New Brunswick seniors who are having afternoon coffee in the fall sunshine.

Life-space intervention is about helping children, youth and families manage the challenges that they experience in their life-space. We can intervene to change the structure of the life-space and the way it looks or sounds. We can teach young people how to change the structure of the space, what to look and listen for, and how to create a quiet space in the environment around them and in their own mind. Taste, touch and smell are also essential to the physical aspects of space. Touch, as an activity, is essential to children's health and development. Its essential nature is not just about the communication of love and caring (part of the mental aspect of life-space) – it also promotes healthy brain development and the development of various social capacities, including healthy attachment (Berscheid, 1999). Changing sensations of smell can create physical reactions in the body and affect the way people live in their life-space. Consider the young person with a perfume allergy, for example. Simply taking a shortcut through the wrong aisle in a department store may cause him or her to experience severe medical stress. Similarly, the physical characteristics of a neighbourhood (a significant physical location within the life-space of a child or youth) can change simply because of the addition of families from different cultures and with different culinary preferences. Taste changes over time. Many young children have particularly sensitive taste buds and develop a wider range of tastes as they grow older. Favourite foods may change, or they may remain strongly associated with particular social contexts, such as family dinners or the snacks consumed in the first bursts of freedom as a teenager.

The physical aspects of life-space, when it is considered as a unified space, are under the control of both the practitioner and the young person. Agency can be exerted through physical intervention or physical activity. Leaving one location to go to another physical location in the life-space and continue living life is an act of agency. Agency can also be exerted mentally, through the agency of your own interpretation or construction of the physical aspects of space. The way young people construct their life-space is often directed by the mental dimension of life-space.

Mental Dimension

We construct the mental dimension of life-space in the thoughts and feelings that are generated in our heads and hearts. These thoughts and feelings are built over time as we develop our understanding of the physical dimension of life-space and its influence on our lives. Helping children manage the changes in the physical and relational dimensions of their life-space occurs in the mental dimension of life-space. Therapeutic strategies such as re-storying through narrative therapy, cognitive behavioural therapy, mindfulness and other approaches are actively applied within the life-space to help young people construct different perceptions of that space. Ungar (2002) suggests that "troubled" adolescents are a construction of their parents and other adults who are threatened by the exuberance of young people. In essence, most adults do not like to have their own life-space disturbed by teenagers. He reminds us that only five percent of adolescents in trouble persist with those troubling behaviours into adulthood. In turn, he believes that young people understand spaces such as jail or the community as locations of safety where they feel good about themselves. These spaces help them cope with feeling unsafe in their home (through abuse) or school (through bullying). These examples illustrate the role of the mental dimension of life-space and the importance of understanding life-space as a single space rather than as multiple physical environments. Within this construction of life-space, the selective deployment of the child and youth care practitioner into one particular location no longer makes sense.

Story: Mental Constructions of Life-Space

The challenge of the new parkour route has chased out the anxieties Andre had been having about school. He's now looking forward to seeing his friends at the youth centre and figuring out what the plans are for the weekend. He's a little flushed when he enters the youth centre, and Denis gives him a high-five and a handshake, commenting, "You look like a red maple leaf. Who's chasing you?" Andre laughs. "Just tried a new route to get here, the railway and the old dam. I saw a few nice maples." Denis raises his eyebrows. "Wrong time of day to be messing with the train tracks; don't you remember the VIA that comes through around now from Montreal?" Andre shrugs. "I was more worried about the dam and how slippery it was," he retorts. "Okay, I'm glad you're thinking about some of the hazards. I wouldn't want to have you disappear on us," says Denis. Andre snorts and walks away. Denis makes a mental note to follow up, thinking that Andre seems a little distracted.

Andre has grown up in the small town and knows only the unique mix of Acadian culture. He brings a fierce Acadian passion to his activities. He was attracted to parkour because of its French roots, and he believes that his training in martial arts helps him to control his temper. Before karate he had a tendency to strike first and talk later, but his training has helped him control himself, and he enjoys the art and precision involved in the *kata*.

Walking to the back of the youth centre, Andre is annoyed with himself for not being able to remember all the colours in French. He can't quite capture the right word for the colour of the sumac trees in English, and he remembers that the word his mother taught him really seemed to describe them. He feels more and more like he is losing her completely. His connection to his father, his uncle and the community, including the dojo and the youth centre, are all strong, but absent his mother or any connection to her. No one talks about her and she has no family in the community, as far as he knows, and no former friends. He wonders again how she could just disappear without saying goodbye or making any contact since then.

The actual effects of the physical dimension of the life-space are largely neutral. It is the dynamic nature of life-space and agency that allows young people to make meaning of their interactions with the physical environment. A history of personal expectations is created and carried into current and future interactions in the life-space. In other words, while young people actively engage with the specific physical environments they are in – playing soccer, rearranging furniture, or smelling the cooking pot on the stove – they also develop a set of expectations and a history of having fun, feeling comforted by a favourite chair, or missing Grandma and her best curry combination. Sometimes these expectations create a sense of safety in the life-space, while other times they create a sense of anxiety or surprise when the life-space does not match their expectations.

To be aware of these expectations, young people require a certain skill and mindfulness. Based on historical expectations, they form judgments and opinions about the present life-space quickly. Young people react emotionally to the environment around them. In familiar environments, such as home or school, these reactions can intensify and escalate in response to the emotions of others. Reactions may be more muted in other environments, but they are still present and can be carried into other locations throughout the life-space. Young people can arrive at school still carrying the emotional vestiges of a bad dream or a night in a homeless shelter, but practitioners in school expect that they will leave these emotional reactions aside and pay attention to the activities of school.

Values and beliefs are constructed within the social context of the life-space and applied to the physical environments that make up the life-space. Values are those things that we think are important – those ideas, items, and feelings that we value or prioritize over other things. Young people develop values and beliefs from the surrounding life-space and from the active application of their own thinking (agency) about the events that occur there. They are agents in the development of their own values and beliefs. Laws represent the institutionalization of values that are thought to be important to society. Policies in a workplace, school or community centre are the values of that organization, and organizational values are part of the structure that is created to surround young people. Conflicting values in the life-space create tension and prompt attempts to exert agency over the structure of the program. Conflicting beliefs about how people should behave and the way environments should be structured also need to be sorted out in the life-space. Statements such as "Home should be safe," "Home requires a permanent address, parents, and a sense of belonging," and "Home is where the heart is" are embedded in the social constructions of culture, and they influence the mental dimension of the life-space of young people.

The ideologies of cultures and institutions extend the idea of life-space far beyond just the environments where practitioners are located. This extension suggests that life-space should be focused on the person, not the structures of the environment. People interpret the environment through their thoughts and feelings, as well as the values and beliefs that they hold and carry into other environments. These mental dimensions of life-space are modified through interactions with the physical environment and the people who are present in these environments. The relational aspects of life-space are central to the interaction between physical and mental dimensions of life-space.

Relational Dimension

Relationships surround us and feed the emotional substance of our life-space. They can support a young person in crisis, or diminish a young person's capacity to deal with challenges in other dimensions of the life-space. Relationships change over time, and they change us and the space that we exist in. Garfat (2008, p. 20) suggests that relational practice focuses "on the relationship, while recognizing and respecting the characteristics of the individuals involved in that relationship," and that relational work "attends to the relationships itself." Within the relational dimension of life-space, the young person or practitioner consciously attends to relationships, to the nature of those relationships, and to nurturing relationships as part of the life-space he or she travels in.

One cannot *not* have a relationship after having met someone (and possibly even before having met them), and therefore the relational dimension of life-space is about what one does with and within the relationship. Relational aspects of life-space include the shared activities that we undertake and the meaning that we make of those. Attending to relationships means caring about other people and thinking about how caring is expressed. It means actively engaging to understand the other person's thoughts, feelings, intents and desires. The relational aspects of life-space are the core of practitioner interventions (explored in Chapters 3 to 6). Before we consider the activities of life-space intervention, however, we will briefly explore the impact that relationships have on how young people construct their life-space.

When a young child enters the schoolyard on the first day of school, the physical environment may be perceived as threatening and intimidating. The school is not yet a place of comfort, and there has been no opportunity to develop a sense of belonging or an expectation that this is a safe place. This is why a parent often accompanies a child to school on that challenging first day. The presence of the parent in that moment does not physically alter the space in any substantive way, but it significantly alters the way the child constructs the space. It is the relational safety afforded by the presence of the parent that mitigates the threat and intimidation of this new place. In fact, being with the parent (the relational context) mitigates virtually all of the emotions and sensations affecting the child in that moment. In addition to relational safety, the child experiences a sense of relational comfort, relational belonging, relational attachment and relational hope within the physical place of the school. This transference of emotional comfort is the result of the impact of relationship on physical place.

As time passes and the child develops relationships with peers and teachers (and child and youth care practitioners), this relational comfort is transferred from the parent to these new relationships. In this way there is continuity within the life-space, whereby the relational presence of others serves as a critical connection between locations and different social contexts. Therefore, home and school can be constructed by the child as components of the same life-space. Young people who struggle significantly in the school environment may be unable to construct the necessary continuity between different locations within their unified life-space. For these young people, the separation of place between home and school is missing a critical relational link. Aboriginal children whose parents were educated and raised in the residential school system struggle through school and often fail or drop out, while their parents are significantly absent in the living space of the school. The expectations of pain and failure associated with schooling means that Aboriginal parents may be absent from the school space both physically and emotionally. Without the capacity to recognize and gain comfort from the relational dimension of the life-space, young people face severe conflict between the physical dimensions of the location and the mental dimension of how they construct the living spaces of the school.

In some social contexts, the relational dimensions of life-space take on even greater significance. If we consider the physical context of a homeless youth, for example, we can readily recognize that there are few physical limits – the space is not defined by physical features such as walls, fences or even buildings. The movement of a homeless youth through his or her life-space is defined primarily by his or her relationships with peers (and perhaps family or other significant others), and the physical characteristics are at best secondary to the evolution and day-to-day nature of relationships. A homeless youth may say, "I live on the streets," without indicating any specific street or address. This lack of specificity is indicative of the youth's mental construction of life-space, in which the streets are not a location but a concept that provides a space for relational engagements.

In much the same way that the physical and mental dimensions of life-space change and evolve, so do the relational characteristics. Therefore, again we must consider the role of agency in life-space interventions. For the practitioner, any engagement with a young person or family affects the relational characteristics of that person's life-space. Thus, it also changes the structural relationships between the physical, mental and relational dimensions of life-space. Similarly, the young person or family can act to reshape or reconstruct their life-space based on how they make meaning of any given relationship. Homelessness, for example, may be a challenging structure in which life unfolds, but the relational characteristics of a "homeless life-space" can present opportunities for caring and engagement even when an identifiable place to meet regularly is absent. In this way, we are approaching another characteristic of life-space that, like relational dimensions of life-space, is place-less. We will explore this next.

Story: Musings on Relational Life-Space

Andre felt very connected and at home in his community. Besides his aunts and uncles, who had watched out for him and looked after him when his dad was off fishing in the first few years after his mom left, there were two teachers from elementary school who made sure to look him up regularly. They both volunteered in the homework program at the youth centre and they sometimes offered to tutor him in math or English on their own time, since he struggled a bit with the material. He was trying really hard this year not to use the tutoring. He wanted to make the grades himself. It seemed like cheating otherwise.

Denis kept saying to him, "Smart people know when to ask for help. Stupid people don't ask. Don't be stupid."

But that Scottish stubbornness and independence that he got from his dad was getting in the way.

Andre had been friends with the same group since kindergarten. Some of them were very poor, and he remembered the fun times they'd had picking bottles in the ditches along the Trans-Canada highway so that his friends could help out their families in between the welfare cheques in the winter. He was really glad that his dad was able to work his way off the boats and into the local packing plant. At first it meant his dad had to work midnights. Now, since his dad was in management, he was away sometimes at the head office, but at least there was year-round income. Andre was tight with his friends, but these days some of them seemed really depressed. They were getting into some drug dealing to survive the depression and make a little money.

Andre didn't want to abandon them, but he didn't much like the pressure they sometimes put on him to participate. Sensei had made it really clear that drugs weren't an option if you were training. Besides, a couple of the local RCMP guys trained at the dojo too, and Andre knew full well that they would know if he was using. They knew everything, even if they let on that they didn't.

(Continued)

Denis interrupted Andre's reflections about the people in his life as he poked his head into the homework room at the Youth. "How's it going?" he asked. "What's the struggle today?"

Andre shook his head. "I have to write this essay for English about something that I'm passionate about. She wants us to use lots of adverbs and adjectives. Then we have to go through and label them. It's stupid."

"What's the struggle?" Denis repeated.

"How am I supposed to use them if I don't know what they are?" asked Andre.

"Yup, that could be an issue."

"I mean, I sort of know what they are, but I don't think I'll get it right. I guess I could just write it, since the computers are open here, and then get Ms. Eddy to help me when she gets here."

"You know what I always say," replied Denis.

"Yah, yah. Smart people know when to ask for help, and I'm a smart guy!" said Andre. "At least some people think so. Will you read it when I'm done? I'm going to write about the free-run I just did. Fall colours, thinking about my mom. . . . Should be lots of adverbs and adjectives in that. . . ."

"I'd be honoured to have a look," said Denis as he withdrew. He was pleased with Andre's initiative and that he'd get the chance to follow up on Andre's pensive look from earlier. Then he wondered if *pensive* was an adverb or an adjective.

Virtual Dimension

It is tempting to think of virtual spaces as spaces that lack concreteness, that are not real, and that therefore do not really exist. By doing so, we immediately negate the very concept of life-space and replace it with living space. Virtual places are very real, so long as we accept that young people have agency and therefore experience their lives in the context of their social and psychological construction of spaces rather than some objective way of defining spaces. As we have just discussed, our "real" life-space is constructed by the complex entanglement of physical, mental, relational and virtual dimensions of life-space. Virtual life-space might include those environments in which we interact and relate to others, but where all the senses are not fully utilized. The virtual space of a social networking site on the Internet is an example. People interact in such a site primarily through visual and auditory (e.g., sound bites in videos) channels, but many of the visual and auditory components of communication (the nonverbal cues of facial expressions and voice tone) are missing. In this example, the virtual-dimension life-space interacts with characteristics from the relational and mental dimensions of life-space but misses many of the physical characteristics that are not captured through the use of technology. Did virtual environments exist before the technological revolution of the late twentieth century? We believe that virtual spaces have always existed, and that the technology of today enhances the impact of such spaces in that it allows us to be engaged and to relationally connect with others as we construct these virtual spaces. But virtual environments existed even before modern technology, including the virtual environment of madness, the virtual environment of the imagination, and the virtual environment of the spiritual world. All of these have always been present in the life-space.

Story: Temporary Madness in the Virtual Life-Space

Andre opened his eyes and looked straight into the eyes of the nurse who was changing the dressing on his forehead. He noted that her third eye was a different colour than the other two, and that there was purple snot running down her chin. He tried to lift his arm and push her away, but he couldn't move. He screamed instead, but she didn't seem to hear him. "Maybe she's deaf," he thought. Then Sahim looked away from the dressing she was trying to remove and realized that Andre's eyes were open.

"Hi," she said. "You're awake." Then, as his eyes got really wide and filled with terror, she pulled back and said, "You had an accident on the dam. You broke your arm, got a big cut on your head, really ripped up your hamstrings, and broke a few ribs."

Andre struggled to understand what she was saying as he watched the flames shooting out of her mouth and the purple goo on her chin turn into a butterfly and fly off. Finally, he screamed, "Get the fire extinguisher – you're going to burn up!"

Sahim sighed and said, "Okay. Close your eyes and I'll take care of it."

She headed off to call the youth worker attached to the Psych unit and let her know that Andre needed some attention. She then called the psychiatrist about the dosage for his pain medication.

Monique appeared by Andre's bed in the ICU within a few minutes of the call. She wasn't freaked out by drug-induced psychosis, but she knew that Andre would be. The sooner she helped him understand and explore this new virtual world, the sooner she could connect the virtual and the real back together for him. Then they could figure out together how to manage his injuries and the short-term effects of the medication, and assess whether there were long-term effects.

"Hi Andre," she said. "I'm Monique. I'm the youth worker here in the hospital. Sahim said you seemed frightened and she was concerned about you."

Andre screwed his eyes shut even tighter. The voice sounded so re-assuring.

"Hi Mom," he said.

"No, I'm Monique, your mom's not here right now. You can leave your eyes closed but tell me about what frightened you with the nurse."

Monique wanted to find out what he was seeing or hearing, and who and what was present in his life. Then she could start to help him make sense out of the accident and the hospital, and get him back to "normal" life as soon as possible. She hadn't read his chart yet – no time – so she had no idea what had happened to him. But he looked pretty banged up, kind of like he'd been hit by a train. She'd heard some rumours yesterday about a near miss on the VIA tracks. She wondered where his family was. There was no evidence of visitors.

A particularly fascinating context for the virtual environment of madness is constituted through the psychiatric disorder known as Munchhausen's syndrome. This disorder is diagnosed when a person articulates experiences and sometimes even an identity based on entirely fictitious circumstances that often include seemingly impossible situations that create symptoms of ill health. The disorder is named after the main character in a German fairytale, the Baron of Munchhausen, who claimed rather famously that he pulled himself out of quicksand by his own hair. Young persons suffering from this disorder without the diagnosis are frequently identified as pathological liars, attention seekers, or even as manipulative. Yet we know that none of the more common behavioural therapies are particularly effective with these youth. From a life-space perspective, we can argue that one reason for this lack of effectiveness is that in dismissing the life-space constructed through the disorder we are imposing a life-space that is simply not real to the young person. Ironically, then, the virtual life-space of madness takes precedence in the experience of the young person over the real spaces more commonly recognized by society. We might recognize similar conflicts and tensions in the relationship between real and virtual spaces in relation to psychiatric disorders such as schizophrenia, mania or even multiple personality disorder. Madness generates life-spaces that are virtual and yet very real for those experiencing them. We do not need to accept how young people construct their life-spaces, but by understanding and entering the life-space, we can recognize the young person's agency over that space and how that agency within the virtual dimension might be usefully employed.

The imagination can also generate constructions of life-space that exist for some but not for others. Within the context of imagination, life-space may have physical characteristics, as we discussed earlier. These characteristics are invisible to anyone else unless there is a relational engagement with the person that includes the exploration of imagined spaces. From a life-space perspective, the imagination is similar but not identical to the mental dimension of life-space. Whereas the mental dimension of life-space is constituted through the mental and emotional interpretations of spaces that are physically in common with and accessible to others, imagined life-space is constituted through the mental and emotional interpretation of spaces that are constructed individually and in unique ways such that they are not visible to others unless they are described. However, even if the space itself is inaccessible to others, it still contains physical and relational dimensions. We imagine relationships with famous people and we imagine ourselves in homes, cars, schools, and other locations that we don't actually go to. The imagination transcends the material reality of people and places, and it allows the construction of relationships and spaces that are uniquely suited to meet the needs of the person in the moment.

Virtual life-spaces based on spiritual factors mirror those based on madness and the imagination in most respects. One crucial difference is that the structures of religious doctrine may be imposed, at least when the spiritual factors correspond to an existing faith or religious movement. In such cases, the agency of the person may be mitigated or reduced by a perceived spiritual imperative that may have controlling or guiding features, and that therefore determine aspects of the virtual life-space and how it affects the person.

Virtual aspects of life-space are powerful and complex. Whether digital, imaginary, a product of madness or spiritual, they are often invisible to others in the young person's life-space, but may be very present for the young person. Our intervention task is to make these virtual aspects explicit and visible. This is particularly important because while they have great potential as a therapeutic tool, virtual constructions of life-space also have

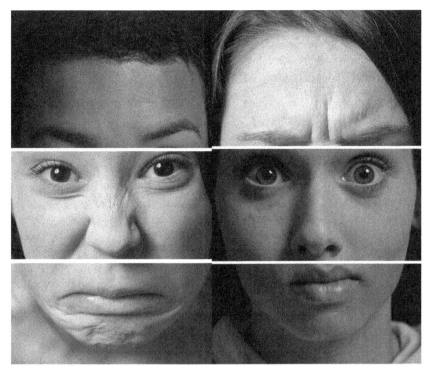

The Virtual Look in the Mirror

Source: Laine Robertson

Whether we are looking in the mirror or contemplating our lives, we see a unified and logically consistent whole. We don't see separated physical locations or varied expressions. In conversation with others, we share and learn about people whom we've never met, developing a relationship with those people. There is a unified life-space. However, just like the faces in this photograph, the face looking back at a young person represents many things. Different ethnic backgrounds (visible or invisible), emotions, ideas, locations, and possible hallucinations all stare back. This is the complexity and variation of the life-space – changeable and yet completely consistent.

great potential as unsafe environments for young people. Historically, there were safety concerns about the isolation and sometimes unpredictable decision-making of individuals whose lives unfolded primarily in the context of madness or within imagined or spiritual life-space. The introduction of new technologies has further compromised the safety of the virtual life-space given, for example, the increasing prevalence of Internet-based predators. Ironically, the incidence of online child abuse may be an indication that predators have a good understanding of virtual life-space.

The questions that need to be explored thoroughly include how we can be present in the virtual life-space of a young person, and how we can ensure connectivity between real and virtual spaces and places. As we discussed earlier, intervention from a life-space perspective must take into account the relative discreetness and connectivity, or the entanglement, of all the places, real and virtual, in which young people live their lives through understanding and engaging with the various dimensions of their life-space.

Learning and Life-Space

Learning is an inevitable byproduct of living, and it is therefore a central activity in the life-space. Wherever and however life unfolds, learning characterizes the experience of moving through space and time. As we proceed to explore the concept of life-space intervention in the remainder of this chapter, understanding learning in the context of life-space is essential.

Learning is typically thought of as something that occurs in school, as a result of teaching. This is a limited view of learning when considered from a life-space perspective. The life-space is an educational "structure," and the manner in which a young person engages the dimensions of life-space offers opportunities for learning. Learning serves to connect the many places where we live our lives, and it allows us to generate new ways of connectivity between such places. What we learn through our experiences in one context transfers to other contexts, and each new experience is tied to the previous ones, notwithstanding changes in time and place. Teaching is present in the social interactions of the life-space but teaching is not "active" in the same way that it is when lessons are prepared in school. Learning is progressive and gradual in the life-space and is "tested" on the basis of how useful it is for managing life, rather than through exams or assignments.

When we approach young people from a perspective of pathology and problem-focused intervention, we negate the possibilities for learning within their life-space and instead focus on closing off or excluding them from certain components of their life-space as a way of protecting them from adversity. Adversity is an opportunity to learn from undesirable behaviours or habits. From the perspective of life-space intervention, excluding young people or protecting them from specific living spaces also results in the disruption of continuity within their life-space. Therefore, it can have the adverse effect of disrupting the young person's mental construction of life-space in many different locations, including "healthy" places. From a life-space perspective, the response to risks and safety concerns about social networking sites is not to exclude young people from participation. Rather, it is to join in developing strong protective measures in the life-space as the young person has constructed it. Learning unfolds regardless of social context, and the practitioner's role from a life-space intervention perspective is to be present within that learning in order to engage the young person in contemplating his or her agency within that life-space, right here and right now.

Story: In the Moment

Monique started with "the moment," hoping to find a way to understand what had happened and discover the various dimensions of Andre's life-space so she could help him figure out his next steps. First, she knew that there had to be a return to rationality (though she wasn't sure what that was for Andre), so the moment was the place to start.

"Tell me about what frightened you a few moments ago," she said.

Andre took a big breath and rushed through a few sentences of apparent gibberish about eyes, rouge, les yeux, purple, snot, butterflies, and a few other incomprehensible terms. Then he concluded with "There was fire coming out of her mouth and the purple butterflies kept getting burned when she talked. She shouldn't talk so much."

Monique agreed. "Yes, Sahim likes to explain lots of things and we might have more butterflies around here if she said less. Butterflies are nice to look at." She decided to do a little reality test with him.

"What did Sahim explain to you about where you are and why?" she asked.

"I'm in the hospital," Andre said, opening his eyes. "Hey, you're not my mom. She was here a minute ago. What did you do with her? She likes butterflies."

"I must sound like her," said Monique. "Is she Acadian?"

Andre screwed his eyes shut again. "Stop with the flames," he said. "You'll burn her."

"Keep your eyes closed, Andre, and tell me what you see."

"There's butterflies coming out of this purple goo in the air and flying through the flames. Where are they coming from?"

"If you can see them with your eyes closed, maybe it's your imagination?" asked Monique.

"No, no, it's really dangerous. I have to save them," he said, reaching out with his arm.

"Okay, we will. I'll help." Monique soaked a washcloth and placed it on Andre's head to cool him off.

"Thanks, the flames are gone," said Andre.

"Why don't you tell me how you got into the hospital?" asked Monique.

Andre proceeded to ramble, partially in French and partially in English, through a story about fall colours, parkour, a train, and the dam. Monique was able to pick out that his uncle was at the hardware store on Main Street and that he was going to the youth centre when he slipped and fell. She knew that the rest of the details were probably only partially accurate, but she was listening for people whom she could call and invite to the hospital. Andre didn't say anything about his mother or father, which she found somewhat curious. She figured that people might pull him from the delusions temporarily and they could start to construct a plan for what needed to happen next, so her first priority was to get some familiar people into the room.

Monique knew that there were going to be some difficult decisions for Andre and the inter-professional team about pain management, drug withdrawal, rehab for the broken bones, catching up and returning to school, and getting back to his normal activities. It was all going to take time. The sooner she got a support team together and they all helped each other understand what Andre was facing, the sooner he could start making some decisions about how to manage his newly revised life-space.

In the closing section of this chapter, we will explore how the concept of life-space as we have described it affects the process of life-space intervention. We believe that our focus on one unified life-space as the framework for living one's life in multiple places and spaces fundamentally changes the direction of intervention. Further, we believe that focusing on respecting life-spaces constructed by young people provides a foundation for ethical child and youth care practice at a time when technology, culture and social change are accelerating well ahead of our understanding of ethics and good practice.

Life-Space Intervention Reconstructed

In Europe, the field of child and youth care is embedded in the field of **social pedagogy**, and in Great Britain it is embedded in the field of social care. In these locations, learning and caring occur in a social context, and practitioners become experts in helping others learn about and manage the expectations embedded in the social structures that surround them, regardless of age, disability/ability, or social circumstance. The focus on social learning, or learning in a social context, is different in Europe than it is in North America. Here, social learning has become associated with the concepts of social learning theory, which postulates that people with power and prestige become agents of social change through reinforcing behaviour that they approve of, and/or "role modelling" appropriate behaviour that is then imitated by those who admire them. Therefore, in North America, behavioural change and the careful development of plans for change using goals, rewards, and critical social reinforcement have become the accepted basis of intervention. In this book, by reconstructing life-space intervention, we have defined **social learning** as being more akin to the European ideas of social pedagogy.

The focus of intervention in the life-space then becomes "learning in the broadest sense," meaning what the young person learns about how to manage the dimensions of his or her life. A balance must be established between the power of the practitioner and the agency of the young person in the process of change. Intervention becomes fluid when we focus on opportunities for learning and relationships that support learning and personal growth – we might call this "pedagogy of upbringing." Such opportunities are created only in a climate of caring, engagement and strong relationships. Intervention, guided by the young person, takes time; it requires multiple players, each with unique roles; and it unfolds in the context of the young person's life-space, well beyond a single physical location. We will explore the ideas of learning, pedagogy and the pedagogy of upbringing in greater detail in Chapter 7.

Thinking and acting to intervene beyond the physical location in which the practitioner and the young person are located opens new possibilities. The obvious possibilities are that the practitioner joins the young person in multiple places, acting as a connector between those places and helping the young person develop and grow within the social expectations of those places. Less obvious possibilities for intervention include helping the young person develop agency, self-advocacy, and an understanding of the need for certain social structures and the possibilities and potential for influencing them. The possibilities for action include responding to opportunities in the current physical environment of the young person's life-space, and responding to the needs and opportunities that arise in locations that the practitioner cannot access, but that the young person must manage.

Additional opportunities and challenges for intervention arise when the virtual dimension of life-space is considered. The technology of today's social world brings new opportunities for connection and learning in extremely different social contexts. Young people can connect across the world with other young people who, in spite of poverty, civil unrest, and political or religious conflict, are reaching into the life-space of those in very different circumstances. Intervention may take the form of facilitating global understanding, discussing cultural ideology, or figuring out cross-cultural social etiquette. These interventions may or may not require communication that is strictly text based. The virtual dimension of the life-space includes the possibilities of the imagination and of spirituality as locations for action and intervention in the life-space. Complexity increases when life-space intervention is reconstructed from this perspective, and the demands on the practitioner for conscious and principled practice also increase. The practitioner's interventions require critical analysis, conscious awareness and self-determination.

The practitioner must be active and engaged in determining the best choices for intervention at a given moment and from a long-term perspective. Active choice or agency in life-space intervention means that the practitioner has an understanding of the young person's social context or life-space, the social structures of the physical places where the young person travels, and the cultural and historical influences on those structures. The question of what society (or the institutions representing society) expects of this young person must be balanced with the immediate needs of the young person for safety, freedom or autonomy. This is a complex task in which the practitioner cannot simply rely on the plans or structures created by someone else. The practitioner must critically engage and analyze the social spaces and structures of the young person in collaboration with that young person.

The agency of the young person is present within the mental dimension of the life-space and, as the practitioner confronts the expectations of the young person, issues related to culture and identity arise. The young person's expectations about the social structure and social norms of an institution where we encounter him or her are embedded in culture and identity, transmitted through the social structures in which the young person was raised. Often, it is in the nexus between these expectations and the expectations of the current social structure that the conflict and need for intervention arises, creating an apparent struggle for power. Intervention can involve imposing social expectations (power over the young person and assimilation into the current social structure) or it can be an opportunity for learning. We suggest that intervention must be constructed as an opportunity for learning, not as an imposition of the social expectations of the current location. When intervention is defined as an opportunity for learning, the focus for the practitioner becomes learning about the culture and identity of the young person, and learning about the social expectations of the current life-space. The practitioner and the young person also focus on mutual learning about each other and the relationship between them.

The need for intervention is identified within the relational dimension of the life-space, which provides the "location" where practitioner and young person "meet," and where the opportunities for learning and change emerge. Practitioners who recognize the multiplicity of relationships that exist for a young person and the social opportunities that they provide for learning about life are no longer "alone" in the intervention process. Instead, practitioners are travellers in the life-space of the young person, and their role is to open opportunities for learning, convey the expectations of our social structures, and engage with young people in their journey through life. The tools of intervention in the life-space are used within the tension between the social structures that impose limits and controls and the agency of the young person, which carries individuality and personal power. The tensions between agency and structure are explored in the next chapter, followed by a more detailed examination of the tools of intervention – caring, engagement, relationships, and boundaries.

Summary

This chapter has introduced an expanded way of thinking about the life-space. Previous writing about LSCI and life-space interviews conceived of life-space as a "place" where the young person and the practitioner are both located, and stated that social interactions within the setting can be used to teach the young person new ways of interacting within societal structures. We describe the life-space as a unified space with physical, mental, relational, and virtual dimensions. This way of thinking about life-space opens new possibilities for intervention. This chapter reviewed the four dimensions of a unified life-space and briefly introduced the concepts of structure and agency.

In a place-based approach to life-space, structure is a primary tool for intervention. However, when life-space is defined as a unified space, the agency of young people and of practitioners is introduced, and life-space becomes the social location for learning about how to manage life. Agency is therefore returned to young people, and practitioners are required to consider issues of power, culture, and identity in their management of the structures within which they work. These tensions are explored further in the next chapter, providing additional background to the consideration of the nature of intervention in the new life-space.

Discussion and Exercises

Reflection in Practice

Awareness of Self and how you create and move through your own life-space is critical to effective and ethical intervention with young people. Reflection in the moment of practice and moment-to-moment during interactions with others is a difficult and learned skill. As you go through the rest of your day, attend consciously to the characteristics of your life-space and consider the four dimensions described here. Try to bring conscious awareness to how they evolve and interact with each other and within your practice relationships.

Reflection on Practice

In the story about Andre, identify or create descriptions of the following:
1. Physical life-space
2. Mental life-space
3. Relational life-space
4. Virtual life-space

Reflection for Practice

Consider a vulnerable young person that you know and apply the concepts of structure and agency as described in this chapter.
1. What are the structures that this young person must deal with?
2. What opportunities are there for agency in the life-space? What actions has the young person already taken to establish agency?

Theory in Action

1. Life-space is an evolving concept, both for the field of practice and as a descriptor for the multiple dimensions of a young person's life. Choose five concepts presented in this chapter. Define them and provide an example of that concept from your practice or daily life.
2. Complete a search of academic journals to find out how the concept of life-space has been defined historically and where it originated. (Hint: Look for the historical writings of Kurt Lewin.)

CHAPTER 2

Agency and Structure in Life-Space Intervention

Jennifer

Source: Kyle Stewart

In this chapter, we explore complex issues in relation to life-space intervention and provide a theoretical foundation for thinking about life-space intervention. We explore these questions: When we intervene with young people, is our purpose to affect the social context of the young people, such as their families, their peer groups, and the rules at school or in the home? Or do we aim to affect the young people themselves, and the decisions they make, the actions they take, and the things they might be thinking about as they manage the multiple life-space dimensions we explored in the previous chapter? We also need to consider this question: How does change happen? If we think that the social context determines how young people live their lives, then we need to change the social context. If we think that young people are able to actually affect their social context, then we can change what young people do and help them shape a social context that is healthier, more supportive and more to their advantage.

For example, we may be assigned to provide in-home support to a family in which the parents are challenged by the difficult behaviours of their teenage daughter. When we meet the family in their own home and have the opportunity to observe how the family members interact, we might notice that the parents are very aggressive and loud, and always redirecting their daughter. We might also notice that the daughter is insulting and rude to her parents. We might ask ourselves these kinds of questions: Is the daughter rude because the parents yell at her all the time? Do the parents yell at their daughter because she is so rude to them? If we focus our intervention on reducing the yelling of the parents, will the daughter become less rude? Alternatively, if we help the daughter be more polite to her parents, will they stop yelling?

We can readily see in this example how our belief about the relationship between the social context and the actions of a young person might direct our interventions. A similar set of questions can be asked regarding the relationship between programs and clients more generally: What effect does the structure of a program have on the actions (including the behaviour) of clients? Conversely, to what extent do the actions of the clients determine how the program is shaped, how it is structured, and how it operates on a day-to-day basis? In other words, what is the relationship between the structures in the life-space of the young person (the way society, the family, and the group home are organized and function day to day) and the agency of the young person (the decisions and actions taken by the young person to exercise control over his or her life-space)?

Story: Hospital Food

Jennifer wasn't one to hold back. "The food here is garbage," she growled at the woman interviewing her. She had been looking forward to giving this feedback all day, after she agreed to participate in a focus group organized by the hospital staff. They hoped to get some feedback from patients about how they liked the service and what could be done to improve it.

Jennifer had been at the hospital's juvenile psychiatric in-patient clinic for the past three weeks. Her parents had discovered deep scratches all over her forearms and even her wrists. Fearing the worst, they had brought her to the hospital emergency room. When she was asked about her self-harming behaviours, Jennifer had indicated a pre-occupation with hurting herself, maybe fatally. In fact, she had no intention of committing suicide, but she didn't know how to articulate the reasons for her self-harm. The attending physician chose to admit her to the locked, in-patient unit where she was to undergo psychiatric treatment.

At first, Jennifer didn't mind being admitted to this unit. It was peaceful and calm here and, in general, the nurses and treatment workers were nice enough. She had expected to be discharged after a couple of days. When she found out that she would have to stay in the unit for at least 30 days, she freaked out, and that night she cut her wrists deeply enough to require seven stitches.

Over the past three weeks, Jennifer had meetings with several doctors, including a psychiatrist who spoke to her very briefly. To her surprise, that brief encounter with the psychiatrist resulted in her having to take a cocktail of medications. She didn't really understand what each medication was for, but she knew that she was made to take them to battle her "depression, anxiety, impulsiveness" and potential affliction with bi-polar disorder.

When Jennifer asked why she would have to stay for 30 days, she was told that it was because of her risk to herself, as evidenced by her cutting behaviours.

"So, if I don't do any cutting, I can go home?" she asked the doctor and some of the nurses. "Yes, you have to prove that you can manage your feelings in more meaningful ways," they invariably responded.

Since there was nothing in her room that lent itself to cutting, Jennifer did indeed abstain from cutting. After two weeks of no cutting, she asked her doctor about an early release date. "Look, I haven't cut myself for two weeks. I'm done with that, so why can't I go home now?" "Well," the doctor responded, "it's not just about not cutting yourself. You have to be able to show that your thinking has changed and that you understand why cutting is not an appropriate way of expressing how you feel."

So Jennifer had been working on developing proof of her new thinking. She paid careful attention to the words used by the doctors and nurses, and she tried to pick up clues from what they said during morning rounds that would help her mount a convincing argument. But no matter how much she tried, her argument was never quite good enough, and it became clear to her that the hospital was going to hang on to her no matter what she said.

When she heard about the focus groups to get feedback from patients, she didn't hesitate to sign up. At first she was glad to be given the opportunity to provide input on how the service was offered and how it might be improved. Just before the group was to start, one of the other youth from Jennifer's unit turned to her and whispered "I've done these a bunch of times, and at the end they might give us a sweet snack for participating. That's why I always sign up."

As the group got underway, the nurse facilitating the discussion explained the process. "I really want to hear your thoughts and opinions on how to make this unit better and more useful, so please feel free to say anything at all. We can't improve the service unless you tell us what you would like to see happen." Jennifer had wanted to talk about discharge criteria, being part of the decision-making and wanting to get better explanations about her meds. But as she was about to start talking, she suddenly had an overwhelming sense of hopelessness. Without hesitation, she switched her comment. "The food here is garbage," she growled.

Structure and Agency in the Life-Space

It is common these days for service providers to engage young people by holding focus groups and inviting those using services or even those who have used services in the past to offer their reflections on that experience. Multidisciplinary meetings and professional conferences invite young people to speak about their experiences and make recommendations for policy or system changes. In some contexts, such as mental health and child welfare, young people are routinely organized into advocacy groups and act as public educators, and they are invited as speakers at annual meetings with high-level agency personnel and other stakeholders. Even within planning meetings for intervention with particular young people, case reviews almost always include time for young people to express their feelings and thoughts about the interventions and the plan for changing their lives (Crowe, 2007; Ginwright & James, 2002).

All of this reflects an increasing understanding among service providers that young people have a voice of their own, and that in spite of some different language conventions, this voice is valuable and therefore must be heard. This democratizing trend in the helping professions represents a declaratory commitment to patient rights, consumer voice and youth engagement as the core indicators of progressive thinking on how services are delivered. Although these initiatives are intended to render services for young people more inclusive and responsive to what young people say they want or need, these initiatives are not really about young people. Instead, they ask young people to speak about the service structures and the agency of service providers, and to make recommendations for improvements within these structures and within the manner in which service providers and individual professionals connect with young people. In other words, incorporating young people's voices into program design and service delivery recognizes the **structure/agency dilemma** of the service system, but it fails to recognize or respond to the structure/agency dilemma of young people themselves. Practitioners and policymakers ask young people to help them do their work differently, structure their programs in more responsive fashion, and adjust legal, policy and system contexts to reflect their interpretation of what young people have said. But they don't ask young people to exercise their own agency in relation to the structures embedded in their life-space.

We argue in this chapter that life-space intervention strategies must be connected to the agency of young people rather than just respond to the voice of young people as they provide feedback on how our service delivery structure engages them. In order to get started, we need to take a moment to define our terms. What exactly is meant by *agency* and *structure*, and in what ways are these two concepts connected?

What Is Structure?

The term *structure* is used in many ways in professional literature and in discussions about programs and service delivery. Terms such as *organizational structure, program structure, family structure* and *policy structure* appear frequently in our professional language. In addition, references to structural change, structural adjustment and structural barriers, as well as restructuring, are popular. Each of these terms can be interpreted in myriad ways. In practice, however, we provide very little context for these terms when we use them. The term *organizational structure*, for example, is often equated with the organizational chart that depicts the departments in an agency and describes the positions people hold in relation to the organizational hierarchy. *Program structure* is often used interchangeably with *program routines*, *family structure* is defined as the membership and roles of people in the family, and *policy structure* is synonymous with the collection of legislation and regulations that influence service provision. Conversely, structural barriers are often thought of as including excessive red tape, inaccessible institutions or poorly thought out legislative or regulatory requirements. Restructuring, within a narrow articulation of structure, is linked to program closure, the shifting of management positions or the appointment of a new supervisor.

All of these ways of describing structure share a focus on the visible and identifiable building blocks in a specific institutional or organizational context (for example, the group home, the child welfare agency, the family or the school). Structure in this context describes the arrangement of individual elements within a group of elements. For example, the structure of a particular family might consist of Mom, Stepdad, the client and two brothers. The structure of the group home could be said to consist of the supervisor, the staff, the residents, the building, the program, and the policies and procedures.

When we apply this method of describing structure to a young person's life-space, we may encounter some difficulties, since life-space is not constituted solely by elements that are visible or easily identifiable. The life-space represents neither an institution (such as a group home, treatment centre or family) nor an organizational context (such as the children's mental health service sector or the education sector). To the contrary, the life-space transcends institutional and organizational categories. As we suggested in Chapter 1, it incorporates physical, mental, virtual, and relational dimensions into one unified group of elements with a focus on learning within the life-space.

The concept of structure is more complex than a simple description of particular elements. Structure not only describes how elements within a group of elements are arranged, but also entails the relationships between such elements (Giddens, 1979; Parsons, 1937). Structure, contrary to our more intuitive understanding, is dynamic rather than static. In addition to representing the building blocks of a complex whole, structure delineates how each of these blocks is related to the others (DiTomaso, 1982). The relationships between the building blocks of structure can be active, such as when decision-making is devolved to the front-line staff, or passive, such as when front-line staff make no decisions at all because in a culture of top-down decision-making they perceive themselves to lack authority. When the relationships are active, the structure is two-pronged. Descriptively, it maintains the elements of hierarchy, but dynamically (or relationally) it transcends that hierarchy by reversing core processes associated with hierarchy, such as the direction of decision-making. When the relationships are passive, the descriptive and the dynamics elements of structure are mutually reinforcing, and the organization operates precisely as one might expect it to given its hierarchical structure.

The concept of structure must be explored along with its mutually reinforcing relationship to agency. Structures are constructed by agency, but structure has a self-sustaining quality that transcends the impact of agency. In society, structure organizes the social lives and activity of the members of society, and therefore is only slowly affected by societal agency. We can identify the various elements of societal structures and have some confidence that these will be in place for some time to come. For example, most societies include an element of government, which provides leadership and enacts the laws (another element of societal structure) we live by. We can also explore the dynamic or relational aspects of various societal structures and have some confidence that the dynamics among these elements will prevail over longer periods of time. For example, we might reasonably expect that government will pay attention to what people want, and people will pay attention to what government does – at least in the Canadian or U.S. context. Describing structural elements in a particular society and observing the dynamic relations between such elements help us understand how societies function. Describing the elements of "government" and "people," and examining how governments and people interact in Canada or the United States, help us understand the foundation of modern democracy.

Structure and Young People

In the context of a young person's life-space, structure is more complex. The life-space may contain building blocks that can be described, such as the family, the school, the group home and the peer group. However, this list tells us nothing about the life-space of any particular young person. Virtually all young people have these building blocks as structural components of their life-space, but the structure of the life-space manifests itself quite differently for each young person. It is in the relational connections between these elements that we can begin to understand the structural context of a young person's life-space.

Such life-space might be structured hierarchically – one building block takes on a dominant role and influences the young person's responses to other elements of the structural context. For example, for many young people the peer group takes on the dominant role in the structure of their life-space during adolescence, and all the other elements become subordinate to interactions within the peer group structure. For some young people, video games have been elevated from an activity to a structural element of life-space, gradually dominating other elements, such as family and even the peer group, to assume a central role in the life-space (Block, 2008; Gentile, 2009). In both situations, we often encounter family conflict and school exclusion as consequences of structural rigidity. The young person withdraws from other structural elements such as school and family in order to maintain the dominant one – in these cases, the peer group or video games (Adler & Adler, 1998; Prinstein & Dodge, 2008). But this does not mean that young people can create their own structures within the life-space at will. Instead, the dynamic or relational context of life-space structure is affected when the young person resists the rigidity of other structures. This resistance is, in fact, the young person's agency.

When we consider the arrangement of various structural elements in the life-space of a young person, additional complicating factors can be identified. The virtual and mental dimensions of the young person's life-space represent structural elements that may not be identifiable to anyone but the young person. Indeed, in the mental and virtual dimensions of a young person's life-space, it is difficult to distinguish structure from agency. In effect, the young person uses agency to create structures that reflect a reality that is not visible to anyone – it is a personal and internal reality within which the young person navigates.

The structural elements of the mental and virtual dimensions of the life-space are no less "real" than those that can be identified and observed by others, but these elements are uniquely real to the young person involved. This puts us, as practitioners, in a very difficult position. Our approach to seeing structure as the combination of visible and identifiable elements in an institutional or organizational context has not prepared us for this kind of more nebulous structural context. While we typically have some experience navigating within the structural context of institutions, including family and peer groups, we are not well prepared to navigate the structural context of a young person's imagination. During in-home family support work, for example, we are able to identify the structural elements of the family membership, and to observe some of the challenges that might be involved in how these members relate to one another (Garfat, 2003). We are not well placed, however, to identify the structure of the family as it is imagined by the young person through whom we became connected to the family in the first place. As we work toward restructuring the ways in which the family members relate to one another, we may or may not be restructuring the subjective reality of the young person's life-space, since that reality may be based on an imagined family structure rather than on the one we encounter in our observation of the family.

This is an important insight into thinking about structure in the context of life-space intervention – structure is not an objective reality to be moulded into what we think will be effective or positive. Instead, structure is the arrangement and relational connection between elements of the young person's life-space as these are created and manipulated by the young person. Structure is, therefore, the product of agency. In the context of life-space intervention specifically, structure is the product of the agency of the young person within the mental and virtual dimensions of the life-space. As we will see later in this chapter, however, even this statement proves only partially viable. Structure may well be the product of agency, but the agency responsible for any given structure is itself an outcome of that structure as well.

What Is Agency?

The term *agency* is not commonly used in child and youth care practice outside of its conventional use referring to an organization. Thus, we speak of the agency that provides family support services, or an agency that is known to be a good employer. Another meaning of this term, however, refers to the capacity of individuals to act on their own behalf and to exert influence on the environment in which they live. Thus, we speak of a person having agency in the sense that the person has capacity to initiate action or respond to the actions of others, to the impact of some outside circumstance, or to the influence someone else is exerting on him or her. An effective way of capturing this meaning of the term *agency* is to think of it like this: People have the capacity to be their own agents of change. They can act to effect change within themselves, to change the context of their everyday lives, or to counteract some outside influence on their lives (Côtèa & Bynnerb, 2008; Woodman, 2009).

The concept of agency is an important consideration for practitioners involved with young persons who face various challenges. Much of the service system has its ideological roots in the belief that human services are fundamentally about helping others to "catch up" in terms of socio-economic status, mental health functioning, educational performance, or behavioural conduct. In this framework, catching up usually refers to the social norms defined by the systemic structures within the context of the young person – education, behaviour, mental health, and so on. Moreover, this ideology has a deeply embedded belief that the helper has the power to improve the lot of the person being helped. Achieving the societal norms in any of the contexts listed above is a function of how well the helper does the job. Here we often encounter a double standard in professional human services. When young people do well (meaning that they come closer to reaching societal norms), the helper gets credit for a job well done; when young people do not do well, it is often framed as their fault rather than the inadequacies of the helper's approach. Thus, we end up with terms such as *doesn't fit the program, unfosterable, resistant,* or even *damaged beyond repair.*

The implications of this ideology are quite significant in terms of how we allow agency to manifest itself among services, professionals and clients. In most of our service contexts, the agent of change is the program or service or, in some cases, a specific helper (professional). It is the helper (the program or the specific professional) who gives life to agency and who takes on the mantle of the agent of change. Programs and professionals exert their influence on the everyday experiences of the people being helped, and they often alter the structural contexts of young people in order to improve their lot in life.

We can identify this dynamic in virtually every context of child and youth care practice. When a young person is admitted to a residential program, it is the effectiveness of the program's structure, the usefulness of the program's routines, and the skills and decisions of the program's staff that ultimately decide the fate of the young person. Where we are assigned to a young person in a school setting, the improved performance can be attributed to the teaching methodology of the classroom or the teacher, the structural features of the environment (lower student-to-teacher ratios, more individual attention, etc.), and how practitioners follow through on performance expectations in spite of the behavioural challenges from the young person. In the context of a community-based outreach service, it is thought that the material offerings of the program (food, clothing, shelter) and the skills of the workers will produce change for the young people involved.

In all of these situations, agency is bestowed upon those who provide help, but not on those for whom that help is provided. When the roles of young people are limited to absorbing the effects of the help that they have been offered then the only room they have for their own agency is to resist the efforts of those trying to help them. Within this framework, the resistance or active engagement against those helping efforts is used to explain negative outcomes. Young people under these circumstances are thought to have failed to take advantage of the opportunities offered or to lack the capacity for improvement.

The consequence of denying young people agency, or the capacity to be the agents of change in their own life-space, is that the engagement that occurs in programs, in services, and with professionals is limited to a form of interference. The virtuous goal of such interference is to effect change in the more challenging areas of the young person's life-space, that is, areas of dysfunction, high risk, lack of safety, or poor performance. In practice, however, such interference can be quite indiscriminate. Areas of potential competence may be diminished or altogether excluded from the process of change and areas of risk or dysfunction may increase. Moreover, this approach makes young people the observers in the shifting dynamics in their own life-space, and, not surprisingly, any new dynamics that are introduced in the interests of change fail to produce sustainable outcomes. When young people are unable to exercise their agency and when the agency of others (programs, services or professionals) is withdrawn, the new dynamics revert to the old ones or morph into something even more problematic and risky than what was there before the intervention occurred.

Working with Agency

Recognizing the agency of young people renders our work more complex but also more meaningful for the young person. Our work becomes more complex because the purpose of our becoming involved with a young person shifts. Rather than helping to effect change in young people's life-space, our purpose becomes to empower their agency and to guide them as they exercise their agency in meaningful ways. What constitutes a meaningful way of exercising agency depends on the structure of the young person's life-space. Recalling that the structure of the young person's life-space has been created by the young person exercising agency (sometimes not entirely consciously) in the first place, we then come to the very difficult and complex relationship between agency and structure, which we have referred to previously as the agency/structure dilemma. In our work with young people we must find ways of providing opportunities for them to exercise their agency in their life-space. However, at the same time, the core reason for our presence in young people's life-space(s) in the first place is to represent the essential functions of societal structure(s) and therefore to mitigate their agency. To the extent that young people's agency sets up battles with structure that are self-defeating or that perpetually condemn them to a place of defensive reaction and social alienation, we must understand the agency/structure dilemma and the process of structuration from the perspective of young people.

Agency, Structure and Structuration

It is very common for child and youth care practitioners to do things not because they want to but because they feel they must. In a residential context, for example, they may impose consequences on young people for using profanity. Although practitioners may use profanity on a regular basis when around peers, and although our society recognizes that the use of profanity is common and generally acceptable among friends, the majority of residential programs throughout North America have rules prohibiting the use of profanity. When a young person breaks this rule, consequences must follow. This is an example of structure determining the actions of practitioners, or, in other words, of agency becoming subject to structure. In the day-to-day work of practitioners, agency frequently becomes subject to structure. There are many ways that employment structures, for example, can limit the possible actions of practitioners. Such structures determine when practitioners work, where they work, how they work, how they report about their work, when they can excuse themselves from work, and so on. Legal structures determine what practitioners must report to child protection authorities, the rights of the young people we are working with, and practitioners' own rights with respect to their employment context. Program structures might determine what practitioners do from moment to moment and how they engage with the young persons in their care, while authority structures set the rules for decision-making, the capacity to circumvent rules, and the role of any given practitioner within the larger, often multidisciplinary team. If we examine closely the role of structure in the everyday work life of the practitioner, it is clear that structure is a determining factor in what the practitioner actually does, and that agency is limited by the commands of structure.

Young people are also significantly affected by the structures embedded in their life-space. The many different places in the life-space each have their own structural configurations. Schools have rules about conduct and expectations about performance. Families have often deeply entrenched hierarchies and role allocations, as well as behavioural and performance expectations. Even peer groups can be hierarchically organized, with some young people taking the leadership roles and others assigned to follower tasks and roles. Young people who are involved with more institutionalized services, such as residential care, hospitalization or office-based therapy, experience structure in overt and often intrusive ways. In those situations, rights and responsibilities are clearly delineated, policies and procedures are outlined from the start, and conduct expectations are vigorously enforced.

A Place for Agency

With the commands of structure constantly hovering, it is sometimes difficult to imagine a place for agency, whether this is the agency of the practitioners in their work with young people or the agency of young people in their everyday life-space movements. For the practitioners, we could argue that agency is present in the relational components of their work with young people. At least in the context of relationships, practitioners can develop their own set of rules and norms that correspond to their comfort zone pursuant to boundaries and the vulnerabilities of Self. Even in this context, however, we find that there are structural limitations in the form of imposed boundaries that are often articulated as policies and procedures or job descriptions. For the young person, however, even in the context of relationship, structure determines agency, because the rules of relationships between young people and practitioners are generally set and implemented primarily by the practitioner.

Within this formulation of the structure/agency dilemma, it appears that structure dominates agency, and that agency exists in small measures but always at the behest of structure. This is the core argument of structural determinism, which has provided the foundation for many major social theories, including structuralism, Marxism and existentialism, all of which draw substantially on the bio-social theory of Darwinism (Cho, 2010; Giddens & Held, 1982). The implication of such a one-directional relationship between structure and agency in the specific context of life-space intervention is very significant. Our efforts to assist young people experiencing difficulties in life will logically focus on the structures within their life-space. Since their agency is either dormant or driven substantially by the commands of those structures, it would clearly make sense for us to aim our interventions at helping young people conform to the expectations of structure so that their experiences of chaos, risk, and severely unbalanced situations and circumstances are minimized. Indeed, some of the dominant clinical approaches in child and youth care practice (as well as in related disciplines) are precisely aimed at doing this – behavioural approaches, cognitive-behavioural approaches, and even family systems approaches take as their starting point the idea that a successful outcome of intervention restores the preponderance of structure over agency by collapsing the young person's resistance to the commands of structure.

It is also possible, however, to formulate the structure/agency dilemma confronting young people using the opposite configuration, that is, a one-directional relationship that privileges agency over structure. Indeed, this has been the core ingredient of most medical models in child and youth care practice. In these models, young people are constructed as the problem that needs fixing – their actions, whether behavioural or mental health related, are the cause of structural imbalances in the various places of their life-space. Family dysfunction is seen as the result of the young people's anti-social behaviour or mental health crises, school failure is the result of their capacity deficits or behavioural escapades, and struggles in institutional care are the result of their disobedience and deviant mind set. The imposition of control over young people requires adding rigidity and inflexibility to the structures (rules, consequences, expectations, physical containment, chemical interventions), and the control and structure are direct responses to the agency of young people. In this formulation of the structure/agency dilemma, the goal is relatively simple: By denying young people their agency, the structural imbalances in the life-space are corrected and young people's conformity to structural commands is re-established (Pazaratz, 2009).

Story: The Sweet Treats

Jerome generally preferred not to accept case assignments in hospitals, partly because he really disliked the food there. But since he had just wound up his work with a young person in a group home, he reviewed the file of the young woman in the hospital anyway. It didn't take long for him to decide that this would be a great assignment. Apparently this young woman had been admitted to the hospital's juvenile psychiatric unit as a result of repeated incidents of self-harm. While she was initially thought to be making good progress on her road to recovery, after about three weeks she took a turn for the worse. Since then, she had repeatedly tried to harm herself using food utensils, bathroom mirrors and even metal bed frames to scratch her wrists and arms. Her behaviour had escalated considerably and she was refusing to engage with any of the interdisciplinary team members at the hospital. In fact, in spite of many attempts on the part of the hospital staff to make her more comfortable in the unit and to engage her positively, her only response was that she hated the food at the hospital.

In response to her behaviours, the hospital psychiatric team had upped her medication dosages and the nurses were increasingly taking a hard line with her, withdrawing TV privileges and confining her to her room more and more. After nearly eight weeks, everyone was at their wits' end. It was decided to contract with a child and youth care professional to provide greater supervision, monitoring and control of this young woman.

Jerome arrived at the hospital with his pockets full of sweet goodies. When he was led to Jennifer's room, he entered partially, leaving the door wide open, and introduced himself. "Hi there, my name is Jerome. I work with young people in places like this, and I was asked to come here and spend time with you." "Well," Jennifer responded, looking directly at him, "you'd better go home again because the food here is terrible." Then she turned away and didn't say anything else. Jerome quietly took out a chocolate bar and placed it on her dresser. "I'll be back later and check in on you," he said before leaving the room altogether.

Surprisingly, it turns out that the one-directional formulation of the structure/agency dilemma has very similar outcomes regardless of whether agency or structure is the primary focus of developing an intervention strategy for young people experiencing difficulties. As practitioners, our goals quickly become shaped in a way that reinforces the preponderance of structure over agency, whether this is driven by a focus on the young person's acceptance of conformity (cognitive behavioural approaches) or by the imposition of control as a way of denying the young person agency altogether (chemical interventions).

The emphasis on structure is problematic from the life-space intervention perspective, because the young person exercises considerable ownership over the life-space even in the face of substantial and sustained challenges to this ownership by adults. As we suggested in Chapter 1, young people are able to circumvent attacks on their physical life-space by reconstructing their life-space within the mental and/or virtual dimensions. Whether young people use social networking sites to create an identity that they are prevented from assuming in the material living space (the group home, the family) or whether they simply imagine a different lived experience compared to what has been constructed for them, it turns out that the structure/agency dilemma for young people contains many more possibilities than the one-directional relationships articulated above.

Structuration Theory

Social theorists in the 1950s, 60s and 70s argued either that structure determines agency or that agency determines structure. In response, British social theorist Anthony Giddens (1973, 1979, 1990) offered an alternative formulation late in the 1970s that has become a core element of virtually all social theory: **Structuration theory**. This theoretical formulation resolves the structure/agency dilemma by suggesting that the two are locked in interdependency through a perpetual dynamic of co-creation. On the one hand, societal agency is indeed directed by structure. However, in responding to structure, members of societies never respond exactly as structure would have it. Instead, the societal actors' collective responses to structure are approximations of the perceived expectations or commands of structure. When ritualized and habitually repeated, the degree of deviation from what structure really would have us do refines the structural norms in its image. The actors' responses to these newly recreated structural norms will again be approximations, and once again the ritualized and repeated manifestation of societal responses will re-refine the structural norms. This process of mutual shaping will go on endlessly, thus creating a perpetual mutual interdependency between agency and structure, a process that Giddens (1979) labelled the process of structuration.

Structuration sounds more complicated than it actually is. By way of example, let's consider a multidisciplinary team, consisting of a teacher, one or two child and youth care practitioners, and a consulting psychologist, who are trying to provide an ordered and safe classroom to a group of adolescents who demonstrate challenging behaviours. To create safety, the team develops structured routines and expectations, using a point and level system to regulate the youths' behaviours. The young people's behaviours do become less concerning over time – this is a reflection of structure determining agency. From time to time, however, a young person experiences behavioural problems that escalate quite severely, and the team is wondering why such behaviours are not being mitigated by the high levels of structure. After some reflection, the team realizes that some behaviours are symptomatic of significant pain on the part of young people, and responding to such behaviours requires that the practitioners on the team develop less control-based relationships with the young people. Thus, the actions of the young people in the classroom determine the direction of change in the structure of the program. Their agency has moved structure into a new and different phase.

In the context of the life-space experiences of young people, agency and structure function in a similarly **symbiotic** relationship. Their agency both shapes the structure of the life-space and represents a response (or reaction) to that structure. For example, most families function based on a constant reinforcement of the family culture. The extent of rules and expectations are based on the outcomes of the children's performance, and that performance both responds to and reinforces these rules and expectations. Parents may, for example, have imposed particular routines related to completing homework while also ensuring that the children participate in social and recreational activities with peers and in the community. The children perform well at school, thus reinforcing the appropriateness of having abundant access to friends and community.

Similarly there is symbiosis of structure and agency within the context of the virtual dimensions of life-space. A highly anxious young person, for example, may manage anxiety by constantly seeking reinforcement from relationships in the life-space as well as by posting updates on the social networking site, or creating "status" statements that demand a response. "All is lost" or "Life is upside down" will prompt enquires and reassurances from friends, thus providing reinforcement that others are present and attentive, and the anxiety will be well-managed and under control.

The mutual reinforcement of agency and structure can also take on **dialectical** characteristics. The culture of a family, for example, may shift from a laissez-faire approach to one that is rigid and intolerant in response to repeated acts of disobedience or irresponsibility on the part of a young person. In this scenario, the structure of the young person's life-space is reshaped based on the outcomes of agency, and the young person exerts agency via responses that are increasingly incongruent with the evolving structures present in the family, which further accelerates the reconfiguration of family structure toward more rigid and intolerant responses and structure. If a young person fails to participate in the established homework routines at home, and obtains poor grades at school, parents may suspend the young person's access to friends and community until the outcomes at school change. The young person, in turn, may resent this shift in family structure and routines, and become increasingly distant from the expectations and rules at the home. Thus, the young person reinforces not the past structure of "give and take," but rather the evolving structure that is becoming less tolerant of the wants and desires of the young person. Similarly, the highly anxious young person may fall victim to the anxiety if the sought-after reinforcement that all will be well is not regularly obtained. The structure of mental health will shift from being well-managed to unpredictable. As this shift unfolds, the inability to predict outcomes will further increase the anxiety.

In a dialectical relationship, agency and structure reconstitute each other, and the process of reconfiguring both agency and structure intensifies as a result of the incongruence between the two. Rather than reinforcing one another through the congruence of agency and structure, in the foregoing examples structure changes agency and agency changes structure in an ongoing evolution.

Consequences of Structuration

Structuration theory provides us with two insights into the dynamics of service provision for young people experiencing difficulties in their lives. First, as the arbitrators of structure, service providers share responsibility for how the young people receiving their services respond. When service providers respond to deterioration in the behaviour or performance of young persons in their care, they may well be initiating a dialectical process of structuration. In more familiar terms, they may be laying the groundwork for a power struggle in which winning and losing are the only two possible outcomes. In the parlance of structuration, one possible consequence is a withdrawal of the right to agency on the part of the young person so that the structure of the service can maintain full control. The other possible consequence is the loss of the young person altogether, manifested by service exclusions, unplanned discharge, or the disappearance of the young person.

In a school setting, for example, the behavioural challenges presented by a young person can lead a service provider to impose consequences such as suspensions and detentions. The intention of such consequences is to reassert the authority of the school environment and to demand compliance of the part of the young person. In some cases, this may well work, and young people will adjust their behaviours to the command of the school, thus giving up their own agency. In other cases, however, young people rebel against the consequences, and over time simply do not show up for school.

Paradoxically, the second insight provided by structuration theory is that young people exercise considerable control over the service provider. Their agency can lead service providers to fundamentally change or adjust their approach to service provision, even if such changes or adjustments are, on the surface, contrary to the young person's interests or desires. When service providers make changes in order to reassert control over young people, what they are really doing is acknowledging their lack of control in relation to the young person's agency. It is the agency of the young people that is controlling the impetus for change, though that agency does not typically affect the direction or substance of change.

In a residential program, for example, the non-compliance of a young person may lead to the withdrawal of privileges and the cancellation of program activities, thus inadvertently changing the nature of the residential program from one that is community-focused and nurturing to one that controls and contains behaviour. The agency of the young person has altered the structure of the program. It has also altered the everyday experiences of the staff on the job, the requirements for follow through on consequences, the expectations for team communication and worker consistency, and many other factors that are affected by the shift from one type of service provision to an entirely different approach. In this way, far from having exerted control, the residential program has been subjected to the control exerted by the agency of the young person.

The Relational Context of Structuration

Virtually all the helping professions – certainly in child and youth care practice – broadly understand that **relationship** is a central component in the interactions with young people (Austin & Halpin, 1987; Brendtro, Ness & Mitchell, 2005; Burns, 1987; Charlesworth, 2008; Fewster, 2001; Garfat, 2008; Parry, 1999). However, the position of relationship with respect to the structure/agency dilemma is rarely explicitly considered. Yet it is precisely the position of relationship that creates the opportunities for life-space interventions that transcend the concepts of control and compliance. Indeed, the relational concept of "the space in-between" articulated by Garfat (2008) is fundamentally about locating relationship within the structure/agency dilemma of the young person's life-space.

Story: Specialty Programming

Jerome knew that his meeting with the hospital team was not going to be an easy one, but he was determined to convince them to ease up on the restrictions on Jennifer. After four weeks of working with her, he had learned a few things about her in spite of her otherwise closed-off posture toward him. For one thing, she didn't really mind the food so much at the hospital. In fact, she seemed to always look forward to lunch and dinner times. Perhaps more importantly, he had learned that Jennifer really did not have any expectations of anything in her life changing. Through language and body posture she was consistently conveying a sense of defeat, coupled with a fierce sense of defiance and non-capitulation.

What others saw as behavioural deviance, Jerome had come to appreciate as Jennifer's logical response to her feelings of disempowerment and irrelevance. Put simply, Jennifer did not believe that anything she did really mattered; ultimately things are the way they are, and she had no power to effect change.

While Jennifer may have felt that she could never get the results she wished for, she wasn't about to let anyone else have it their way either. The more the nurses and doctors tried to control her, the more out of control she would behave. Her ultimate goal was to matter again. If she couldn't achieve that goal by doing things that might improve her situation, then she would pursue that goal by doing things that would adversely affect everyone else's situation. And this, she had learned and Jerome certainly could confirm, she was very good at.

Jerome opened the meeting by talking about Jennifer's conduct over the past few weeks. He was very careful to align his description of any incident with the timing of consequences and restrictions for previous incidents. Then he simply stated what needed to be said. "I would like you to consider restoring her privileges, including TV, common room access, and group involvement." "Why would we do that after all of the incidents you just described?" the psychiatrist asked rather cynically. "You're suggesting that we reward her for her behaviour? Can you tell me what kind of theory this approach is based on?" Jerome responded calmly. "Jennifer has been rewarded for her behaviour for weeks now. She has become so special that you have even given her her very own program, with her very own program routines, and you are doing everything differently than you normally would just for her. The restrictions you have imposed reinforce her behaviour, and her behaviour reinforces the restrictions. This will not end until one side re-assesses their approach. If this is difficult for you, I suppose I could ask her...."

There are many possible positions for relationship in the structure/agency dilemma. Most obviously, we can position relationship as a component of the structure of a young person's life-space. In this way, relationships are considered a part of the structure of the program or service that is being provided to the young person, and they are integrated into the performance expectations of staff members.

In many cases, services are organized to position relationships in precisely this manner. In residential programs, for example, one staff member is often given the role of primary worker for a specific young person, a role that is designed to generate a special connection between that staff member and young person. Similarly in schools, one-to-one workers are assigned to particular young people as part of the service delivery structure. Relationships in these contexts reflect not so much the agency of a staff member but rather the structural organization of the service. From the staff member's perspective, the relationship exists because the job requires it to exist. From the perspective of young people, these relationships have little value outside of the role assigned to the practitioner within the (perceived) structure of the young person's life-space. Young people know that their agency in relation to these relationships will affect the structural elements of their life-space; the staff member involved in the relationship is really just an extension of that structure in the first place.

However, relationships can also be positioned in the realm of the staff member's agency, set against the structure of the service itself. In this case, the relationship may become an ally to the young person's agency within the perpetual mutual regeneration of the structure/agency dilemma. This can happen, for example, when practitioners advocate on behalf of a young person in their own service. Alternatively, the relationship may become an entirely new structural element within the life-space of the young person, disconnected from any specific service but mimicking the dynamics of the structure/agency dilemma in an entirely new context.

Relationships that are based entirely on the agency of a staff member and that are disconnected from the structure of the service pose multiple problems. For one thing, almost all service provision is based on the concept of a service plan in which a variety of individuals fulfill different elements of an otherwise unified treatment plan. It is therefore important for staff members to abide by the elements of such service plans, including those elements that reflect not so much the personalized services for a particular young person but rather the organizational culture of the service provider. Exercising agency within relationships, therefore, threatens established organizational structures regarding boundaries and engagement. Beyond this, however, practitioners are expected to act in support of a given service plan, even if they themselves are not entirely convinced that this is appropriate. While some level of advocacy is acceptable, acting contrary to a service plan is usually not acceptable.

From the perspective of the young person, relationships that reflect the agency of the staff member rather than the structure of a service may sabotage the service altogether. The staff member is, after all, a component of the service's structure, and the staff member is present in the life-space of the young person because of employment with the service provider. If the staff member's agency is incongruent with the structure of the service, the young person learns that dialectical agency, or active opposition, is an acceptable response to the structural commands of the service. In this case, the relationship provides little value to the young person who is facing his or her very own and very personal structure/agency dilemma.

Relationships and Agency

It is clear that the relational connection between practitioner and young person can neither unfold disconnected from the structural context nor reflect an extension of that structural context. Instead, this relational connection must be located alongside the young person's structure/agency dilemma rather than within it. The relationship itself becomes a navigational tool for young people that assists them to find their way through the complexities of the ever-changing and mutually reinforcing interplay between agency and structure. Moreover, the relationship aims to empower the young person's agency while at the same time guiding it toward a meaningful engagement with structure rather than a dialectical movement in which agency and structure are in constant conflict.

For example, a practitioner who engages a young person in an in-home support program operated by a child welfare agency faces several structural elements embedded within this scenario. These include the institutional and policy structures of child welfare agencies, as well as the structures related to the constitution and culture of the family unit. In addition, the practitioner is limited by the employment structure, including factors such as how many hours can be invested in this assignment, when work is scheduled, and various rules and regulations pertaining to boundaries, communication requirements with other professionals, and so on. Faced with an increasingly rigid structure in the life-space, the young person rejects the assistance offered, thereby moving precariously close to being subjected to more imposing structures, such as being removed from the home and placed in a residential program.

The relationship between practitioner and young person in this scenario must carefully avoid becoming an extension of movement in either direction within this dialectical process. This means avoiding both of the following messages: "You cannot continue to refuse to do what your family and the child welfare organization ask, and therefore I am here to help you comply with these demands" and "You are a victim of your family and the agency, and I am here to help you fight to have it your way." The first message creates a relationship that is an extension of the structure, while the second message represents an alliance with the young person's agency without attention to the realities of structure. In either case, the dialectical movement within the structure/agency dilemma (from the perspective of the young person) is reinforced, and the relationship will move the scenario toward the point of crisis and rupture. Instead, the relationship between practitioner and young person must be positioned so that it reverses the dialectical movement of the structure/agency dilemma without limiting either the young person's agency or the requirements of the structure. An appropriate message to frame the relationship therefore could be "This is where you are by yourself; let's see where we can get to together." This message frames the relationship as a possibility for change, but it does not impose a particular content or direction for that change. The structural realities in the life-space of the young person are maintained and continue to influence the young person, who is empowered to exercise influence and agency over these structural realities in ways that might create outcomes that are acceptable to and/or desirable for everyone involved.

The relationship itself provides opportunities for the young person to exercise agency in a more reflective and strategic manner. The practitioner's presence in the life-space becomes a resource for the young person rather than another imposing structure to be fought, resisted and ultimately rejected. For the practitioner, the guiding question becomes "How can I interest and assist this young person in re-establishing congruence within the structure/agency dilemma?" Given the focus on both the structure of the life-space and the young person's agency, the practitioner avoids the temptation to be the one responsible for generating change. Rather than imposing change within the structure of the young person's life-space (for example, insisting the parents change the household rules such as extending curfew or reducing homework time) or trying to change the behaviour of the young person (or example, imposing rewards and consequences, level systems, or other types of incentive programs), the practitioner focuses on the relationship itself and on the role of the relationship as a resource in the young person's struggle to manage the structure/agency dilemma.

Story: Stepping Back

Although Jennifer had significantly improved her behaviour in the unit over the past few weeks, Jerome was not entirely happy with the way things were going. He wasn't accustomed to having to work so hard to make a connection with a young person. On the one hand, he had fought hard to get the unit to stop its ever-tightening, control-based regime around Jennifer, and this strategy had produced the effect he had hoped for. Jennifer stopped escalating her behaviours almost immediately and, for the most part, began to display a much more pleasant disposition toward the nurses and even the doctors. On the other hand, Jennifer now frequently approached Jerome with further requests to "get things" from the unit. Somehow she seemed to think that Jerome's role was primarily to negotiate on her behalf. This relationship didn't seem quite as equitable as Jerome had hoped for.

After some reflection on his part, Jerome decided to approach Jennifer with his concerns. "I am worried that you are using me to get the things you want, but that you don't really care much about connecting with me on a deeper level. We don't seem to be able to talk about anything other than how to get the unit to change the rules or ease up on expectations This is not making me feel very good."

Jennifer seemed puzzled by this comment. "What are you saying, Jerome, you don't want to be on my side anymore?" At first, Jerome didn't know how to respond to this; he had been prepared for a comment of this nature, but now that she had said it, he was temporarily tempted to go on the defensive and to reassure her. Without such reassurance, he thought, their relationship would take some major steps backwards. But he caught himself just in time, and he knew that "getting back on her side" was not the answer to the current dilemma. So instead, he said, "I want you to take some time and think about where your side is and where you want me to be. Ultimately, you have talked about wanting to get out of here, but also wanting to feel confident that once you are out you'll be able to handle yourself in a good way. So how can I help you get out of here without robbing you of your confidence? Do you think what we are doing together right now will get you there?"

Are You Insane???

Source: Laine Robertson

Life-Space Interventions and the Structure/Agency Dilemma

So far, we have established that young people are subject to a structure/agency dilemma in which they are influenced by the structure of their life-space while also maintaining influence over the specific manifestations of that structure. Conflict arises when structuration (the perpetual reshaping of the structure/agency dilemma) becomes incongruent and takes on an increasingly dialectical character. Within this dynamic, agency continues to reshape structure. However, this reshaping results in an ever-increasing divide between the requirements of structure and the desires of agency.

Therefore, the building blocks of an intervention strategy include at least three fundamental principles:

- The goal of intervention is to re-establish congruence within the structure/agency dilemma.

- The relationship is positioned alongside the structure/agency dilemma rather than within it.

- The intervention itself is directed at the process of structuration rather than the structure itself or the agency of the young person.

In support of these three principles of life-space intervention, we can identify four core concepts that will shape the everyday presence of the practitioner in the life-space of the young person. These are the concepts of caring, engagement, relationship and boundaries. These four core concepts have in common a passive, or non-intrusive, position in relation to the structure/agency dilemma of the young person. This is not to be confused with the concepts themselves being passive. On the contrary, caring, engagement, relationships and boundaries are active concepts that render the togetherness of practitioner and young person a dynamic and ever-evolving experience. Yet their active character does not require an alliance with either structure or agency, nor does it mitigate the roles of either structure or agency. Each of these concepts allows structure to exist in response to the agency of the young person while also empowering that agency to influence the structures to which it responds.

In addition, these four concepts encourage interventions that are firmly positioned in the life-space experiences of young people. Recognizing that structure represents one component of that life-space, these concepts empower young people with agency to exert influence over their life-space in ways that will shape their everyday experiences within that life-space. Further, each of these concepts provides opportunities for life-space interventions that take into account the various life-space dimensions outlined in Chapter 1. As we suggested there, a young person's life-space is not limited to the physical places where life unfolds – it also includes the virtual, mental and relational spaces that shape everyday life. One of the challenges of dealing with a dialectical movement within the structure/agency dilemma of a young person is the multiple articulations of that dilemma that are possible given these dimensions in the life-space. It is, after all, entirely possible that while there are incongruencies in the structure/agency dilemma of the young person as we see it, the young person has created congruencies by shifting the focus of agency to the virtual dimension of the life-space. Life-space interventions in relation to the structure/agency dilemma of a young person therefore require not only a focus on what we see, but also a focus on the young person's articulations of the life-space that we cannot see. While we will devote separate chapters to the concepts of caring, engagement, relationship and boundaries in the context of life-space intervention, the roles of these concepts are briefly highlighted here, specifically in relation to the process of structuration.

Caring

Young people are almost always suspicious about the substance of our caring. They question whether we really care about them and they observe carefully how we care for them. Young people are acutely aware that our caring for and about them takes place in the context of being paid to do so. In their minds, this significantly alters the value of our caring, and it certainly raises questions about the integrity of that caring. Verbal reassurances that we genuinely care ring hollow, especially early on in our relationship with the young person. Therefore, practitioners have to work hard to convey their caring for and about the young person in ways that are meaningful and sincere from the young person's perspective. There is frequent temptation to align oneself with the struggles or challenges articulated by the young person. The intended message of this approach is "See, I really do care about you and you can trust me." However, giving in to this temptation commits the practitioner firmly to the agency of the young person in spite of the structures affecting life and the practitioner's role. Such an approach is likely not sustainable, because the time will come when practitioners have to either position themselves against the agency of the young person (in response to high-risk behaviours or predictably undesirable outcomes) or realign themselves with the structures of the young person's life-space and the practitioner's employer. When this happens, not only is the message of caring undermined, but it is exposed as insincere. From the young person's perspective, the experience is best captured by "See, you didn't really care about me after all," thus further diminishing openness to relational engagement.

Caring in life-space intervention and in the specific context of the structure/agency dilemma must therefore be targeted differently. Specifically, practitioners have to position their expressions of care (both in the context of caring about and caring for the young person) in relation to the ongoing dynamics of the structure/agency dilemma and how the young person is experiencing this dilemma. This means that caring targets the life-space experiences of the young person rather than the current dilemmas in any component of the life-space. Targeting these experiences requires us to be open to exploring the whole spectrum of life-space experiences, including experiences embedded in the mental and virtual worlds of young people, such as mental processes, the imagination, virtual technologies, and experiences in a variety of relationships. In other words, caring is expressed by providing opportunities for young people to be honest about how they looks at things, where they spend their time physically and virtually, and how they construct their agency in relation to the structures affecting them every day.

Caring requires a curiosity and interest in how young people try to affect the structures within the life-space, and how they respond to the impact of these structures on their own agency. Our caring is directed at acknowledging, but not judging, their approaches to structuration.

Engagement

At the beginning of this chapter, we pointed to a number of engagement strategies that have become common in service settings for troubled young people. These include engaging young people in developing strategies for change, asking for their feedback on how we provide our services, and including them in the development of intervention plans and strategies.

Engagement in this context is always well-intended, but it invariably mitigates the agency of the young person because it ultimately seeks to impose change within the structure/agency dilemma facing the young person. In practice, this approach to engagement attempts to either enforce new standards and directions (additional structure) onto the agency of the young person (behaviour modification strategies, rewards and consequences, incentive programs) or alter the structures surrounding the young person in such a way that his or her agency is forced to respond differently (out-of-home placements, adding one-to-one supports at school). This approach to engagement is not congruent with the approach to caring cited above. While we are open to allowing young people to present life-space experiences and their approach to structuration, we then move to control these experiences and this approach in order to reconfigure the structure/agency dilemma, thus mitigating agency and the ability to act on the structures that affect young people.

Fundamentally, the role of engagement in the context of life-space intervention is to challenge young people's agency by identifying with them how their agency affects the structures embedded in the life-space. Such challenges cannot simply be limited to young people's actions at home, at school or in the community. They must also incorporate the virtual dimensions of the life-space and reinforce the foundation of caring we have already created in relation to the experiences of the structure/agency dilemma.

Relationship

Caring and engagement are without a doubt the core ingredients of relationships, but they are not the only factors that affect our relationships with young people. Indeed, rather than being constituted by caring and engagement, relationships provide a context for our caring and engagement – it is within the context of relationship that our presence in the life of the young person becomes meaningful. Meaningful relationships in this context require more than a coming together of two individuals; they require a framework for being together physically, mentally, relationally, and virtually.

Young people exercise agency in their relationships with practitioners in much the same way as they exercise agency with respect to the structures of their life-space. The relationship with the practitioner is one component of that life-space, but it is one that stands apart from the everyday structures of the life-space. The goal of the relationship within the context of life-space intervention and the structure/agency dilemma faced by the young person is to ensure that the young person has a way of reflecting agency in relation to structure. This means that the relationship is a safe space for the young person to explore the possible effects of agency. In this way, the relationship transcends the physical concept of being together and evolves into a much more complex and comprehensive structure in the life-space of the young person. A relationship that is open to the young person's life-space experiences, including those that are virtual and therefore less visible and identifiable, provides opportunities for the young person to explore approaches to structuration and provides feedback in a non-judgmental and non-directive manner.

Boundaries

All aspects of the life-space are subject to boundaries. Fences, for example, mark physical boundaries in the life-space that a young person travels in, and, for some people, strong cognitive structures limit or place boundaries around painful memories and experiences. Relationship boundaries set by practitioners are often part of the structure imposed by policy directives or organizational cultures. However, to the extent that practitioners exercise agency in the setting of interpersonal boundaries, these reflect the practitioners' sense of Self and their experience of the relationship with the young person. In the context of life-space intervention, specifically as it pertains to the young person's structure/agency dilemma, one important consideration with respect to the setting of boundaries is the acknowledgment that the young person also sets boundaries. Given the importance of allowing the young person to exercise agency in the relationship, respecting the boundaries set by the young person is paramount.

Boundaries, however, are not static and dormant – they are an active component of the process of structuration. Interpersonal boundaries are negotiated in the context of relationships. As relationships evolve and the parties are experiencing one another in ever-changing contexts and situations, the relationship itself becomes a microcosm of the structure/agency dilemma. Boundaries will affect the relationship, but the relationship simultaneously affects the boundaries. This is one of the reasons why meaningful relationships between practitioner and young person cannot be governed entirely by boundaries set through policies and pro-cedures or organizational cultures. Relationships that cannot accommodate evolving boundaries are not sustainable over time and are inherently limited in their role as a reflective resource for the young person (Gharabaghi, 2010). Reflecting on and examining boundaries and the process by which the young person exercises agency over boundary structures becomes a significant part of the focus of life-space intervention.

Moving from Theory to Practice

In this chapter, we have explored in some detail the role of structure and agency in the life-space of young people, and we have suggested that there is an ongoing dynamic that relates to how structure and agency are connected to each other. The core lesson of this chapter has been that one cannot meaningfully engage in life-space intervention without recognizing and respecting the agency of young people. Life-space interventions generate sustainable change in the everyday experiences of young people and use the agency of the young person as the core resource to generate and sustain such change. Young people are recognized and promoted as the agents of change in their life-space. The role of the practitioner is to empower young people to exercise their agency wisely.

At the same time, the connection between structure and agency articulated in this chapter provides opportunities for practitioners to guide young people through the many reality checks provided by life's ups and downs. Taking responsibility, planning ahead, recognizing natural consequences, and practising discipline and perseverance all signifi-cantly affect the process of structuration. Young people must find their way through these lessons as they exercise their agency. What is important from the practitioner's perspec-tive is that these lessons cannot be imposed through the agency of the practitioner, nor can they simply be inserted into the structures of the young person's life-space.

All of this theoretical contemplation is relevant in everyday practice. It speaks to the importance of really thinking about core concepts of life-space intervention in multi-dimensional and complex ways. Concepts such as caring, engagement, relationships and boundaries are often taken for granted and interpreted in superficial ways. In reality, it is at the level of these concepts that life-space intervention takes shape. Therefore, the seemingly mundane and routine tasks associated with these concepts must be subjected to a renewed and critical consideration in order to ensure that life-space interventions are sensitive to the complex possibilities presenting themselves for young people and their pathways to adulthood.

Discussion and Exercises

Reflection in Practice

Consider a time in your professional practice when you felt powerless. Choose a time when you had no control and you were told what you must do, and yet you fundamentally disagreed with or failed to understand the logic of the "rules" that were defined for you to operate by.

1. What was your reaction? Consider and describe your feelings, thoughts, and actions in this circumstance.

2. How did you reassert your control or power? Did you use legitimate or illegitimate means of influence?

3. How did the rules change? Was there a direct change? Or was it indirect and subtle (or slow to occur)?

Reflection on Practice

In the story about Jennifer, identify examples of the following:

1. The rules and structures of a hospital adolescent psychiatric program, and the intent of those rules relative to keeping young people who are in the program safe

2. How Jennifer exerted agency on the hospital social system

3. How Jerome focused on the structure/agency dialectic that Jennifer was engaged with

Reflection for Practice

Consider a young person you know who is engaged in a dialectical struggle between agency and structure. Reflect on how you might begin to intervene in the life-space of that young person.

1. To begin, apply the following six questions to the young person that you have in mind.

   - What is your reaction to this young person? Consider and describe your feelings, thoughts, and actions in this circumstance.

   - How do you reassert your control or power with him/her? Do you use legitimate or illegitimate means of influence?

   - How have the rules changed? Was there a direct change? Or was it indirect and subtle (or slow to occur)?

   - What are the rules and structures of the program? What is the intent of those rules relative to keeping young people who are in the program safe?

   - How is the young person exerting agency on the program social system?

   - How can you focus on the structure/agency dialectic that the young person is engaged with?

2. Once you have identified the structure, the young person's agency, and the elements of the dialectic as you know them thus far, reflect on the dimensions of the life-space and on how the young person structures his or her life-space. Take some time to consider where you need to explore further:

   (a) Physical

   (b) Mental

   (c) Relational

   (d) Virtual

3. Consider how best to approach that exploration in a way that focuses on the process of structuration.

Theory in Action

Structuration theory postulates that people are at the same time the creators of social systems and created by a social system. Freedom to act and the constraints of the social norms and rules are delicately balanced in the creation of a functioning social environment.

Consider the concepts that are part of structuration theory and identify examples of them in your day-to-day life-space.

1. What are the norms and rules that you follow? How do they change from location to location? Relationship to relationship?

2. What freedoms are "given" to you by key players in the social system? What freedoms do you "act" to take within the social system(s) that you are in?

3. Over which social system do you have the most agency? What have you influenced there?

CHAPTER 3

Caring: The Foundation of Life-Space

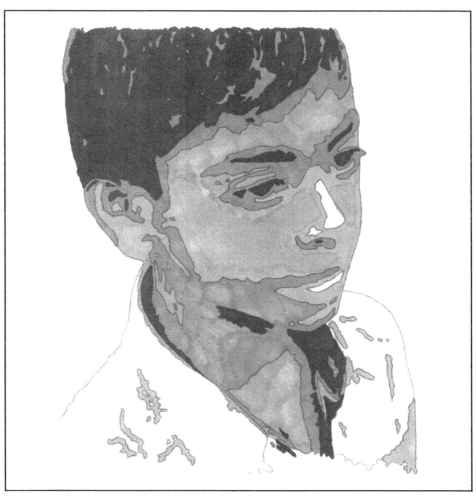

Mehdi

Source: Kyle Stewart

In spite of its prevalence in our professional language, the concept of caring is under-developed in child and youth care practice. While we might acknowledge the importance of caring for the young people we serve, we typically spend very little time exploring what caring actually means. Beyond the common usage of the term, which indicates a sense of concern for and attention to a particular child or youth, there has not been a great deal of deeper contemplation of the concept in our discipline. Yet caring, arguably, is the very core of what we do, and once we begin to explore this concept from the perspective of life-space intervention, we quickly realize that it is also one of the more complex aspects of our work.

The concept of caring is often articulated as an emotional disposition toward the other (Ainsworth & Fulcher, 2006; Bosworth, 1995; Brannen, Mooney & Statham, 2009; Mandell, 2008). In this sense, caring for the other is a function of our Self. It is an expression of our emotional response to the other as a particular person, or to the context in which the other's life unfolds. Thus, we might care about a young person because we are triggered by specific characteristics, personality or vulnerabilities. Or we might be expressing empathy, recognizing that the situation is a difficult one, perhaps harmful, painful or otherwise representative of a broad range of challenges. The social construction of childhood innocence further promotes a generalized form of caring. We are emotionally responsive to childhood vulnerability, struggle and trauma. On the surface, such a simple construction of the concept of caring makes it a virtuous one – caring reflects our humanity and our capacity to express empathy and deliver nurture. However, simple constructions of core concepts may result in our taking for granted the caring values and processes that, in fact, are not present.

When we limit our conscious understanding of the concept of caring to one that focuses on an emotional response to the vulnerability of a young person, we risk becoming less responsive as we become accustomed to the vulnerability of the young people we encounter. Our repeated (perhaps chronic) exposure to young people who have been neglected, traumatized or abused, or who are challenged by their unique functioning or limited capacity, creates pressure to re-evaluate the strength of our emotional responses in order to maintain our own health and well being.

"Be sure to take care of your own Self" is good advice for new practitioners. Caring deeply about young people simply because they are vulnerable is not sustainable over time. In child and youth care practice, high levels of vulnerability among the young people we serve are the norm – this is why we are there in the first place. But we cannot limit our understanding of caring to an emotional response to vulnerability. When we come to recognize or accept vulnerability as the norm, our emotional responses flatten out and our capacity to care is diminished. When or if this happens, our caring becomes limited to the extraordinary circumstances of those young people who have out-of-the-norm stories. While we might still care about the others too, caring is no longer an active, conscious process that is a significant component of our life-space intervention.

Presence

We can conceptualize caring in a different way – one that explicitly reflects the life-space context of our work. The concept of **presence** can help us transcend the emotional qualities of the caring process. Being present in child and youth care practice creates an emotional readiness and a deep desire to relationally engage the everyday life experiences of the young person, including the spaces and places where these life experiences unfold. Our presence is reflected in part in our physical coming together with the young person at home, in school, in the community or in a residential setting. However, it is also reflected in our engagement with the life-space itself, whether or not the young person is physically present. This is a critical component of caring in child and youth care practice. Young people experience their lives not only in relation to where they are physically located at any given moment, but also in relation to how they perceive their role and place in informal and formal settings, such as the family, the peer group, the group home, and the community. Therefore, our presence within their understanding and memory of these settings contributes to a relational connection that extends beyond our scheduled time together with the young person (Anderson-Butcher, Cash, Saltzburg, Midle & Pace, 2004).

Story: Mehdi's Big Move

Mehdi's anxiety was boiling over as he and his social worker pulled into the driveway of the group home. Only 13 years old, Mehdi knew that this was the beginning of a major journey. He could never return to his family's home after all the shame and embarrassment he had caused them by getting arrested for breaking and entering into the neighbour's home. All of that just to find some alcohol. Now he was kicked out of home, violently so, and the social worker told him that he had to live in a group home for a while. She couldn't tell him for how long though. "We'll have to see what happens," she said. The group home looked like a normal house in the neighbourhood, except for all the cars already in the driveway, and for the teenagers hanging out on the front porch smoking cigarettes. Everything looked scary to Mehdi, and he tried hard to cover up the fact that he had been crying just minutes ago.

After they entered the group home, a guy introduced himself as one of the staff and asked them to come and sit in the office for a bit to talk. Mehdi followed along, trying hard not to look around for fear of what he might see. "Get me out of here," he thought to himself. When they got to the office, the guy said his name was Mike, and then he pulled out some cookies and a soft drink from one of the cabinets. "I know I always feel better with some sweets when I get anxious," he said to Mehdi with a smile. "I wonder what you are thinking right now," he asked, still extending the box with the cookies to Mehdi. "Cookies?" thought Mehdi. "I get arrested and kicked out of my house and the guy offers me cookies?"

Mike interrupted his thoughts and started laying out what the afternoon would look like. "All right, Mehdi, I won't tell you not to worry, because I know you will anyway. And I won't tell you to relax, because you won't for a while. But over the course of the afternoon, we have to figure out together what you want your bedroom to look like, the kind of food you like, and what activities you like. We also need to know who in your life you're missing the most right now – your friends, your relatives, or whoever – so we can start right away to figure out how you can maintain all of those connections. So what do you say, do you want to talk here or would you like me to take you around the house a little and talk while we're looking around and meeting some of the other people in the house?"

Therefore, caring in our everyday practice becomes less an emotional concept and more an action-oriented concept. The desire to be present in the life-space of the young person is translated into active engagements with the multiple dimensions of life-space. These include tangible and material places where the young person is physically engaged; virtual spaces, such as social networking sites, where the young person experiences community; and imagined spaces, such as the young person's daydreams, visions and fantasies. In this sense, our caring is targeted at the space between the young person and ourselves, rather than at the young person. The space between us is where caring finds its relational foundation, and this is where caring requires an invitation to the young person to share (and explore) the life-space together. The message is not "I like you" or even "I care about you." It's "I am here with you" or "We are here together."

Understanding caring in terms of being present in the life-space significantly expands the possibilities for life-space intervention. In practice, one of the limitations for practitioners is time – very rarely do practitioners have the luxury of physically being with the young person around the clock. Even in the 24/7 context of residential group care, shift schedules and employment standards dictate the patterns of presence between young person and practitioner. When caring is seen as an emotional response requiring a physical presence with the young person, the constant shift from presence to absence based on work schedules creates stress, and may highlight the isolation of the young person during times of absence. In contrast, when practitioners actively seek to be present in all of the dimensions of life-space – including those with no material basis, such as the mental and virtual dimensions – they remain relationally connected to the young person even when physically absent. Young people experience their lives through spaces and places in which they are not present; that is, they think about family, peers and other settings while preoccupied elsewhere. When young people's reflections on these settings can include the practitioner and the young person's connection to the practitioner, life-space intervention is no longer limited by logistical issues such as work hours.

It is critical to understand the notion of presence beyond the physical context. We are also present in a young person's life-space symbolically, whether we were aiming to be or not. Unfortunately, our unintentional symbolic presence often has negative implications because it is often characterized by our absence. We are missed. The more successful we are in creating a connection with a young person through our physical presence, the more likely our absence in other settings is noticed and lamented. Ultimately, then, the experience for the young person of our physical presence may be suspect. As we provide the young person with the experience of being cared for only when we are physically together, we inadvertently create a framework for the young person through which all other life-space experiences can be interpreted.

For example, imagine a young person participating in an after-school program and feeling cared for and connected to a particular practitioner. In this specific component of the life-space, the young person experiences the benefits of nurture and a sense of belonging. Upon returning to the home environment, where such nurture and sense of belonging may be less evident or even be absent, the contrast to the experience of the after-school program is strong. If the practitioner has not somehow engaged the home component of the young person's life-space, either through a symbolic presence or through a physical representation such as a **transitional object** (a photograph, a card, a special object that connects the young person to the practitioner), the young person experiences a rupture within the life-space.

This rupture means that there now are identifiable but unintended boundaries between components of the young person's life-space. Within some borders, there is caring and nurture, but once the boundary is crossed physically, these experiences vanish and the young person returns to an experience of isolation and alienation.

Ruptured life-space is a source of tension and stress for young people. The various components of life-space become increasingly disconnected and the emotional response to the experience of life-space becomes dispersed. To navigate through ruptured life-space, young people must change their disposition in response to different components (settings and relationships) of the life-space. Sometimes they must be guarded; at other times they must confront aggressively and sometimes withdraw.

Caring in child and youth care practice is about unifying the life-space experience for the young person. We can do this by ensuring that the practitioner is present physically and symbolically throughout that space, thus creating continuity and safety for the young person to develop a personal identity while exploring the life-space.

Exploring Places in the Life-Space

When meeting a young person for the first time, one of the tasks for the practitioner is to put into action a caring response, one that reflects a deeper understanding of caring, by initiating a mapping process. Mapping entails exploring a young person's life-space – the locations of importance to that young person, including any virtual settings, the relationships that preoccupy the young person's heart and mind, and the spatial dimensions of thoughts, dreams, fantasies and imagination. From a life-space intervention perspective, caring means that assessing the young person's behaviour, performance and conduct are secondary to gaining an understanding of the person's life-space. Caring is expressed through this exploration, or mapping, of the life-space and all the engagements of this life-space that follow.

It is not enough to simply identify places in a young person's life-space. Frequently, identifying such places is already partly done through the process the young person participated in when formally beginning the relationship with the practitioner. These intake processes typically gather information about the young person's school, home life, and sometimes community involvement. They may also address important current or historical relationships with other practitioners. However, most of this information is descriptive, and the descriptions reflect the perspective of whoever received the information and made note of it. The descriptions often miss the mental and virtual dimensions of life-space that are more subjective and less likely to be recorded.

Mapping a young person's life-space is a much more complex process through which the practitioner finds access points to engage the young person rather than simply describing a particular place or relationship. The goal of this mapping process is to uncover spaces and opportunities for the practitioner to become present. For example, when young people talk about their social networking sites, practitioners can explore that space together, and perhaps create a connection to their own pages (becoming "friends"). This is one way to become present in this virtual dimension of the young person's life-space. In the physical dimension, such as the school setting, the practitioner may visit the school after school hours with the young person, simply to create a presence within this component of the life-space. Symbolic representations of presence can be found in the memory of a game of tag or catch, or simply the memory of walking and exploring the grounds together. Similarly, the practitioner may explore a young person's home environment, including the bedroom and the common areas, the video games, the neighbourhood and the local convenience store. Meeting the young person's friends and developing a connection with that peer group, however superficial and distant, will allow the young person to communicate about particular experiences with that peer group – "You know my buddy Eric? He got suspended" or "Remember Shiva? I think she's good looking." If the practitioner did not try to be present among the peer group, the young person likely would not share these experiences within the life-space – what is the point of speaking about a friend the practitioner has never met?

Using our presence as the basis for caring cannot be limited to engaging with physical places, peer or family relationships. People of any age are often preoccupied with virtual or imaginary spaces rather than the physical places through which they move. Mapping the life-space, therefore, also entails exploring these nonphysical spaces from the perspective of the young person. In particular, the practitioner may explore the dreams,

Story: Mehdi's Nightmares

"They're just dreams, Mehdi," she said casually from the office chair where she had been sitting all morning. "Don't worry about it, and make sure you get your morning routines done before you leave for school."

Mehdi liked Sandra, the staff member who most often worked the morning shift at his group home. She rarely dished out consequences, never raised her voice, and he thought she really liked him. What he didn't like was that she was too casual. She always minimized the issues he wanted to talk about and her response was pretty much the same every time: "Don't worry about it; focus on what you have to get done; it'll all be all right in no time." A while ago, Mehdi had woken up from a nightmare early in the morning, and Sandra came running into his room. When he told her that he had had a nightmare, she again reassured him that dreams are not real and that he

would be all right. In her usual casual tone, she said, "If you have another nightmare, just remember I am here. Call me if you need me." "That's the problem," Mehdi thought to himself as he drifted back to sleep, "she is out there, but she's not in my nightmare to help me out when I actually need it."

Later that afternoon, Mike had come on shift. Mehdi had casually mentioned his nightmare to Mike. Mike wanted to know what it was about, and so Mehdi told him. After that, Mike was preoccupied with some other issues, but he came up to Mehdi's bedroom that night with a hand-drawn poster of himself and Mehdi holding big Viking swords and looking angry. "What's that?" Mehdi wanted to know. Half seriously and half jokingly, as he taped the poster to the wall above Mehdi's pillow, Mike said "Well, just in case those bastards from your nightmare come back tonight, we'll be ready for them."

The Nightmare

Source: Talia Jackson-King

anxieties, fears, hopes and aspirations of young people, and how these are manifested visually in their minds. It is not simply a matter of asking, "What are you hoping to do for a living when you grow up?" The practitioner needs to join the visual imagery of a young person's future, to learn how fantasies are manifested, anxieties contemplated or fears coped with. The practitioner is seeking to engage (but not intrude on) spaces that are central to the young person's experience of the life-space, but that remain invisible to outside observers. For example, finding a presence in a young person's anxieties about failure acknowledges that the anxiety is real and legitimate. It also invites the young person to work through it with the support of the practitioner rather than camouflage it through behaviour, aggression or withdrawal. An abstract or simple drawing of the practitioner and the young person shielding each other from the anxiety monster (for young children) or a gift of a worry doll or stress ball (for teenagers) creates a presence for the practitioner within the experience of the young person's anxiety.

In this way, exploring real or imagined places that constitute the life-spaces of young people becomes an expression of caring that transcends the limitations of an emotional response. Moreover, using one's presence in the life-space of the young person avoids the pressures associated with sustaining emotional connections, not only for the practitioner, but also for the young person. For the young person, the fear of disappointing a caring practitioner is mitigated through the ongoing presence of the practitioner in the life-space.

The caring connection is not a function of emotional attachment and its continuous hunger for reaffirming experiences of such attachment. Rather, it is manifested by the togetherness of the individuals, and their affirmation of a common interest in and engagement of the space between them. In short, caring in child and youth care practice means to be present, fully and completely, throughout the life-space.

Shaping Place and Space

Earlier we identified caring as an action-oriented concept, based on our intentional presence in the life-space of the young person. It follows from this that caring is an active and intentional process, and therefore our presence in the life-space is not a passive presence. On the contrary, we give life to this presence by shaping the life-space wherever possible. We do this because the young person's experience of the life-space provides the foundation for both developmental growth and identity formation.

It is important in this context to articulate clearly the difference between shaping the life-space and simply exerting control over the young person. This is especially important given how easily we resort to imposing control as a way of mitigating safety concerns or self-destructive behaviours on the part of the young person. In light of the vulnerabilities of young people and how easily these are exposed, imposing control in order to avert further harm and possibly even trauma seems reasonable. However, we also know that young people accomplish very little in developing a sense of Self, an identity, and the capacity to manage the unpredictable nature of everyday life, when they are subjected to external controls over longer periods of time. Our focus on safety may, in the long term, be counterproductive (Ungar, 2008, 2009), and our need for compliance and conformity from the young person likely reflects our own insecurities and needs more than the young person's needs (Fox, 1994; Phelan, 2008, 2009).

Shaping the life-space is not about controlling the young person. Instead, it provides opportunities for the young person to explore the life-space and, in a context of emotional safety, nurture and an ongoing experience of feeling cared for, understand how to respond and manage the various entanglements that are present there. Under conditions of extreme vulnerability, it is difficult for young people to pause long enough to consider their options for next steps or future directions. For many young people, the need to remain on a set path, no matter how self-destructive, results from the everyday stress and tension experienced in the life-space. Very often, and perhaps ironically, this stress is amplified by conflict and tension in those components of the life-space that are designed to set the young person on the right path – the group home, the special school, or the probation office. This often happens because practitioners, following the structure of the program, fail to distinguish between imposing control on the one hand, and their capacity to shape the life-space of the young person on the other hand.

From the life-space intervention perspective, there are always opportunities to express caring and give the young person an experience of being cared for. In the context of the young person's everyday experiences of the life-space, the warmth and humanity associated with shaping the physical environment and the relational connections of the young person convey a mutual respect and a foresight with respect to the young person's needs in the moment. As we will demonstrate below, the practitioner finds opportunities for bringing caring to life by shaping the life-space of the young person. Indeed, using proactive, preventative and interventive approaches to shaping the life-space of the young person is the core of child and youth care practice. It is, perhaps, even a prerequisite for all other engagements with the young person (Ainsworth & Fulcher, 2006; Bath, 2008; Krueger, 2009).

Proactive Shaping of the Life-Space

Although more associated with a particular branch of the American psychology movement of the 1960s, the German term *gestalten* captures very closely the essence of the proactive approach to caring in life-space intervention. *Gestalten* literally means "rendering," and is typically used in German to describe the purposeful creation of a particular mood, atmosphere or physical appearance in order to accomplish a particular goal. When throwing a birthday party for a pre-teen youngster, for example, parents often spend extraordinary time, energy and resources to create a particular mood or physically dramatic set for the children attending the party. For example, if the party is based on fairy tales, parents spare no expense to ensure that the cake, napkins, balloons, and even the paper plates and disposable cups represent the fairy tale theme. In this sense, the parents are engaged in the process of *gestalten* – they are taking purposive actions to convey a particular feeling, mood, and atmosphere for the party.

Child and youth care practitioners can also proactively manifest caring in the life-space of a young person. In the context of a group home, for example, the young people's bedrooms can be decorated in accordance with their interests and preferences, and they can be offered a cup of hot chocolate on a cold day without having to ask for it. These are examples of proactive ways to make the physical space one that involves nurture and the experience of being cared for. Being proactive to ensure that components of the young person's life-space reflect caring is a critical element of child and youth care practice. However, it is often neglected, since practitioners take on a reactive stance instead. Being proactive really means anticipating the opportunities for caring experiences on behalf of the young person by always remaining conscious of a young person's experiences in the life-space, regardless of what the specific setting in the life-space might be at any given time. Such proactive engagement with the life-space sets the tone for the relational presence of practitioner and young person.

Setting tone as a function of child and youth care practice is not always an obvious process. As we discussed in Chapter 2, practitioners often deny themselves their own agency in the ever-evolving "dance" with structure. In particular, the physical environment is easily mistaken for a structural element of the work with young people that the practitioner is thought to have very little control over. In fact, this is not accurate. Exerting influence on the physical environment to create a more caring environment simply requires additional consideration for the role of tone in practitioner–young person engagements. Tone manifests in the way in which a young person experiences presence in the environment while being engaged with the practitioner. Tone can be anxiety-provoking and tense, or it can be nurturing and safe. Practitioners exert considerable influence on the direction of tone in their interactions with the young person. The previously cited example of decorating the bedrooms of young people according to their preferences creates a structural element in the setting of tone. Further, the implications of having done so together create a constant presence for the practitioner in the life-space of the young person.

It is also possible to proactively affect tone in the moment. Offering hot chocolate on a cold day without being asked to do so is just one example of setting tone in the moment. Other examples might include offering a jacket while walking through the park on a cool evening, or offering food during the admission process to a group home. In these examples, the specific act of rendering the physical environment is temporary, but it incorporates into the presence of the practitioner a connection to the physical environment that the young person experiences as a gesture of caring.

The critical element of proactive approaches to caring in life-space intervention is recognizing that young people are engaged with practitioners in a spatial context. Especially in the earlier stages of the development of relationships between practitioner and young person, the young person remains highly conscious of the physical context of relational interactions and, often for good reason, maintains a guarded and protective coping mechanism. It is unfortunate that in many situations practitioners are unaware of the importance of tone setting and expose young people to experiences of the physical environment that are anxiety-provoking, threatening and altogether alienating. An obvious example is the admission process to a group home. In many cases, particularly when this takes place on a crisis basis, this process is an exercise in paperwork in which the young person is asked to sign off on various documents, is given a summary of rights and responsibilities, and is escorted to an impersonal and probably scary bedroom. Even when practitioners are making an effort to sound caring and considerate, and are actively trying to ensure the young person is as comfortable as possible under the circumstances, the experience is still exceedingly difficult for the young person. Setting tone is not about being polite and considerate. It is about intentionally and proactively generating a relational presence in the life-space of the young person that provides the first indications that the environment itself is caring, and that caring experiences are associated with engaging with the practitioner.

Although the proactive approach is premised on the commitment to recognize young people as unique individuals with their own ways of experiencing caring, it is possible to generalize beyond our engagement with a specific young person. Proactive approaches to caring that extend beyond individual relationships require a focus on at least two concepts that are essential aspects of life-space intervention: Nurture and aesthetics. Nurture is not simply well-meaning and caring gestures by individual practitioners. It also unfolds continuously on the basis of the emotional and even physiological experiences a person has in relation to the physical environment. We know, for example, that physical spaces characterized by significant disorder induce stress and anxiety. Some research has also been conducted on the effect of colours on mood – bright colours are stress inducing while earth tones have a calming effect. Sights, smells and sounds all influence the nurture experience of a physical space. Although there are differences in how a specific person may experience particular sights, smells and sounds, as practitioners we have some control over ensuring that the physical environments in which we interact with young people exude as much nurture as possible. In a residential care setting, choices about decor are far more significant than simply whether they reflect personal tastes and preferences. We can use what we know to maximize the experience of nurture on the part of young person. Paying careful attention to the lighting in the home (poor lighting contributes significantly to the intensity of seasonal affective disorders), the quality of mattresses we ask young people to sleep on, and even the materials used for flooring (carpets contribute to allergic reactions, which induce stress) are all essential components of nurture and proactive caring.

Similar measures with regard to smells and sounds are also proactive approaches to life-space interventions, particularly to the caring expressed through our presence. The preparation of food in a residential program or a young person's home can create a nurturing smell, especially if we have some knowledge of the preferences of the young people occupying the space. Some research has demonstrated the calming effects of classical music and jazz on the mood of persons experiencing stress. Conversely, there is considerable research indicating that the sounds of television and talk radio add stress to an environment and increase the intensity of agitation and discomfort in people. Practitioners equipped with this knowledge can shape the physical environment proactively by gradually shifting its nature to reflect these findings.

Beyond maximizing the nurturing content of the physical environment, practitioners need to reflect on the aesthetics of space and place. The opportunities to proactively shape spaces aesthetically in partnership with young people abound. Aesthetics is more personal and subjective, and therefore less guided by research findings. This creates openings for the practitioner to engage young people in the ongoing development of aesthetics. Discussing trends in colour, choosing visual art in a variety of media (photography, sculpture, painting), and designing common room arrangements or a flower arrangement for the table are all aspects of aesthetics that young people and practitioners can share to create a beautiful environment in the common places in their life-space. This too is a form of caring in the life-space of the young person and, once again, the outcomes of aesthetic reshaping reflect the practitioner's caring and presence.

Preventive Shaping of the Life-Space

Much like the proactive approach to shaping the life-space, the preventive approach seeks to render components of the life-space as conducive to the young person's experience of caring as possible. Unlike the proactive approach, however, the preventive approach focuses specifically on our mapping of the young person's life-space and our understanding of specific triggers or challenges in that life-space. We can target how we shape the life-space based on our connections to the young person through the life-space. Three preventative strategies are pre-empting tension, creating transition and escape routes, and "caring to control."

Preventive approaches shift the focus away from the physical environment toward the relational and virtual components of the life-space that are often imaginary. For many young people, tensions arise not so much from being physically present in a particular place, but from the relational associations – real or imagined – that the young person creates regarding particular places in the life-space. The home environment, for example, provides opportunities for proactively shaping the life-space through the decor, smells and sounds of the home setting. This does not, however, address some of the relational sources of tension that often take precedence for young people.

Pre-empting tension requires practitioners to be present in the real or perceived relational conflicts of the young person. For example, a young person may experience chronic tension as a result of constant comparison and under-performance relative to a sibling. The tension is carried throughout all of the experiences in the many settings of their common and individual life-spaces. The practitioner can find opportunities to be present in sibling rivalry in various ways, including addressing the problem head-on with both siblings, reducing the frequency of triggers by limiting the opportunities for head-to-head competition between siblings, or simply acknowledging the burden associated with living with an overachieving sibling. Recognizing that a particular relationship is a source of tension in the life-space of the young person provides the opportunity to acknowledge the young person's struggles and challenges. It also ensures that such tension does not become the foundation for a pattern of responses to others who trigger feelings about such competitive tensions. More importantly, it provides the young person with an experience of being cared for, inasmuch as the practitioner has found a way to be present in an ongoing area of conflict for the young person.

In addition to pre-empting tension in the life-space of the young person, practitioners can also shape the life-space by creating **transition paths** and **escape routes**. These are critical elements of preventatively shaping the life-space, since the identification of tension and potential sources of conflict alone does very little to help the young person develop effective coping mechanisms or resolutions to such tensions and conflicts. Given our articulation of life-space as a unified space in which experiences in one setting are carried through to other settings through the virtual or relational dimensions of the life-space, it becomes very important that the road map for navigating one's life-space include options for a wide range of routes and paths. A relational tension at home that influences the young person's functioning at school points to a transition through these components of the life-space that has failed to mitigate the emotional impact of the tension at home. New transition paths are required that allow the young person to convert the relational tensions at home into manageable discomforts that can be temporarily sidelined in order to focus on functioning effectively in another setting.

Without a commitment to understanding young people in the context of their journeys through their life-space, practitioners often inadvertently push them through transitions that offer no comfort or prospect of resolution. Instead of acknowledging the presence of tension from a different setting in the young person's life-space, practitioners focus on persuading the young person to sever the connection between the settings and to view the unified space as a collection of discreet spaces, each disconnected from the next. Such transitioning is ineffective, and the young person experiences this advice as uncaring. In such a case, the expectations of the practitioner have become primary and, having provided much input, the practitioner is now waiting for the young person to make a chronically unsuccessful transition path successful.

Similar to transition paths, escape routes are essential features for managing the life-space of a young person. It is not reasonable to expect a young person to successfully resolve all points of tension in the life-space. Instead, some tensions can be avoided, so long as an escape route readily presents itself. As practitioners, we must remain vigilant about the escape routes for young people. It is useful in this process to take inventory of the possible routes a young person has access to when tension is encountered in the relational life-space. For example, where a young person has a history of getting into trouble when associating with a particular peer group, what alternative activities are available to that young person to limit or avoid altogether interactions with that peer group? Practitioners can provide escape routes more easily than most other people in the young person's life-space.

Offering an alternative activity, such as going to a movie, at a time when the young person feels pressure to attend to this peer group is just one example.

In order to render the provision of escape routes sustainable, practitioners can also consider introducing the young person to new settings for his or her life-space. Recreational clubs, extracurricular activities and the like all ensure that, at any given time, the young person has alternatives to engaging with situations and relationships known to cause tension. Since the practitioner initiates the development of escape routes, thus creating presence in the young person's experience of these routes, the young person's experience of being cared for is reinforced.

Finally, and closely related to escape routes, is **caring to control** when necessary. In reality, even when transition paths and escape routes have been developed, there are still situations and moments when the preventive measures already taken to shape the life-space are not enough to prevent a significant problem or crisis. In these situations, the presence of the practitioner is required and, especially in the earlier stages of engaging the young person, the presence must be physical.

There are times when the best prevention strategy is imposed control. Caring cannot always be based on a conscious effort to mitigate the power differential between practitioner and young person. However, it is possible to impose control using the power differential embedded in the adult–child relationship rather than the practitioner–client relationship. Adult control of young people's activities is not in and of itself contradictory to the concept of caring. In fact, there are times when the imposition of control is the only caring alternative, and the young person might experience anything else as uncaring. There is safety and comfort in having someone else make the decision and in being prevented from getting into further trouble. While imposing control can unfold as a preventive approach to shaping the life-space, in enforcing such control we are moving closer to an interventive approach to shaping the life-space. This is what we will explore next.

Interventive Approaches to Shaping the Life-Space

Although conceptually child and youth care practice has moved significantly from its behavioural roots, in practice much of what child and youth care practitioners actually do still involves responding to behaviour and encouraging positive performance. In many cases, the programs in which child and youth care practitioners work are structured to provide external controls in the containment of young people's behaviour. Therefore, programs use techniques and methods that might involve point and level systems, token economies, and other ways of predictably imposing punishment for nonconformity and offering reward for compliance. In many other cases, especially where practitioners work with young people in a nonresidential context, behaviour and performance management are less overtly based on control but still involve measures that connect "growth" to the young person's behaviour and performance. In a school setting, for example, the influence of the practitioner's work is measured in relation to academic progress and the number of visits to the principal's office, the number of suspensions, or the number of significant incidents. Even when practitioners engage young people in their own homes, such as in a family support or preservation program, the progress of the young person is measured based on performance within family conflict and on following parental or guardian expectations.

Life-space intervention, or interventive approaches to shaping the life-space, does not require the practitioner to abandon behavioural or performance expectations entirely. On the contrary, expectations related to behaviour and performance should remain firm and high. Unlike behavioural approaches, however, interventive approaches to shaping the life-space do not simply use reinforcements for behaviour or performance as the intervention. This is because we recognize that challenges and troubled moments may be the norm, and such challenges and moments influence the young person throughout the life-space rather than only in the particular setting where they occur. The focus of an interventive approach to shaping the life-space is on building the capacity of young people to learn from the experiences along the journey and find ways of applying such learning throughout the life-space, especially to those dimensions that have no material basis, such as the thoughts and emotions that define their daydreams, imagination and the anticipation of what might happen next.

The foundation of interventive approaches to shaping the life-space is caring, much in the same way as caring is the foundation for virtually everything that unfolds in the relational engagement between the practitioner and the young person. Making the experience of intervention a caring one from the perspective of the young person, while we intervene to protect or redirect, requires that we be prepared for the young person's inevitable resistance. This resistance reflects the young person's projection of the consequences of intervention throughout his life-space. For example, if the practitioner intervenes in a young person's plans to hang out with peers who have previously been involved in criminal activity, the implications of the intervention extend far beyond the forbidden access to the peers in the moment. The young person may also be concerned about what other friends will say or do, self-image, and a more generalized resistance to control. The young person may worry about stories and taunting at school for having failed to meet up with this peer group, and may also need to imagine the activities of his peers in his absence. All of this adds up to significant implications in the life-space in spite of the practitioner's unquestionably protective motivations.

This intervention by itself is therefore not likely to be experienced as a caring one by the young person. Within the broader context of life-space intervention, the substantive content of caring is contained in the practitioner's acceptance of his **power to care**. The practitioner accepts the role of power in the life-spaces of young people and, in spite of having to manage resistance and any behavioural response to an intervention, the practitioner cares sufficiently for the young person to exercise the power to intervene appropriately.

In the example below, the intervention is directly linked to the practitioner's presence in the life-space of the young person, including prior connections to the peer group. Thus, the practitioner is able not only to impose restrictions on the young person's access to a particular peer group, but also to personalize this restriction because of specific knowledge of and connection to that peer group: "You may not hang out with Eric and Mohammed today, because I know that Eric especially is not thinking too straight these days," rather than simply "You can't see your friends because they're bad news."

While young people rarely greet restrictions with enthusiasm, at least in this case the restrictions are explained based on specific knowledge of the situation and those involved. The behaviour or performance of the young person is not necessarily the issue, but the circumstances of specific members of the peer group as they relate to the protection of the young person are specified. In this sense, the young person might experience this imposition of restrictions as symptomatic of the practitioner's presence in his life-space.

While protective restrictions are one important component of an interventive approach to shaping the life-space, not all interventions need be protective. In many instances – particularly where safety is not acutely threatened – the young person may be encouraged to discover the consequences of decisions, even if the practitioner anticipates negative outcomes. In these situations, the target of the intervention is the after-the-fact response to the negative outcomes. Instead of focusing on punishment and imposing consequences, the practitioner's concern is to assess and provide guidance to the young person in coming to terms with the outcomes. Sometimes, the intervention may be made to absorb the shock of the negative consequences on behalf of the young person.

When the young person's capacity to accept responsibility for the consequences of his or her actions is not yet fully developed, or when it is subject to high degrees of anxiety, fear or some other mental health–based response, absorbing the shock of the outcome may include strategies such as allowing the young person to take cover behind the practitioner, or even rescuing the young person by resolving the problem to mitigate the negative outcomes. An example of this in the context of community-based child and youth care practice is the possible response to a young person who has been caught shop-lifting. For the practitioner, the range of possible responses extends from allowing the process of the victimized shop to unfold, even if it results in criminal charges for the young person, to advocating on behalf of the young person that police not be involved, and perhaps negotiating a form of restitution to be carried out by the young person. From a life-space perspective, involvement with the criminal justice system affects many other components of the life-space, including family dynamics and access to school programs and part-time employment. It also creates embarrassment and shame for the young person. Whatever consequence is ultimately negotiated, the practitioner's capacity to intervene is, for the young person, forever associated with the practitioner's presence, thus again reinforcing the experience of being cared for even in the face of poor decision-making.

Interventive approaches to shaping the life-space derive much of their action-oriented content from the debriefing that follows. The goal of intervention is to ensure that the behaviour and the intervention are explored in the context of the full life-space of the young person rather than just in the narrower experience of a particular setting. The practitioner's concern when shaping the life-space through active intervention is primarily the path of the experience through the **material and non-material components** of the young person's life-space. Questions of immediate relevance are those that explore the experience in relation to the young person's self-image, daydreams, mental health, imagination and fantasies. Also of immediate relevance are questions that try to find a place for the experience in both material and virtual settings, such as school, the peer group, and online social networks, and the cellphone. If a young person becomes involved with the youth criminal justice system, for example, the debriefing process might consider how the young person communicates this involvement through various channels with his peer group, family and other significant persons. Furthermore, it could consider how the choice of communication format reflects the young person's self-image and real or imagined role and reputation among others. Again, by directly exploring the implications of specific outcomes in relation to the life-space, the practitioner ensures a presence in the long-term memory of the incident.

Story: The Amir Affair

Throughout his stay at the group home, Mehdi had maintained regular contact with his best friend, Amir. Amir was one of the boys involved in the break-and-enters that set off the chain of events resulting in Mehdi's placement in the group home. Mike had met Amir on several occasions. Mike seemed to like him, and he generally supported Mehdi's continued relationship with him.

One afternoon, Mehdi was very upset because that morning, a meeting with his parents to discuss their possible re-involvement in his life had not gone very well. In fact, the way Mehdi had understood his parents, they were basically saying that he would never be allowed back into the home – the shame he had caused them was just too great.

This caught Mehdi off guard. He had had a string of successes in the past few weeks, including getting a better-than-ever report card and landing a part-time job at the local Tim Hortons coffee shop. The job was an especially important success, because his father was always preaching about how back in Pakistan, kids of Mehdi's age supported the family household financially. Mehdi had tried to get a job for some time, but the local Starbucks rejected his application several times, in his mind because of where he was from. During the family meeting, none of his successes seemed to make a difference, and his parents seemed closed off to any possibility of giving him another chance.

In the early afternoon, Amir had called and asked Mehdi to join him in a secret adventure. Mehdi knew this was code for a drug deal, because Amir had been getting deeper and deeper into trouble around drug use and even dealing. Mehdi was in a rotten mood, preoccupied by his thoughts about his family situation. As a result, he agreed to meet Amir.

Mehdi was getting ready to leave just as Mike returned from grocery shopping. "Where are you off to?" he asked. "Just going to meet up with Amir," Mehdi responded, sounding annoyed and unfriendly. Mike paused for a moment, and then he simply said, "No, actually, you're not." "What the hell?" Mehdi responded, raising his voice considerably and uncharacteristically.

Mike stopped what he was doing, looked Mehdi straight in the eyes, and spoke slowly using his deep voice. "The meeting this morning didn't go as you had hoped, and I know what disappointment like that can feel like. I also know Amir and I've met some of his other buddies, and today is not a good day for you to hang out with them. End of story, you are not going!"

Mehdi was getting frustrated, half knowing that Mike was right and half resenting that he was being told he couldn't go. "Who the hell are you to tell me I can't go?" he yelled at Mike. "I'm going anyway." "Well," Mike said, suddenly smiling, "I have told you clearly that you can't go today. But if you choose to go anyway, I might choose to come with you. And you know, buddy, I'm feeling a little goofy today, so there's no way of telling what I'm going to do once we meet up with your friends."

The final element of an interventive approach to shaping the life-space is the goal of restoring confidence and health in the young person's experience of any particular incident or negative outcome. The memory of such incident stays alive for the young person, and the practitioner has a significant role in determining the nature of that memory. Will it be carried as a memory of failure and deficit, or will it be shaped as a memory of a meaningful response to a significant challenge, a successful instance of problem-solving, and a path toward restored confidence and health?

This restorative component of life-space interventions is what sets such interventions apart from other, more behavioural interventions. Behavioural intervention ends with the completion of punitive measures. The evaluation of the young person's response to these punitive measures is based on whether the offence reoccurs, or on a generalized impression about the young person's commitment to conformity and compliance with societal expectations. In this approach to evaluating growth and change, the absence of a reoccurrence can be interpreted as evidence of change. However, there is really no reason to believe that the young person has absorbed any meaningful lessons that can be transferred to the journey through the life-space. Life-space interventions, in contrast, ensure that the practitioner's relational engagement of the young person is present in the long-term memory of the situation. Restoring confidence and health means that the presence of the practitioner is associated with a positive outcome rather than with the typically negative experience of accepting the punishment. In addition, the focus on restoring confidence and health prepares the young person to carry on with the journey through the life-space without constant reminders of failure or deficit. Resolving the tension within the life-space that results from problems in a particular component or setting is critically important. Without such resolution, any intervention is one of the moment, but not one that carries forth beyond the moment and the specific setting.

Caring for the Virtual Life-Space

The association of the concept of life-space with physical dimensions in the life of young people has limited practitioners' opportunities to convey the experience of being cared for. When practitioners limit their presence to the "real" places in which young people are located (the family home, school, or residential program), much of the young person's experience of life is missed, and therefore the practitioner cannot convey caring in the virtual and mental dimensions of the experience.

Like most of us, young people spend a great deal of time imagining other worlds, other roles for themselves in the world, and a wide range of circumstances pertaining to how their daily lives unfold. For example, many young people imagine a life in which their families are different, or in which they are star performers in school, or even in which they have friends and relationships in Hollywood or the music industry. For young people, daydreams about their version of success and recognition are important coping mechanisms for the everyday experience of hardship, trauma or sadness, and the daydreams help them to establish an identity. In some cases, psychiatric disorders may further contribute to "unreal" or virtual components of the life-space that are of considerable importance to the young person. The degree to which a young person is functional in those spaces is not the primary concern. Instead, it is critical to recognize that the young person's life-space extends beyond the visible, and that its many components that are invisible and far removed from the reality of the practitioner are very real to the young person.

On the one hand, the imagination and other virtual spaces are rightfully the private realm of the young person, and not necessarily spaces where the practitioner should try to have a presence. On the other hand, when such spaces are created specifically as a way to cope with negative experiences in "real" physical places and relationships, these imagined spaces provide important connections – and perhaps synergies – for the young person's capacity to manage in the "real" places in the life-space. In this case, the practitioner's presence in imagined spaces provides an opportunity to extend the experience of being cared for beyond the trauma and emotional turmoil of the experience in the physical world.

More than ever before, it is now possible to identify the transitions between the physical and virtual dimensions as imagined by the young person. With the introduction and widespread use of communication technologies such as social networking sites and gaming, there has been a gradual shift from the in-person persona toward a persona that reflects varying degrees of accuracy and reality mixed in with a desire to breathe life into imagined persona. The ability to create a social networking profile allows young people to reflect on their actual profile and make changes, additions and deletions based on a version of the ideal profile under the circumstances. Even socially isolated young people, for example, are able to convey a sense of social connection by adding friends and generating a high level of activity on their personal site. The world of gaming takes this one step further by allowing young people to choose personal profiles based on characters that mix reality-based skills and attributes with those that are based in fantasy. More complex games allow young people to create a simulated life-space that includes everything from multiple settings where life unfolds to a wide range of interpersonal relationships. For the older youth, these games even provide opportunities to create and evolve their sexual identity. In this way, young people can take on the persona of the hero, the villain, the martyr, the superstar, or even the fighter for social justice (Crowe & Bradford, 2006).

Our knowledge of gaming addictions and other mental health concerns arising directly from participation in gaming and social networking sites confirms the importance of the virtual realm of a young person's life-space. Not only are young people active in this virtual life-space, but the safety and risk elements of their participation take on an entirely different dimension, with outcomes that frequently include self-harm, emotional breakdown and even suicide.

In many respects, the importance of such imagined worlds in the young person's life-space should come as no surprise to us. While these components of the life-space offer possibilities for personal development and identity formation that are far more complex than what is offered to the young person in the physical world, the level of guidance, supervision and debriefing in this virtual dimension is often non-existent. It is therefore not surprising that young people find themselves overwhelmed by their own creations, which emphasizes the importance of the practitioner finding a way to have a presence in the imagined world.

Whether it is in the development of a profile for a social networking site or in the context of simulated gaming, the need to perform, meet expectations of others, take action, and sustain or sever connections prevails. Measures such as the number of online friends and the level of activity on the site, or the level achieved in the game, all affect how young people experience their involvement in the virtual world as much as in the physical world. Therefore, anxiety and fear, mixed with uncertainty and the fantasy of being different (a fantasy within the fantasy) also prevail. While the virtual places of a young person's life-space may arise from a desire for something different, the identity of the young person is influenced in ways that must also be cared for. The risks of the virtual dimension are intensified when the experience of being cared for is absent, so the practitioner must ensure a presence in these virtual dimensions of life-space as well.

Ensuring a presence in the virtual dimension of a young person's life-space can take many forms. For example, taking an interest in the gaming involvement of the young person by either directly participating or becoming acquainted with the characters of the game, is one way of ensuring presence. One of the important opportunities presented by the young person's involvements in the virtual space is the possibility of reversing, or at least mitigating, the inherent power differential between the young person and the practitioner. The virtual world, driven by the personalized decision-making of the young person, is one space where the practitioner is not the expert. Thus a shared presence in both the physical and the virtual dimensions of life-space provides opportunities for mitigating issues of power and control, and for making the life-space one in which caring is experienced as genuine and democratic rather than strictly professional and elitist.

The opportunity to care for others genuinely and democratically raises further issues about how caring is operationalized in the life-space of young people. We will explore how caring is manifested in issues related to social justice next.

The Social Justice of Caring

Many of the young people we engage with are subject to multiple forms of disadvantage. While some disadvantages, such as learning disabilities, cognitive problems and mental health issues, are not themselves the outcome of social inequity, the social responses to such issues often fail to include considerations of social justice. Young people may experience discrimination, social stigma or difficulty with access to programs and services, or they may be marginalized and socially alienated as a result of prejudice and judgment about their situations. The challenges faced by these young people have root causes in poverty, racism or other forms of injustice related to human rights.

As child and youth care practitioners, we are unable to eliminate some of these barriers to social justice faced by the young people we work with. We can, however, be present in the struggles to make the world a better place, and work to improve the social conditions related to the challenges faced by the young people we work with. The broader responses of the social system(s) to inequities that are relevant to young people are very much a part of their life-space, and our presence in the debates surrounding these challenges is another opportunity to convey our caring to the young person.

For example, if we are working with a young person who encounters difficulties at school as a result of nonconforming behaviour, we can address the school's concerns while also advocating that the school uphold its responsibility to provide an education. By doing this we ensure that our presence creates an opportunity for the young person to experience our engagement in the life-space. Such advocacy is not difficult to undertake in the specific life-space of a young person with whom we have a relationship. In addition, the same kind of thinking and initiative ought to inform how we advocate for issues that are not directly related to the young person we are working with, but that reflect the issues and challenges all young people may encounter. For example, participating in social dialogues related to poverty, racism or gay rights, volunteering at the local food bank, participating in political rallies related to social justice issues, and helping with fundraising to enhance neighbourhood recreational activities all connect our presence in the life-space of the young person to a broader presence in society. These connections and our presence there reflect our concern and caring about the issues of inequity affecting young people in similar circumstances.

The importance of thinking and acting beyond the day-to-day circumstances of the young people we are currently engaged with reflects the openness of life-space intervention. Once we accept the challenge of engaging a young person in the life-space, we must recognize that we cannot map out or delineate this life-space as a closed system. In fact, the life-space is never a closed system – it interacts, expands and contracts in accordance

Story: The Ongoing Connection

April 25, 2012

Hey, Buddy!

So here I am, on this beautiful island enjoying the sunshine. My first vacation in years. I just had dinner at this nice restaurant on the beach. The view was great, but tell your mom that even here the food isn't as delicious as that Pakistani meatloaf she made when I was over at your house. I am still savouring that one.

Can you believe that you're back home with Mom and Dad? Remember how you told me you thought it would never happen? Well, there you go – sometimes it's good to be wrong. Did you take that trophy we won at the gaming competition with you? Where did you put it in your room? I think it should go right on the dresser next to your bed. A place of honour (lol)! Hey, we fought hard to win that thing.

How is your buddy Amir doing? Still getting you in trouble, I suspect. Well, you can tell him from me that I love his new tattoo, but he needs to keep you out of his nonsense. Maybe when I come back the three of us can go do something together

Guess what I did yesterday? As it turns out, on this island there are lots of homeless kids who have absolutely nowhere to go. And without a home, they are not allowed to attend school! Can you believe it? So I joined a rally to demand changes to those crazy laws. You would have loved to be there. People were singing traditional songs and dancing, and they had made these incredible signs and posters – not quite as skillful as your art, but still really cool.

Anyway, I hope your nightmares are getting better. Remember, when those big guys come after you, just picture me there with a big baseball bat chasing them away!! Not that I would encourage violence, though . . .

Take care buddy, and I'll see you as soon as I get back.

Mike

PS: Saw your pictures on Facebook! Very funny!

with social dynamics at the local and global levels. Young people themselves are attentive even if such dynamics appear far removed from their daily reality. Global economic, environmental, political and spiritual crises are sources of anxiety and uncertainty for all people, and we often underestimate the impact of these issues on the life-space of the young. Given their preoccupation with seemingly more trivial issues, we take for granted young people's ignorance of these more complex global dynamics, forgetting about the invisible structural components of life-space in which these issues are often present. Whether it is through fleeting thoughts or more active engagement with these issues, young people need to know that we are present in the broader social issues, and that our presence reflects our caring for and about the challenges and anxieties associated with being young.

Summary

In this chapter, we have argued that caring is a central element of child and youth care practice that is often taken for granted. In the context of life-space intervention, caring is represented in the practitioner's ability to be present in the places where the young person's life unfolds. Such places include not only the physical settings where the young person spends time (such as the school, the family home and the neighbourhood), but also the relational spaces such as peer groups; virtual spaces, including social networking and gaming sites; and even spaces such as the imagination, fantasies and daydreams. The practitioner's task is to find ways to be present in all of these places and spaces. Such presence can take myriad forms, including those that are proactive, those that are oriented toward preventing tension and conflict in the young person's life-space, and those that are interventive.

The core of caring in life-space interventions is shaping the life-space using strategies that focus on the specific characteristics and identity of the young person. In so doing, the practitioner must consider how young people experience and interact with expressions of caring in the physical, virtual and mental components of the life-space. This complex task requires using the sights, sounds and smells of physical settings to promote nurture and safety while also engaging with the intricacies of being present in the virtual life-space. Caring interactions are manifested with the young person's peers and family, as well as through participation in gaming and social networking sites. In addition, practitioners must be present in the local and global issues related to social inequity and social justice that are relevant to young people who are facing similar circumstances.

Ultimately, caring in the life-space transcends the emotional responsiveness commonly associated with the concept of caring. Instead, it provides an intentional, strategic approach to ensuring that young people experience their relationships with practitioners as caring.

Discussion and Exercises

Reflection in Practice

Recalling that caring is more than an emotional response to vulnerability, and that it requires presence in multiple dimensions of the life-space, assign yourself a Self-care time. As you go through that time – whatever it looks like for you – monitor and attend to your thoughts and emotions. Try to answer two questions:

1. How does caring for your Self feel?
2. When were you most present to yourself?

Reflection on Practice

In the story about Mehdi, identify or create examples of the following:

1. Proactive strategies for caring
2. Preventative strategies for caring
3. Caring interventions, such as
   (a) Protective power
   (b) Deflecting punishment
   (c) Restoring confidence

Reflection for Practice

Consider a young person you know who is vulnerable.

1. Identify the specific conditions of social inequity that contribute to the young person's vulnerability.
2. Reflect on your own commitment to local and global social justice to identify what actions in your own practice you can take to influence at least one of the following: Poverty, violence, human rights, racial hatred, gender bias.

Theory in Action

As described in this chapter, caring is not a concept involving emotional connection. Rather, caring involves action through our presence physically, metaphorically and virtually. Presence entails active engagement with multiple dimensions, including tangible and material places where the young person is physically engaged, virtual spaces such as social networking communities, and imagined spaces such as the young person's daydreams, visions and fantasies. The "subject" that the practitioner cares about is not the young person as an individual, but the space within the relationship. The message is not "I like you" or even "I care about you." The message is "I am here with you" or "We are here together."

1. Write a story about caring for a young person to illustrate these ideas.
2. Complete a search of academic journals to find out how the concepts of caring and presence have been defined by other professions or disciplines.

CHAPTER 4

Engagement Strategies for Life-Space Interventions

Johannes

Source: Kyle Stewart

Early descriptions of engagement in child and youth care practice originated from the intense 24/7 context of residential care. Early writers in the field, including Redl, Bettleheim, Maier and even Bronfenbrenner, attributed behavioural problems among young people to a lack of engagement and cited boredom as one of the core causes of disruptive behaviour.

The push for a more dynamic approach in the residential care context escalated during the 1980s and the 1990s, when writers such as Lorraine Fox and Karen VanderVen argued strongly for increased recreational and therapeutic activities for young people in residential care. The obvious argument that young people need to be engaged in activities has still not entirely taken hold in residential care settings. VanderVen (2004, 2003) still writes extensively about the need to enhance the capacity of staff and the organizational resources so that engagement in therapeutic activities unfolds as part of best practice. Gharabaghi also points to this chronic challenge in child and youth care practice:

> It is a strange profession indeed when one of the great contributors of knowledge within the profession, Henry Maier, apparently felt it necessary to remind child and youth workers that one of the things they ought to do each day is "say hello" to the children and youth they work with. One would not think that it is necessary for child and youth care practitioners to be reminded of such a basic element of civilized human interaction. (2010, p. 1)

In current practice, the focus on behaviour modification (Pazaratz, 2009) in many programs equates engagement with young people to the imposition of program expectations through point and level systems, consequences, and program routines. From this perspective staff are engaged with residents because they catch young people in their deficits, such as breaking the rules, not following through on routines, or failing to perform according to expectations. Engagement, by this definition, has limited interpersonal content and is a form of control. This type of engagement is disempowering to the young person. Practitioners engage to restore their power differential, which was violated when the young person made some personal choices.

Perhaps more frequently, engagement means interaction, including any exchange of words. In this definition, a simple exchange such as "How was school?" "It was fine" is considered engagement since the staff member has initiated a conversation and the young person has responded. Such everyday interactions between staff and young people are indeed important. However, without a more nuanced understanding of the concept of engagement, these interactions are ineffective as practice tools. In addition, they can undermine the nature of the young person's experience and confirm that it is best to avoid a more complete and sincere approach to being with others. Engagement that is superficial or fiduciary reinforces distance and separateness and therefore contributes nothing to relational child and youth care practice.

We can compile an endless list of examples of engagement that never quite transcend the superficiality or disempowerment of such interactions. What all of these examples have in common is the lack of mutuality in the experience of engagement they describe. It is essential that we move beyond an understanding of engagement as a discreet event (a redirection, a conversation, an interaction) to an understanding in which engagement is fully integrated into the experience of the young person in the context of the life-space. Thinking about engagement requires that we expand the temporal and spatial dimensions of agency and structure when we are present with a young person. Since this is a very complex idea, we will examine it in some detail by breaking it down to its core concepts, starting with the concept of mutuality. We'll follow this with an examination of the role of Self during engagement and some discussion of how practitioners can engage with young people's life-space, taking into consideration both issues of power and the process of first encountering a person, developing the relationship, and then disengaging from the relationship.

Story: Moving Again

Johannes knew that this day, the day after his fourteenth birthday, wasn't going to be a very good one. His foster parents had made it clear that they would not be able to care for him anymore given their age and health problems, but they had delayed his move until after his birthday.

Johannes had arrived in Canada from Germany three years ago with his parents, but no sooner had they arrived than his parents died in a car accident, leaving him orphaned. The local children's aid society placed him in a foster home with the elderly couple that was about to retire from fostering altogether.

The past three years were a blur for Johannes. He was far from past the grief about his parents' sudden death, but he also had to face the challenge of a new country, a new language, and his transition from pre-adolescence into adolescence. Although he liked his foster parents, in reality they provided him with little more than a safe place, some care for his basic needs, and sometimes opportunities to get involved in various recreational activities. Over the past three years, Johannes had been experiencing many troubles at school, and he had taken up smoking and recreational drug use. He also occasionally got into trouble with the law for mischief, minor theft and a couple of fights.

As a result of these troubles, his social worker had requested extensive psychological and psycho-educational testing. The results revealed a boy of high-average intelligence with possible post-traumatic stress syndrome, ADHD and an oppositional defiance disorder (ODD).

Today Johannes was to meet with his worker and a new foster family. While he had already prepared himself for the move to another foster home, he was a little anxious about one particular aspect of this new home. His worker referred to it as a "treatment foster home," and this apparently meant that in addition to foster parents, this home had a child and youth care practitioner who would want to work with Johannes. Johannes had experience with child and youth care practitioners at school; one of these workers was responsible for the behaviour contract that the principal at the school was so fond of putting in front of him whenever there was a problem. "Damn," Johannes thought to himself, "not another one of these know-it-all workers who's going to restrict my life and get everyone to mess up my plans."

Engagement and Mutuality

In Chapter 2 we explored the idea of agency as it is held by young people. The agency held by young people must be given at least equal weight in relation to the choices we as practitioners make about how to engage young people on a moment to moment basis as well as in the longer term. When we accept that young people have agency, we become open to being engaged by them rather than always engaging them. Therefore, engagement becomes a reciprocal process, or a process characterized by mutuality.

Mutuality refers to a common interest in something, whether that is a topic of conversation, an activity or an experience. Even within this very simple understanding of mutuality, we can adjust how we engage. For example, instead of asking how the young person's day at school was, we might more specifically ask how he or she did at the track-and-field meet that day. Few young people are interested in general conversations about school, but most are interested in some specific aspect of what happened at school. Therefore, asking about the track-and-field meet, a particular peer, a math test or recess increases our engagement with the young person's life-space. Mutuality targets our attempt to engage young people toward the aspects of their experience that are of most interest to them. Getting to know a young person's interests, and the hierarchy of these interests, is therefore an integral part of engagement. Paradoxically, getting to know what the young person's interests are requires engaging with him or her, since the most reliable information about interests will very likely come from the young person. Ideally, we would simply ask the young person when we first meet about interests and activities and use this knowledge in all future interaction. Realistically, however, young people are hesitant to tell us their interests (at least not in any detail) until they know us and believe it to be worth their while to do so. In other words, engagement presupposes that we have a relationship.

Just because we know that a young person might be interested in sports, however, does not mean that every instance of engagement can, or even should, focus on this particular interest. In fact, mutuality goes beyond discovering and discussing interests per se. It extends to the exploration of the moment, and any given moment presents an entirely different (and momentary) hierarchy of interests for the youth. Mutuality therefore requires that we be knowledgeable about the young person's interests; that we are astute and observant about the preoccupations of the moment for a young person; and that we are present with the young person to absorb whatever is important in the moment and enters the conversation as young people engage us. The risk of being overly enthusiastic and engaging with young people based on our knowledge of their current interests is that we impose our own ideas about previously determined interests and priorities, thereby negating the principle of mutuality.

There is an apparent paradox in the techniques of engagement as we are describing them – engagement requires some understanding of the young person's interests, but we must engage the young person in order to gain that understanding. This makes it difficult to determine where to start. The agency/structure complex discussed in Chapter 2 provides some guidance.

The very process of engagement is agency, and the knowledge we have of the young person's interests creates the structure. Therefore, the continuous and mutually reinforcing dynamic of agency and structure recognizes that learning about the young person's interests and engaging the young person are simultaneous and mutually reinforcing processes. These processes do not exist or unfold independently of each other, and they are inherently self-perpetuating. Our understanding of the young person's interests and the depth of engagement between us moves incrementally toward richer and more complex dimensions. Initially this process requires more initiative from the practitioner, but it eventually becomes a reciprocal process in which agency and structure relate to both the practitioner and the youth. Within the context of mutuality, the young person also learns about the practitioner, and is therefore able to engage with the practitioner based on the young person's understanding of the practitioner's interests. This evolving engagement comes incrementally closer to completion in the perpetual process of structuration. Within the process of structuration, the impact of engagement extends well beyond the moment and shapes the nature of the relationship (see Chapter 5) and the ongoing evolution of boundaries (see Chapter 6). Indeed, the ongoing evolution of relationship and boundaries is of interest to both practitioner and young person, and is a topic around which they can engage.

Since the development of a relationship is a component of engagement, the early stages of engagement look and feel very different than the later stages. When Maier (2003) implored practitioners to "say hello" to the young people in their care, he offered a brief but powerful reminder of the long-term importance and depth of the foundation on which engagement rests. The simple act of greeting provides the first opening to discover mutuality, since that greeting acknowledges the mutual presence of both practitioner and young person. As discussed in Chapter 3, expressing and demonstrating caring in both the physical and the virtual dimensions of the life-space further supports the building of a foundation for engagement. Caring acknowledges the mutual presence of practitioner and young person, and furthermore celebrates that presence through purposeful action on the part of the practitioner. Thus, caring is engagement, but it is engagement at the foundational level, which builds the opportunity for strengthening mutuality.

So far we have discussed mutuality with a focus on the perspective of the young person in the process of engagement. Recognizing the young person's interests ensures that engagement is not simply a matter of initiating interaction. However, mutuality is a two-way process, so it is critical that we explore the practitioner's side of this dynamic as well. With this in mind, we now turn our attention to the role of Self in the engagement process.

Engagement and the Role of Self

Engagement is both an action and a condition. We cannot experience engagement (the condition) with a young person without doing something, be that starting a conversation, participating in an activity or simply ensuring we are present in the young person's life-space. Beyond our initial action we must be prepared for Newton's third law: For every action, there is an equal and opposite reaction. When we initiate engagement with young people by asking questions about their day, for example, the response may range from an acceptance of our initiative ("I'm glad you asked") to complete withdrawal or perhaps even a counter-initiative that represents rejection ("That's none of your business"). Young people have an internalized way of receiving our initiative and we have an internalized way of receiving their responses. Practitioners need to maintain some level of control over this action/reaction dynamic. We cannot respond to rejection with rejection, since such a response would essentially confirm for the young people that we are not interested in them and their experience of their life-space. In fact, when young people hesitate or do not respond positively to our efforts at engagement, this reflects a healthy and meaningful sense of caution. It is in the best interests of young people to test out the integrity of our actions. Are we engaging them for who they are (or perceive themselves to be), or are we are simply incorporating them into a predetermined expectation of social interaction in the context of our employment (the classroom, the group home, the family home)?

The role of Self in the dynamics of engagement demands that we explore the very same question. Why are we seeking to engage this young person? Are we prepared to accept the response to our initiative as is, or are we determined to "work the relationship" until we get the response we expect?

For example, imagine a young person new to an after-school program who spends the first few moments separated from the group and isolated. To engage the young person, we might ask, "Why don't you join us for dinner at the table?" to which the young person might respond, "I don't eat with losers." This is a moment in which the practitioner has to make some decisions about the path of engagement – the response from the young person opens up several possibilities. We might respond sharply to the poor choice of words on the part of the young person and redirect the behaviour. Alternatively, we might ignore the young person's response and proceed with our dinner with the group. Either decision has a significant impact on the meaning of our first initiative. Redirection would confirm to the young person that we do not want an honest response to our question but instead expect a response compatible with the behavioural and social norms of the program. "Why don't you join us for dinner" ought to have a response such as "Thank you for asking, I would love to" or at the very least "I would rather not right now." If we choose to ignore the young person's response, we confirm that the young person's expression of momentary thoughts and feelings is irrelevant. The most engaging response might be one that acknowledges that our initial effort was sincere. We must also be clear in our own mind about why we asked the young person to join us for dinner in the first place.

Meaningful actions that engage young people require continuous evaluation of the degree to which we have been conditioned by the culture of our employment context. We cannot escape such conditioning altogether, but we can mitigate it by continuously reflecting on our Self in relation to these expectations. In the example above, our invitation to the young person to join the group for dinner requires a moment of reflection on the questions "What if I don't like the response?" and "How will I respond in this case?" Without reflecting, we miss the opportunity to complete this particular initiative. A response to the young person should acknowledge the young person's feelings in the moment rather than our own expectations related to the program culture. Responses such as "Fair enough, this might all be a little too new for you," or "With time, I hope you'll feel differently," or perhaps even "You know, many of us felt that way at first, but gradually we've grown to like each other" might be effective and could be complemented with "The invitation stands if you change your mind" or "I really don't want you to go hungry, so what would you like to eat?"

Ultimately, we cannot fault young people for responding in a way that is true to how they feel in a specific moment. However, we must be prepared to acknowledge the young person and balance our expectations of appropriate language and conduct with young people's need to express themselves in whatever manner feels intuitively right and meaningful. The role of Self during the dynamics of engagement is to provide the foundation for meaningful and respectful experiences and to counteract our preconditioned responses based on program structures and program cultures.

Up to this point, our exploration of engagement has been limited to a context of practitioner and young person, as if this concept of being together were unfolding in a vacuum. In reality, the practitioner never engages a young person outside of the young person's life-space. Engagement therefore requires not only focusing on the young person in front of us, but also exploring the young person's connections to the life-space and exploring that life-space itself.

Story: The Soccer Shirt

Safid's wife looked at him with curiosity, but eventually she couldn't contain herself anymore. "Why are you wearing this soccer jersey to work? Don't you child and youth workers have any dress code standards?"

Safid just smiled, knowing that there was no response that could satisfy his wife at that moment. In fact, Safid had struggled significantly this morning when deciding what to wear to work today. He was scheduled to attend a meeting at a foster home. A 14-year-old boy was going to be introduced at the home, and the plan was to move him there within a few days. Safid was the "treatment worker" for that foster home, and his role in the meeting today was to introduce himself to the boy and explain how the home operated.

Safid had some prior information about the boy, and he knew that in addition to the usual issues associated with a placement change, this boy had experienced considerable trauma when he lost both his parents in a car accident shortly after immigrating to Canada from Germany. Safid had read through the file in only a cursory manner, as he always did in order to balance his desire to know something about the kids about to move into his foster home while at the same time avoiding developing too many biases and wanting to avoid any preconceived notions before they met in person.

In this case, Safid had noticed that the boy had already had numerous life-altering experiences that were pretty much outside of his control. First the emigration from Germany, then the loss of his parents, and now the change of placement because his current foster parents were about to retire. Such experiences were not entirely unfamiliar to Safid, who had arrived in Canada twenty years ago as a refugee from Iran. His parents were still alive, but they lived in Iran and he was unable to return there to see them. As a refugee, Safid often had the experience of many things happening to him without his input.

"I wonder how to start the conversation with this boy," Safid had thought to himself this morning as he was getting dressed. "What if he just tells me to get lost? I don't really have a good response to that, especially because that is probably what I would have done under the circumstances."

Then Safid had an idea. "Forget explaining the program to this kid. He's from Germany, and that's where I am going to start the conversation without saying a word." Luckily, Safid found the Germany jersey he had bought during the 2006 World Cup of soccer in the bottom drawer of his dresser.

Engaging the Life-Space

Engaging the life-space of young people involves four core concepts that collectively help practitioners avoid the pitfalls of engagement that result from the imposition of rules, program routines and social expectations. These four core concepts are choice, exploration, connectivity and influence. We will briefly examine each of these below.

Choice

Engagement that is a direct result of imposing structure and routine is not based on a purposeful exploration of mutuality and common interests. The enthusiastic response of young people to recreational activities should not be confused with mutuality. Participating in an afternoon soccer game at the custody facility, for example, is indicative of compliance (not engagement), even if the young people enjoy the game. This is not to suggest that recreational programming is without merit or counterproductive; it simply means that activities based on program expectations do not in and of themselves reflect mutual engagement between the practitioners and young people. The young person has little choice, since refusing to follow the program expectations usually brings some form of consequence. Even where there is an option not to participate, the young person may see no alternatives, and therefore intentionality and **choice** are absent.

Instead of thinking about program activities as the core of engagement, we can allow young people to direct our movements. A request for a walk in the neighbourhood, sitting with a young person to review a photo album, spending time playing a favourite video game, or even meeting up with peers in the community are all ways to ensure that we are not directed by the structure of the program and that the young person can exercise agency to determine the specific context for engagement. Other examples of ensuring choice for young people include considering aspirations for the future, which may seem unrealistic under present circumstances. We still need to avoid pointing to the barriers and redirecting such aspirations to more realistic grounds, because aspirations are part of the life-space that we must engage. Similarly, young people frequently introduce themselves to us through the medium of lies, half-truths or fictional stories, which are important alternative versions of the young person's identity within the life-space. Rather than correcting the stories or labelling the lies, our focus should be on engaging with these imaginary dimensions of the life-space without necessarily endorsing them or exposing ourselves as impossibly naïve (Burrow, O'Dell & Hill, 2010).

Exploration

Engaging in ready-made activities does not require any exploration. Although the activity is presented as an opportunity to participate (or not), there is no process of exploration prior to arriving at the decision to participate. Such activities are the product of program structure, and thus young people do not have the opportunity to exercise agency. Mutuality cannot exist without agency. The activity itself may be interactive and even enjoyable, but unless there is a mutual exploration of the options possible and a true choice on the part of the young person, it is not inherently engaging.

Exploration is often absent in institutional forms of engagement, and yet it is of great importance. It is through this exploration that we mitigate the safety and logistical barriers that occur as a result of young people's agency. For example, young people may want to engage with dimensions of the life-space that are unsafe, such as the gang they belong to or a place known for its drug consumption. Similarly, young people may choose a form of engagement that is unrealistic for the institution's budget, such as spending the afternoon at the amusement park or attending a musical concert. We cannot always simply accept the desires of young people, but we can always engage in a discussion and negotiate how to proceed. Indeed, engaging young people is much more about the exploratory process of getting somewhere (real or imagined) than it is about arriving at the destination.

Exploring Connection
Source: Talia Jackson-King

Connectivity

Recreational and therapeutic activities in institutions are disconnected from the full extent of both the physical and the virtual life-spaces of young people. Unless activities unfold within the life-space, they do not connect to existing or future experiences. At the risk of being obvious, participation in a game of soccer at the custody facility does not involve playing soccer with friends or family, nor does it build an association with a particular physical setting.

Therefore, games at the facility differ considerably from pick-up games played in the young person's community. In the community games, young people encounter friends or enemies whom they also encounter in different contexts. Relationships develop, sometimes in very small increments, as a result of regularly participating in the pick-up games at the community soccer field, and the soccer field itself becomes a space of considerable importance. The associations related to the experience of playing there extend beyond the moment of the game to the relational dimension of the life-space. These associations might include who was watching the game and who was missing. There are also associations with the virtual aspects of the life-space, such as the imagined impact of a young person's performance on his or her status or reputation among the peer group, status among potential romantic interests, new friendships, and conflicts. The same game in an institutional context lacks this connection to the everyday life of a young person – girlfriends or boyfriends won't be there to watch the play, peers are there only by the happenstance of custodial disposition, and the field itself carries no important and pleasant memories.

Connectivity is a core characteristic of life-space intervention. Engaging with a young person requires exploring the connections between the moment and the life-space. We hope to engage young people as they appear in front of us, and to engage the spaces and places of their life-space. Activities such as introducing ourselves to family members, peers or other significant relationships of a young person, or visiting important places in the life of the young person such as the school, the community centre or the shopping mall, are part of this focus on connectivity. When we engage the life-space of the young person we can be present in the life of the young person beyond the circumstances of the moment. For example, rather than greeting a young person after school with "How was school today?" we may instead ask "Did you hang out with Sarah today and how is she doing?" Thus, we engage the experiences of young people in their life-space instead of imposing a specific location for engagement that is limited to where we work. We can focus on connectivity when engaging young people not only to solicit interaction, but also to encourage performance. For example, if we are concerned about a young person's motivation to complete homework, instead of engaging with a request to complete the homework, we can connect our intention to improve school performance to the life-space: "After you finish your homework, I will battle you on the Wii."

Influence

Program-based activities intended to engage young people have no influence on what happens next. Whether the young person participates in the soccer game does not influence the remainder of the day – whatever routines are scheduled to follow will indeed follow. This is a peculiar dynamic that differentiates the institutional structure from the life-space experience. Being engaged requires ways to exercise agency over what follows, but participating in institutional programming is discreet from the everyday happenings and routines. Thus, such experiences provide little opportunity to build a stronger sense of identity or belonging, or to develop extended relationships. The commitment to such activities is therefore limited – there is no influence over future events, circumstances or relationships. Participation is relatively devoid of consequences and therefore does not reflect a "change" in the practitioner–young person relationship or in the manner in which the young person experiences the life-space. Initiating change in the practitioner–young person relationship, however, is an essential goal for life-space intervention.

Unlike preprogrammed activities, engagement in the context of life-space intervention focuses on new possibilities and opportunities for what might happen next. When we engage a young person about some chronic problems with a peer group or with a particular peer, we must be open to pursuing a range of strategies that emerge from this engagement. A discussion about alternative ways to handle being bullied may (or may not) influence what we (or the young person) do later that day. Similarly, discussing a fight or conflict between a young person and a parent may result in the youth engaging with that parent. There may not be any immediate action associated with engaging a young person on a particular topic or circumstance, but engaging forms a foundation for future discussion about the same topic or circumstance. In other words, engagement is dynamic and evolving, and there is always some influence being exerted on what happens next. Moments of engagement are not discreet or disconnected events, and in the process of engagement we try to ensure that each moment has value beyond the momentary time and space.

Story: Signing Up

Johannes was frustrated and a little scared too. As summer was approaching, his school had made it clear that in spite of his academic difficulties, he would be advanced to high school next year. Tomorrow he was to select his courses at high school, and Johannes was feeling very under-equipped to do so. "Why bother selecting courses I am going to fail anyway?" he said to himself. He knew he could ask Safid to help him get through the paperwork that was required for the signing up process, but that too seemed problematic. If Safid helped him select courses, he would expect Johannes to do well in those courses, and Johannes really didn't want that kind of pressure. At any rate, he still didn't trust Safid, since he had only known him for a couple of weeks.

But Johannes did have to admit being interested in getting to know Safid. Somehow, that guy seemed not at all like some of the other workers he had met at school. Safid didn't do that much and he often didn't say that much, but he always seemed very interested in what Johannes had to say. Sometimes Safid surprised Johannes by following up on something that Johannes didn't realize Safid had even heard him talk about.

Just as Johannes was contemplating these issues, Safid approached him with some papers in his hand. "Hey buddy, I've got some good news. I checked with the high school about whether they offer German as a course option for Grade 9, and they do. I remember when we first met you told me that speaking German was important to you, so I figured you might be interested in taking that course. No pressure, but it would lighten your load next year, especially since you're already a better German speaker than most of German teachers at high school!"

One of the risks of engagement within the life-space context is the comprehensive nature of our presence in the life of the young person. When we hold such a significant presence, we are inadvertently creating the possibility of entrenching a real or perceived power imbalance. It is therefore necessary to reflect on the power dynamics of engagement before outlining some of the possible strategies for engagement.

Engagement and Power

So far, we have discussed the concept of engagement primarily from a theoretical perspective. We hope that this has created a foundation for discussing real strategies for engaging young people that are responsive to the theoretical premises just explored. Engagement is the core of our active presence in the life of the young person. Before we proceed with the next component of our analysis, we must pause for a moment and consider the role of power and **power imbalances** in the context of engagement strategies.

Power is particularly important in child and youth care practice, since the role of the practitioner is socially constructed as that of the helper while the role of the young person is constructed as that of the one in need of help. Practitioners must therefore remain conscious of the power differential that is automatically established in our relationships with young people "in need of help." In the helping relationship, our power emanates from prior knowledge about the young person's life, social history, material resources, knowledge, competencies and, perhaps most dramatically, an agenda for how our relationship will, or at least ought to, unfold. Young people, in contrast, are left at the margins of power in this circumstance. They know nothing about the practitioner, have limited involvement in the early stages of setting the helping agenda, and have already been disempowered because they are identified as someone in need of assistance. In many cases, broader social issues may also come into play, including poverty, lack of education, developmental deficits and a history of problems. The ultimate symptom of the power imbalance between practitioner and young person is found in how we evaluate the success of this relationship. If the young person demonstrates growth and improved performance in basic social functioning, credit goes to the practitioner. If, however, the young person fails to make progress (as defined by professionals, school personnel or family members), blame is assigned to the young person and the practitioner is absolved of responsibility.

We will now turn our attention to the strategies for engagement in a variety of contexts in which practitioners and young people come together. We will differentiate between engagement within an established relationship and engagement during a first encounter, and suggest different approaches to engagement in each circumstance.

The First Encounter

There is a world of difference between engaging a young person that we have known for some time and with whom we have a relationship, and engaging a young person we are meeting for the first time. This difference is reflected in how we choose to engage and get started on the path of building a relationship. Conversation, which is the most obvious means of engagement, is also intrusive and demanding; therefore, it should not be central in our early efforts to engage young people. Conversation requires a degree of mutual interest and trust. Furthermore, it requires that young people commit to articulating their personal thoughts and feelings to someone who is essentially a stranger. For practitioners who think of ours as a "talking profession," this can be challenging, since conversation may be one of our core tools for being with young people. A closer exploration of how we can engage a young person whom we have just met will help to illuminate some of the other tools we have in our tool kit of engagement strategies.

As a first step, we highlight four themes that create a context for how we approach a young person. It is critical to remain conscious of these themes as we proceed to be present with a young person.

Clarity

The young person probably lacks a clear understanding of the purpose and rationale for our meeting. Whatever events might have led up to this point, from the perspective of a young person our introduction into the life-space feels puzzling and confusing. In most situations, professionals involved with young people and/or their families have a prior conversation about how to introduce their presence into the young person's life-space.

For example, a pre-admission meeting for residential care or a family meeting to set up in-home supports are typical approaches to introducing the young person to a relationship with a child and youth care practitioner. When we actually appear in the young person's life-space, however, whatever explanations were given previously fade into the background. The young person's life-space has been altered through an initiative from outside, which is invariably confusing and difficult to come to terms with.

No one likes intruders, and for young people, our presence is an intrusion into the private realm of their life-space. Young people wonder about our real intentions, our sincerity and our motivations. They also wonder about our allegiances and loyalties. Even if we were assigned to be present specifically for the young person, they still wonder whether we will inform parents, other workers or other structures in the life-space (such as school) about their activities, concerns, and dreams. The initial offer of assistance is interpreted as a threat by most young people. They often do not believe that they need assistance. Rather, they typically externalize any perceived problems and assign blame indiscriminately to those who affect their life-space. As a result, our offer of support and assistance is interpreted as a threat to a young person's material and virtual belongings. What will we take away? Will we attack a peer group, reduce access to the community, and impose restrictions and regulations on the everyday dynamics of life? Along with the suspicion that nothing good can come out of any association with us, there may be a significant amount of resentment that we are there in the first place. Do we really think we know better? Who do we think we are, entering their personal life-space and starting to manipulate how things work in it?

Relevance

Whatever challenges are present in the life of the young person, it will not be clear that our presence will be helpful. The young person will have met other adults who were interested in helping, but things may not have improved. Almost invariably, young people have low expectations that others might improve the circumstances of their lives, partly because in spite of promises and commitments made things have not changed substantially. The challenges they have are their challenges, and young people who do not have much do not easily relinquish ownership over what they do have, including their challenges. Young people have many questions about the relevance of our presence. What could we possibly understand about their challenges and everyday experiences?

Fear of Disappointment and Abandonment

In spite of all the negative intuition regarding our relevance to their lives, young people may still harbour faint hope that we can help or at the very least provide something positive in their lives. However, such hope is potentially dangerous and almost certainly will result in disappointment in the minds of young people. Young people may fear that there is no objective rationale for us to care about them, and therefore no reason why we would make a commitment to them once we realize that they are not always easy to get along with or once we become aware of their issues and true identities. Their fear is that by making room for us in their life-space they will face abandonment down the road, which will only exacerbate the challenges they face.

Our first encounter with a young person takes place in the context of these barriers to engagement. Practitioners are not always aware or conscious of these barriers, partly because we have not experienced them and we can only assume them to be present. At times, practitioners may not realize that they are present in a young person's life-space, since the young person often enters the practitioner's work space in circumstances in which the young person is enrolled in a residential program, a school program, or any other program with a discreet physical location (Cunningham, Duffee, Yufan, Steinke & Naccarato, 2009; Raftery, Steinke & Nickerson, 2010; Smith, Duffeee, Steinke, Yufan & Larkin, 2008). The mandate of the practitioner's workplace is clear about the reasons for being involved with a young person and defines the organizational process and culture that contextualize the work. The practitioner explains this first encounter from pre-established guidelines related to the eligibility for the program and the reasons that young people are there. The encounter from the practitioner's perspective is not at all personal or private – instead, it is just another moment in an already established pattern of greeting new clients. In contrast, the young person is looking for an understanding of the encounter with the practitioner from a very personal and private perspective.

Suspicion is an important consideration pursuant to the practitioner's approach to engagement. In group-based programs such as residential care and alternative schools, embedded concepts such as the *honeymoon period* imply that the practitioner should be cautious about accepting as "real" the conduct of a young person on a first encounter. If the culture of a program cynically views young people in general as problematic, then practitioners will exercise their cynicism freely and consistently, and thus will have limited ability to engage the young person with sincerity and integrity on a first encounter. Within cynical program cultures, suspicion is centred around how a young person might influence the degree of control the practitioner currently has. In a more accepting program culture, such suspicion is typically absent, and the practitioner's primary concern is to help young people assimilate into the existing program culture and routines (the period of orientation). The process of accepting a young person to a program almost always includes a planned orientation of the young person to the program but virtually never involves a planned orientation for the practitioners in the program to the young person's life-space.

Practitioners rarely question the relevance of the program or what it offers. Relevance is present simply because the young person has been accepted to the program. Similarly, the fears of disappointment and abandonment are also absent for the practitioner. The introduction of the practitioner into the life-space of the young person is of great significance. In contrast, the introduction of the young person into the work space of the practitioner represents little more than a continuation of an established pattern. The first encounter with a young person does not represent a potentially life-changing experience for the practitioner.

A first encounter between practitioner and young person is thus laden with invisible inter-personal dynamics that are felt much more acutely by the young person than by the practitioner. When we engage a young person for the first time, we cannot assume that we are operating from a blank sheet or in a relational vacuum. In fact, first encounters are relationally crowded spaces in which the path to engagement is easily obscured. It is essential for practitioners to tread carefully, move slowly, and exercise a great deal of patience in their search for the most appropriate path to engage a young person. This is one of the reasons why engagement in the context of life-space intervention must always be a reflective process. A great deal of effort and consciousness are required in order to transcend the triviality of the moment created by program and employment patterns and to do justice to how profoundly important that moment of first encounter is from the young person's perspective.

First Encounters and the Life-Space

From the perspective of young people, their first encounter with us can be a major adjustment to their life-space. When we encounter a young person in a specific program location, such as a group home or a school program, the new "place" – with all of its physical manifestations and social relations – requires that young person to integrate an overwhelming amount of new information, relationships and experiences into his or her life-space. Even when a specific physical place is absent, as it is, for example, when we first encounter young people in their own homes, the addition of a new social relationship requires them to make adjustments to their concept of life-space (Garfat, 2003). As we discussed in earlier chapters, making these adjustments is not simply a matter of becoming familiar with a new physical location or even a new social relation in a familiar physical location. An encounter with a practitioner changes the way in which all social relations in the young person's life-space unfold. The encounter changes the "story" the young person tells about life because a new character, with an as yet undefined role, has been added to this story.

It is important that the practitioner accept the role as a new character in the **life-space story** of a young person and work to ensure that this new character is not labelled a villain right away. The task is to introduce the new character to the story of the young person in such a way that possibilities for character development are not closed off from the start. We must acknowledge from the beginning that we are entering an already unfolding life-space story and that the young person maintains ownership of that story. The risk of disempowering a young person is high as we engage, and mitigating this risk necessitates respect for the young person's life-space.

Therefore, engagement is about exploring the life-space story of a young person rather than setting an agenda for change. In order for our character to take on a meaningful and influential role in a young person's story, we have to learn how the story works, who the other characters are, what locations are central, and how the main character – the young person – creates a role in relation to all of the other characters, the settings and the various plots and subplots in the story.

When we come together with young people, our respective life-spaces are affected very differently, and remaining conscious of this difference is essential to a successful first encounter. The introduction of a young person to the life-space story of a practitioner is a relatively minor event, and the character that the young person assumes in our life-space story is at best a minor role that affects only one place in our story, the workplace. For the young person, however, this coming together is a major change in the plot of the life-space story. The practitioner is a major character whose role intersects with virtually all aspects of a young person's story.

First Encounters and Mutuality

For a first encounter, the concept of mutuality has a more subtle meaning than that discussed earlier. As our new role in the life-space story of the young person evolves, and if we respect the young person's ownership of the story, we must also allow the young person to exercise agency in how our character evolves. Exercising agency is not synonymous with maintaining full control. Rather, there is a complex and nuanced process of negotiating a role for this new character so that both the young person and the practitioner can accept and evolve the character. Our character exercises agency within the structure of the story and is simultaneously affected by that structure. This takes us back to the process of structuration we discussed in Chapter 2, in which the character and the story mutually shape one another to arrive at new plot lines.

In order for young people to absorb the new character into their life-space story, they must quickly gain some insight into the nature of the new character. First encounters are a time of great uncertainty and anxiety, and a mystery story is not particularly useful. Instead, we need to develop an opportunity for the young person to get to know something about the new character. We cannot maintain absolute boundaries and remain closed off to young people while insisting that they expose their stories to us.

This exchange of information between a practitioner and a young person is a narrative and experiential togetherness that explores the space between them; the exchange is to acknowledge the approaching togetherness, a process that in German is called *Annäherung* (gradually coming closer together).

Annäherung is not a forward or one-directional process all the time. There are times when we have to take a step back and reposition ourselves in order to acknowledge that we may have overstepped the boundary of the young person. This is a major shift in the usual approach to engagement, in which we are often concerned only with our own boundaries and presumptive about the boundaries of the young people we encounter. But young people are constantly evaluating their safety and comfort zones with adults, and demonstrating respect for their boundaries is a critical element of engagement based on mutuality. We can therefore add to the process of *Annäherung* a concept from the world of soccer. In soccer, the attacking forward is said to be offside when a pass to him is made at a time when there are no defenders between him and the goal. Similarly, we might find ourselves offside when we engage young people by overstepping into their life-space story, thereby leaving them with no defences and no possibility of retreat.

Engagement during a first encounter is an enormously complex process with many nuanced and subtle details for the practitioner to consider. Such engagement is a dynamic process involving agency on the part of both the practitioner and the young person. In the next section, we will explore strategies that might be useful for initial engagements. Specifically, we will articulate some fundamental principles of early engagement set in the specific context of life-space intervention. These principles preserve the integrity of the engagement dynamic with all of its subtleties and nuances.

Principles of First-Encounter Engagement Strategies

There is no blueprint for first encounters because each engagement takes place in the context of each young person's unique life-space story. Strategies to engage must be personalized even when in the early stages of coming together we really do not know very much about that young person's life story.

The first principle of engagement, therefore, is choice. Providing choices to young people allows them to personalize the engagement dynamic based on how they see their life-space story unfolding. From the choices they make, we can learn about their approach to decision-making in relation to their life-space. If, for example, we are admitting a young person to a residential program, we can offer choices about which bedroom to assign, what food to offer during the admission process, and what kinds of items to display in the bedroom. This allows the young person to mitigate the inevitable feeling of disempowerment by gaining some authority over structuring the physical dimensions of the life-space. If we encounter the young person in a community setting, we might have the young person choose our initial activities, invite a peer to come along, or schedule our initial visit(s). In a classroom, we may offer choices about where the young person sits, what colour the binders are, or even how we might approach providing assistance with school work. Choice is a core principle of first-encounter engagement in order to ensure that young people are clear about how important their agency is in their life-space story. Even though this agency is mitigated by the structure of the program or the limitations of circumstances (protection concerns, custodial issues, school exclusion, etc.), it is still critical to ongoing engagement with young people.

A second core principle for first-encounter engagements is transparency about ourselves. While this principle may be affected by organizational or employment-related stipulations related to boundaries such as self-disclosure, it is very important that young people gain an impression of who we are so that they can begin to assign us a role in their life-space stories. We don't need to disclose our innermost secrets and personal affairs, but we can allow the young person to understand our reasons for being present in this moment, and the scope of our prescribed roles and functions in the program or in the current employment context. For example, a common element of the initial admission process into a residential program is to explain the rules and expectations of the program – how the program functions, what the day-to-day routines are, and what is expected in terms of participating in such routines and following the rules. It is much less common to also explain what the role of the practitioner is, and what the young person can expect from the practitioner in terms of support, authority and engagement. This lack of explanation makes it difficult for the young person to imagine the role of the practitioner in this new chapter of the life-space story, and therefore enhances the need for defensiveness and self-protection.

A third core principle of first-encounter engagement strategies is that of life-space connectivity. Our work with young people should transcend the moment and the material space where we meet and instead subsume the physical and virtual dimensions of the life-space of the young people as much as possible. This approach requires that we establish connections to the life-space from the beginning to avoid situations in which young people compartmentalize our meetings in the context of a particular place and moment. Creating such connectivity can be complicated when programs and services limit the inclusion of other characters from the young person's life-space story in the services we offer. However, such limitations can be overcome or at least mitigated. Early explanations of how the program operates and our role in the program should always include openings for the involvement of others who are important to the young person. When a young person is encountered in a community setting or an in-home support program, it is relatively easy to ensure that the initial activities include invitations for a peer or a sibling to participate. In more institutionalized settings, such plans may be more difficult to arrange, but using technologies such as social networking sites or online gaming can overcome any concerns about the inclusion of others in the program site. Establishing connectivity in our early engagement strategies is critically important because it makes the coming together of practitioner and young person relevant from the young person's perspective and mitigates the isolation experienced by the young person.

These three core principles of engagement for our first encounter with a young person already provide a great deal of opportunity to substantively structure our first few moments with the young person. We can derive from these principles a list of dos and don'ts that can help us mitigate the young person's anxieties and fears about the moment of engagement.

Story: First Contact

When Safid entered the room to join the meeting, Johannes was already in hyper-defensive mode. He had resolved not to engage with any of the people present and instead to just let this meeting unfold as it might. Johannes felt almost irrelevant, and he knew that whatever was planned for him would happen regardless of what he might have to say about it.

This was one of those occasions when Johannes dreamed of his parents and of the life he thought he would have just three short years ago when they had come to Canada. At that time, everything seemed full of promise and he had already planned out how he would adjust to life in Canada. His dad and he would take English lessons together, and eventually he would join the school soccer team where surely he would impress everyone. He was from Germany after all, and soccer was in his blood. He had daydreams of being recognized as the soccer star and of peers wanting to get to know him based on his dominance on the field. He would be modest but also bask in the glory. And after really big games, his mother would surprise him with German cookies and Brause, a German soft drink similar to Kool-Aid.

As the meeting got underway, Johannes' worker talked about the need for the new placement and her expectations of Johannes in terms of behaviour. The new foster parents explained how their home worked and promised rewards for good behaviour. They stared at him as they were talking, checking him out, assessing his promise as one of their placements in their home. To Johannes, it felt like they were already establishing the rules and expectations as a way of saying clearly who will be in charge.

Then this guy walked into the meeting and sat across him. The guy didn't say anything, but Johannes noticed his shirt. It was a Germany jersey from the 2006 World Cup, when Germany surprised the world and placed third overall. As Johannes stared at the guy's shirt, the guy apparently noticed and he placed his hand on the national flag of Germany on the top right of the jersey, looked at Johannes, and gave him a very mild smile and a barely noticeable "thumbs up." In spite of himself, Johannes smiled back. And that was all; the guy didn't really say anything else during the meeting, except that his name was Safid and that he worked at the foster home.

As the meeting came to a close, Johannes had once again withdrawn into his daydream about soccer stardom. He was at home with his parents, eating German cookies and looking at the team picture that had just been distributed. And there in the back row, way to the left, was Safid, the team's coach, smiling and giving the thumbs up.

However, engagement is not a one-time activity limited to first encounters. On the contrary, engagement is the central embedded dynamic in the unfolding of the relationship between the young person and the practitioner, and it is therefore necessary to consider strategies for engagement beyond the first encounter. Specifically, we want to reflect on the changes that occur over time during our engagement with the young person, and how such changes affect the meaning and nature of engagement in the broader context of life-space intervention.

Engaging the Relationship

As our relationship with a young person takes shape over time, the nature of engagement and the role we play in the life-space shifts from finding a role to giving life to our character by connecting the various dimensions of the life-space. Relationships form between the practitioner and other characters in the young person's life-space story (such as peers, family members, teachers, and other professionals), the practitioner physically enters various places within the young person's life-space (such as the school, home, community centre or favourite mall), and the practitioner actively begins to make connections among components of the young person's life-space during day-to-day interactions with the young person.

This ever-deepening connection between the practitioner and the young person's life-space story is a process of **transcendental engagement**. Within this process, our engagement strategies are not limited to the young person. Instead, we begin to transcend the material context of our presence with the young person by engaging non-material dimensions of the young person's life-space story and becoming part of that story as it continues to unfold.

For example, having engaged the young person's connections to peers, the school and family, we greet the young person returning from school with a complex and transcendentally engaging "How did your buddy Eric do at school today? Did you steer him clear of trouble?" While the more generic "How was school today?" engages the young person with respect to performance at school, it is not a very interesting topic for most young people. By engaging with the much more complex constellation of relationships and experiences the young person has at school, we transcend the two locations (school and home) as well as the peer relationships, making our role one that is present to the activities of friends in many locations, even if we are not physically present. Our focus is the young person's experience of relationships with peers as they unfold in the context of a particular place (in this case the school), and the young person's role in both the relationship and the place. We can transcend the life-space components of the young person even further by adding complexity to our greeting: "How did your sister deal with her issues with your buddy Eric today? I know your mom is concerned about that, so did you help them figure out their conflict?" In this greeting, we have transcended life-space components ranging from relationships with peers, to relationships with siblings and a parent, to an experience related to the physical context of school.

The concept of transcendental engagement is about being present in the life-space of the young person by mitigating the compartmentalization of that space, which is often promoted through the limitations of our workplace. In the context of a residential program, for example, our day-to-day interactions with the young person are often limited to implementing program structure and routines. This may create a false perception that we are engaging the young person when we impose the program routines. However, routines are not by themselves engaging, and often have quite the opposite effect. As a result, our interactions with the young person become disengaged from the totality of the life-space altogether, since they are not connected in any way to the other components of the life-space and thus they do not have a role in the continuous unfolding of the life-space story. The opposite of the transcendental approach to engagement, therefore, is discreet engagement, in which being together with the young person is located in a discreet space that is disconnected from the young person's otherwise unified life-space. When this disconnection becomes entrenched, young people experience themselves as being outside of their life-space, with limited agency and within an otherworldly experience. Therefore, not only do they have limited agency, but they also have limited responsibility for their actions.

Transcending the Virtual Dimension

Since we have used the term *life-space story* throughout this chapter, it is necessary to contemplate the role of the virtual dimension of life-space more concretely. Stories are always in the purview of the virtual, since agency in a story is derived from the mental, imaginative and creative impulses of the story's owner. Now that we have become a character in the life-space story of the young person, we are faced with the task of engaging with the young person about ourselves. We need to check in on how our character is doing in the young person's story, and therefore we must think about relationships in the context of *being in* relationship rather than *having a* relationship. When you *have a* relationship, you are the owner of that relationship and the young person's agency to shape the development of your character and how you are represented in his or her life-space story is negated. Yet clearly young people have the capacity to assign our character whatever role they choose. When we acknowledge our *being in* relationship with the young person, we also acknowledge our shared agency with regard to how our character evolves as part of the young person's life-space story.

We can imagine, for example, a situation in which the practitioner has to impose consequences on the young person. In the ensuing conflict, the practitioner may attempt to re-engage the young person by getting past the conflict and initiating a distraction, such as "I know you weren't happy with me yesterday, but let's go to a movie tonight and get past this." This is a positive re-engagement strategy that tries to mitigate prolonged negativity. In most cases, such a strategy will work to rekindle a functional togetherness characterized by getting along and continuing the pattern of interactions already established. However, this is an incomplete engagement strategy. In fact, the very concept of re-engagement is somewhat of a red herring.

Conflict in the relationship is not a symptom of the end of a process of engagement that we must restart. Instead, such conflict reflects a retrenchment of the practitioner's character in the life-space story of the young person from the material dimension of the story to the virtual dimension. Engagement during conflict requires the practitioner to explore how the conflict affects the young person's virtual life-space story. By asking a question such as "I had to be pretty hard on you yesterday, so where am I in your thoughts now?" we are giving the young person a chance to continue exercising agency over the life-space story; indeed, we are encouraging the young person to do so. We are not re-engaging the young person; we are helping to evolve the young person's life-space story, exercising our own agency, engaging the young person's virtual life-space, and creating opportunities for ourselves to evolve the character we represent in the young person's life-space story.

Given that conflicts are typically governed by emotional responses that may exacer-bate the conflict, it is sometimes wise to transcend the material and virtual dimensions of the young person's life-space by creating a virtual presence for ourselves rather than a physical one. Particularly with the availability of virtual technologies such as social networking sites, email and even texting, opportunities abound for being present in the life-space of young people as they contemplate a shift in our character's role. We can, for example, use neutral text messages such as "I know yesterday was difficult; just thinking about you right now" to ensure that the young person remains conscious of our presence and commitment even during times when face-to-face contact might not be desired.

Moving Toward Disengagement

As we have seen throughout this chapter, our engagement with young people is both complex and ever-evolving. We have discussed first-encounter engagement strategies and relationship-based engagement. Within the broader context of life-space intervention, we have developed the concept of transcendental engagement in order to emphasize the importance of avoiding discreet engagements that are outside of the life-space experience of the young person. Our core objective in engaging a young person is to connect our presence to the whole of the life-space, or to the life-space story as it is being developed and manipulated by the young person. The foundation of our approach to engagement is to continuously reinforce the young person's agency in our being together. The young person has the right and capacity to shape the meaning and the path of our engagement, as much as we have the capacity to provide an impetus for the young person to use the character we represent in the story to reshape, evolve and re-inspire relationships, experiences and actions throughout the life-space.

However, our involvement with young people is not permanent. We do not forever assume the role of child and youth care practitioner designated to guide the young person's development. In fact, given the enormous variations in programs and services, our engagement might be limited to a few encounters over a relatively short period of time, or it might span several years of the young person's march toward adulthood. Occasionally it might even continue beyond that transition to adulthood. These variations in our man-dated presence in the life of the young person raise questions about the need for disen-gagement strategies. Fundamentally, we have to grapple with the prospect of separation as our involvement with the young person approaches the end.

From the perspective of young people, separation is as much of a revolution in their life-space as our original coming together. The life-space story must accommodate the departure of a major character, and much like fictional stories, movies and soap operas, such a departure can cause considerable turmoil to a story, resulting in chaos and uncertainty about how the story will continue. Questions about who will take the place of the departed character and how all of the other relationships in the story might be affected without the presence of that charac-ter emerge, creating anxiety and fears. Much as in those other genres of storytelling, there is always a faint hope (or fear) that the departed character might reappear, perhaps in secret ways initially and then building up to the fantastic public exposure. But let's face it – in a sud-den reappearance, the character is never quite the same as we might remember that character from his or her first role. Almost invariably, our fantasies about that character are not fulfilled, and the feelings associated with the presence of that character in our lives are never quite the same as those that we remember from our first round of being together. This should come as no surprise, since the story has moved on, the plot has changed, characters have come and gone, and our own experience as the storyteller has shifted. The particular space occupied by the departed character no longer exists, and trying to reinsert that character into a long vanished space in our life-space story is certain to fail.

Story: The Hockey Jersey

Safid just couldn't help himself. From time to time, he felt the need to check out Johannes' page on the social networking site. As he was looking at the latest photo album Johannes had posted, Safid resisted the urge to post a comment on one picture depicting Johannes being greeted by his extended family at the airport in Germany.

Safid remembered well the last time he had been face to face with Johannes. After two intensive years of being together, Safid had announced to Johannes his impending move to the west coast of Canada. Johannes was initially very upset, but then became excited for Safid because he knew that the lifestyle Safid was pursuing would have a better chance of coming true there. They had talked about staying in touch via email and letters, which they had done for quite some time. But most importantly, they had talked about Johannes' plans to pursue re-connecting with his family in Germany, something that he had resisted ever since his parents had passed away. Safid had helped him write a letter to one of his father's cousins who Johannes thought would be the best relative to connect with. Together they had worked hard to convey the message that Johannes had mixed feelings about reconnecting. On the one hand, he wanted to have a family again and maintain some connection with his parents' past. On the other hand, he was still very upset about the lack of involvement of his extended family when his parents had their car accident.

The response to their letter was immediate and overwhelming. His relatives wrote back to him en masse, expressing their joy that he wanted to reconnect and inviting him, at their expense, to come to Germany for a visit.

It had taken quite some time to make all the arrangements and for Johannes to be ready to take this step. He wanted to ensure that his family understood he had moved on from the past, in spite of his interest to reconnect. The last thing Safid had said to him face to face was "There is no better way to demonstrate your new identity than to wear a Canada hockey jersey when you arrive at the airport!" It was meant to be a funny comment, but now Safid was looking at the picture of Johannes being swarmed by his relatives, wearing an oversized and very distinctive Canada hockey jersey from the 2010 Vancouver Olympics Gold Medal team.

Safid and Johannes had not had any contact for about a year now, and Safid was conscious that it was not for him to re-establish such contact. Johannes had moved on in his life, exploring new relationships and adventures. But as the picture of his arrival in Germany clearly demonstrated, a silent and inactive relationship was still finding ways of making its presence known.

Disengagement in the context of child and youth care practice is not really about say-ing goodbye or about becoming absent. Instead, it is about relinquishing the space occu-pied by the character we represented in the young person's life-space story so that the story may evolve in new and exciting directions. Fundamentally, disengagement is about respecting the ownership and agency of the young person with respect to the life-space story. But unlike engagement, disengagement does not have to abide by the principle of mutuality. We may not be able to continue our efforts at mutually shaping the role we play with the young person, but the young person can continue to engage the character we have become in the story. As we disengage, our presence moves from the young per-son's material life-space to the virtual dimension, where it is committed to memory and accessible by the imagination through daydreams and fantasies. The young person may ultimately miss us terribly or be glad we are gone, but the memory of our presence will continue to engage the life-space. Over time, the memory may fade, but it will already have spurred new developments and new twists in the life-space story.

Summary

In this chapter, we have explored the concept of engagement within the broader context of life-space intervention. The core feature of engagement from the perspective of life-space intervention is that it requires agency on the part of both practitioners and young people. Engagement must be distinguished from interaction or the imposition of rules and structures as part of routine program expectations. Instead, we think critically and metaphorically about engagement as the evolution of a story being told by the young person about his or her experiences in the life-space. The practitioner is one character in that story, with the ability to influence, but not dominate, the development of that char-acter. As is the case in any character development scenario, early encounters between practitioners and young people must ensure that approaches to engagement reflect the unknowns and the often-unspoken fears, risks and anxieties experienced by young peo-ple. Only as relationships evolve can we begin to breathe life into what we have termed transcendental engagement, whereby the practitioner seeks out opportunities for being present in multiple dimensions of the young person's life-space.

Discussion and Exercises

Reflection in Practice

Before your next encounter with a young person, review the section on engagement and the Self. As you engage with the young person, monitor and attend to your thoughts and emotions, and try to answer three questions.

1. What is the (genuine) reason for engaging this young person?
2. What are your emotional and physical reactions to the young person's responses toward you?
3. Was your counter-response genuine and authentic, leaving open the space for mutuality?

Reflection on Practice

In the story about Johannes, identify or create examples of the following. Add examples of your own strategies, and compare them to the strategies used by Safid.

1. Strategies for engaging the life-space based on principles of
    (a) Choice
    (b) Exploration
    (c) Connection
    (d) Influence
2. Strategies for engagement during the first encounter based on principles of
    (a) Choice
    (b) Transparency of the Self
    (c) Life-space connection
3. Transcendental engagement within the relationship
4. Strategies for disengagement within the relationship

Reflection for Practice

Consider a young person with whom you are currently engaged.

1. Identify the sources and locations of power differentials that were present before you even met this young person. These will be present in the context of your "assigned" relationship and the structures of the program that employs you.
2. Describe strategies that you might use to mitigate the existing power differential.

Theory in Action

Engagement reflects both an action and a condition. We cannot experience engagement (the condition) with a young person without *doing* something, be that starting a conversation, participating in an activity, or simply ensuring we are present in the young person's life-space.

1. Describe the difference between engagement as an action and engagement as a condition. Consider the issues of mutuality, power, and Self in your discussion.

2. Complete a search of academic journals to find out how the concept of engagement has been defined by other professions or disciplines.

CHAPTER 5

Relationships: The Fabric of Life-Space

Tabitha

Source: Kyle Stewart

In this chapter we discuss the concept of relationship within the life-space in the context of therapeutic change. We begin by first defining and then exploring *relationship* as it is understood in child and youth care practice. In particular, we focus on some of the differences in how we think about relationships among practitioners, young people, and families. The thinking about relationships and relational practice is evolving. Relationships, particularly interpersonal relationships, are essential tools in practice, but being consciously relational is an approach to life and practice in the life-space of others. Garfat

(2008, p. 20) suggests that relational practice focuses "on the relationship, while recognizing and respecting the characteristics of the individuals involved in that relationship" and that relational work "attends to the relationship itself." In essence, relationships are objects that can be described, and they create the substance of the relational dimension of the life-space and the relational practice that we engage in.

Story: Relating with Tabitha

Tabitha was home alone again while her mom was working at the neighbourhood café. The extra money from the job was nice, but Tabitha missed her mom, especially on Saturday night. They used to make Jello with whipped cream and watch a movie while it "jelled" and then eat it just before she went to bed. Today Tabitha had screamed at her mom when she woke her up. "I'm the only one that has to be awake before lunch. It's Saturday – why can't I sleep in? That's what 13-year-olds DO. I don't want to vacuum the apartment. It's not fair."

Since Tabitha's parents' divorce last year, Sarah's work at a full-time but low-paying office administration position wasn't enough to make up for the lack of financial support from Tabitha's father. Tabitha preferred not to visit him because of the way he treated her mother, yelling and insulting her. The court left this decision to her, given her age. Now she was feeling lonely, with nothing to do on Saturday night. Her mom was working and wouldn't allow her to go out. She thought about phoning some of her old friends, but decided against it. She'd only feel hurt again that they weren't including her.

Tabitha had some good friends in Grade 8 whom she had hung out with since Grade 5. They went to local movies or rented DVDs or video games, went to dances at the community centre, or went skateboarding at the local skate park. They watched each other play soccer or compete in swim meets. Everyone received an allowance or was just given the money they needed to send them to the local movies and enroll them in sports. After the divorce, Tabitha had stopped speed swimming because her dad had been paying the fees and now her mom couldn't afford it.

When Tabitha started high school this year, some of her friends came with her, but others, including her best friend, went to a different high school. As the old friends blended with a new crowd, Tabitha found herself regularly not able to afford to go to the movies or shopping with the girls. They were all interested in buying name brands and Tabitha knew that she couldn't afford that, so she started dressing in a style that was anti-brand name and shopping at the thrift store. She got some pretty good bargains and had a unique style going on, but her friends put her down for it, especially the girls that she didn't know well. She started hanging out at the local youth centre. They charged a small annual membership and a dollar to come in and use the gym, the indoor skate park, video games and computers. "The Youth" as it was called, attracted the local kids who didn't have much money.

Defining Relationship

The term *relationship* simply indicates an association between two (or more) things. The study of relationships is of interest in most disciplines. Mathematicians study numerical relationships, scientists and researchers consider direct and inverse relationships between variables, psychologists study interpersonal relationships, sociologists are interested in social relationships, and biologists examine symbiotic plant and animal relationships. Our interest is in the role that relationships play in the young person's life-space. Caring (explored in Chapter 3) is an important characteristic of our relationships in the life-space. Engagement with young people (explored in Chapter 4) occurs in the context of our relationship with them. As practitioners, we must understand as fully as possible the nature and role of relationship in the pedagogy of the life-space.

Young people have relationships with objects, animals, and even concepts, and they carry these relationships in their life-space. In particular, the physical, mental, and virtual dimensions of life-space must enter into our understanding of relationships. As the cognitive abilities of young people develop, their interaction with and relationships to various aspects of their life-space change. Studies of infant development, for example, indicate that babies develop the capacity to remember or represent a physical object in their mind with some permanence somewhere around their fourth month. They develop "person permanence" much earlier, and to some extent person permanence facilitates object permanence (Santrock, MacKenzie-Rivers, Leung & Malcomson, 2003). These are indications of their relationship with the physical dimensions of their life-space. They reach for objects and people, and smile and laugh in exchange. They also exhibit social smiling, stranger anxiety, and fear in response to the reactions of a parent who perceives an unsafe environment. These are all indicators of the infant's relationship to the physical and emotional dimensions of the life-space. The cognitive ability to understand virtual worlds and virtual reality doesn't develop until adolescence, which means that younger people have a different relationship with a virtual world. The intensity and reality of fantasy play is stronger for younger children, and therefore the relationship to the virtual dimensions of life-space is more real and less unreal. The relationships that a young person has to people, objects, fantasies, imaginary friends, and abstract concepts such as the legal system or mom and dad's work are what unify the life-space into a singular concept.

The Contribution of Relationship to the Life-Space Dimensions

Young people learn, grow and develop in the context of human relationships in the life-space. Once we meet someone, it is impossible not to be in relationship with that person. Even the smallest interaction – a bump on the street, a momentary introduction after which you forget who you just met – becomes incorporated into your life-space. You learn tricks to remember names and be better at it or make the person aware that you won't remember them when next you see them. You apologize for the bump, or you get angry. The association between yourself and that other person goes forward in time and may be refined, reviewed, or reflected on. Through those processes, you learn.

In the first encounter with a young person, when we engage and initiate our relationship, we want to understand the relational character of his or her life-space and the nature and types of relationships that stitch it together. We want to "become" one of those stitches – possibly one of many that will support the young person and his or her family.

The young person brings into our relationship aspects of previous relationships and the life-space that we also need to understand.

As we notice in Tabitha's story above, the fabric of our life-space is made up of relationships. Relationships bring together the various dimensions of the life-space, connecting physical location to physical location and appearing in virtual spaces. Relational work means that we seek to understand the kinship between people, as well as the way they relate to and make meaning of the various other dimensions of their life-space. As relational practitioners, we must understand how young people and families make meaning of their relationships in their life-space. We also need to understand the potential influence of the life-space on our relationship(s) with young people, and the systemic and cultural contexts that limit and direct the character of relationships. Before considering the methods by which relationships support interventions in the life-space, we will explore further the nature of various interpersonal relationships.

Young people have relationships with teachers, friends, family members, neighbours, members of their religious or spiritual community, boyfriends or girlfriends, sporting teams, shop owners, Internet gamers, and many others. Some of these relationships come with predefined roles and expectations based on culture and social context. Teachers, for example, transmit the formal knowledge that society at large has determined is essential for growing up. They are respected and acknowledged as learned members of society, although perhaps more in some other countries and societies. In some social contexts family roles are specifically defined, along with appropriate behaviour and sanctions for not following tradition. The extent to which a family follows socially prescribed definitions of specific relationships varies, but examples such as the following may be present in young people's life-space:

- East Asian women may be expected to accept an arranged marriage or to live under the protection of their parents.

- Italian boys don't cook and are cared for by the woman in the family.

- Canadian Aboriginal people speak of "our ancestors who are watching over us," believing that many generations of grandmothers and grandfathers are present in the life-space, protecting and guiding them.

Culture develops from the fabric of a common life-space within particular communities. As members of a community form relationships with other members, a web of social interaction is created and a set of rules or norms develops for getting along together and exerting social control on the membership of the group. What begins as a simple relationship becomes a set of norms for group members and eventually creates a culture or way of being in the world that distinguishes that group from others. The hierarchical organization of gangs and the gradual process of inducting new members involve relationships that often include objects and symbols (such as gang colours) that have strong personal meaning for young people.

Human beings are social creatures and participate dynamically in relationships as part of the ongoing construction of our life-space. We experience relationships in the physical and virtual dimensions of our life-space through emotional responses and mental representation of the space. We make meaning out of the activities we engage in with others and feel an emotional bond. We review photos of people in albums, on cellphones, and on Facebook. Even if we don't know the person, we connect with people and make meaning of their Facebook pages. Facebook even has a place to indicate your "relationship status." What a complex question!

We cannot *not* have a relationship when someone enters our life-space. Therefore, the relational dimension of life-space is about what we do with and within the relationships that are present in that life-space. In the intersection between the virtual and relational dimensions of the life-space, there is potential for connection and potential for harm. For example, Grace and Anna might be "group-home sisters," who met five years ago and have stayed in touch, occasionally going out to party together and eventually as Facebook friends. Grace is currently working for an escort agency in Toronto and Anna is in first year university with support from her Children's Aid Society. When Anna receives a Facebook request to be friends with Grace's boyfriend Paulo, accompanied by the comment "We met last year at the Halloween party at Clinton's Bar, your profile photo is smokin', let's get together after exams," she must assess the potential risks. Anna has a context, a prior face-to-face meeting, and photos. Relationally, Paulo is part of her life-space and she will respond in some manner, but her risk in accepting him as a friend may be too high.

By using technology and the virtual dimensions of the life-space as well as the physical dimensions, we can bring others into the relational dimension of our life-space. We hope that vulnerable young people are cautious about the relationships that they create as the virtual, physical and relational dimensions of their life-space intersect. However, as child and youth care practitioners we must engage in "relational practice" within the life-space of young people (and our colleagues) to create relationships and to explore the nature of those relationships, thus being "relational" and influencing how the life-space is managed.

The Nature of Impersonal Relationships

As we have said, people have relationships with objects, groups, systems, communities, and organizations, and therefore impersonal relationships within the life-space are also a consideration. Since Lewin's (1948) original concept of the life-space included both the person and the environment, it is natural to extend the concept of relationship to the objects, ideas and collectives within our environments and to explore the nature of those relationships within the life-space of young people.

A young person may say, "Pets [cats and dogs] don't make any demands on you, they can't hurt you, and they just love you unconditionally." This is a statement about relationships, not a statement about pets. Relationships with objects and with animals can carry powerful meanings in a young person's life-space. Pets provide an opportunity for important learning about relationships. Often they are the first living things that have been dependent on a young person for survival, and they are devoted and forgiving. Relationships with pets provide an opportunity to experience and explore power, mutuality, dependency and responsibility, and they allow practitioners to explore some of those concepts with young people without personal reaction or involvement. Service dogs have unique relationships with their owners that seem to reverse the usual pet/owner relationship; they care for the owner and provide safety and security.

Our relationships with objects in the life-space can be complex and dynamic. Transitional objects and transformational objects (Beker & Maier, 1988) provide comfort to children, youth and adults as they go through changes in their lives. Transitional objects maintain a connection with previous environments and with previous relationships during a time when new relationships might be unstable. High school yearbooks carry memories into adulthood as friendships change and young people move. Our possessions, a favourite blanket, the winning baseball, a vial of sand from a special holiday, or the soil of our home-land all carry mental and emotional representations of our Self and our identity. They are also a representation of the relationship that we have with that physical space. Gifts that we provide to others represent our relationship with that person. Hostess gifts say, "Thank you, I appreciate your hospitality." Gifts can be chosen quickly or with careful attention to the personality of the recipient, and the relationship between the giver and the recipient.

We also have relationships with collectives, or systems. Statements such as "My rela-tionship with work is a little shaky right now" indicate the abstract relationships that are present with systems and organizations. The nature of a relationship with systems is gov-erned by the values and beliefs that underlie the organizational operation and their consis-tency with our own identity. If the organizational value system is different from our own, it is harder to form a relationship with the organization. These aspects of employment relationships are governed by the rules and the people with authority who make up the collectives. While people who have interpersonal relationships create and agree to the rules, our relationship with an organization is sometimes more impersonal and focused on the rules and structure of the organization. Regardless, interpersonal relationships are the foundation for changing systemic relationships, they form the core of the relational dimension of the life-space, and they are an essential construct of practice. When agency is present and possible within interpersonal relationships in a system, the impersonal rela-tionship that we might have with organizational structure is mitigated.

Having explored the definition of relationship and attempted to distinguish it from the concept of relational, we will now turn to the conscious implementation of relationships as a construct in practice.

Relationship and Practice

As soon as the practitioner's life-space encounters the life-space of a young person (whether physical or virtual), they are in relationship. The practitioner then focuses on nurturing the relationship, attending to the relationship, and helping the young person exercise the same conscious attention to relationships, their nature, and the importance of nurturing them in the life-space. This is the nature of being human: We are social, and life unfolds in our social space – the life-space.

There are a number of questions we could consider to help us understand how rela-tionship is integral to our practice. The following questions help to frame the relational work we do with the life-space:

- How do various people and relationships move between the physical places and the virtual spaces that the young person inhabits?
- What makes a relationship supportive, destructive or unsafe?
- What is the young person learning about managing life?

- How do the relationships of a young person and the relationships of the practitioner create influence, and who do we (the young person and the practitioner) need to influence?

These questions form a structure within which we can understand how to enter a young person's life-space to form a relationship, how relationships can prevent young people from engaging in risky activities, and how the active nature of relationships helps young people learn to manage their life-space differently.

We will explore this idea of relational practice in the life-space further, but first let's follow Tabitha's story into her first encounters with child and youth care practitioners.

Story: Professional Relationships

Janice was at the thrift store replenishing the supply of winter clothing and other items that they kept at the Youth for young people who needed them or were temporarily homeless. Part of her job as programmer and youth worker was to keep the supply cupboard full, and winter was just around the corner.

She noticed a pair of designer jeans for $5 and thought immediately of Tabitha. The jeans were the kind that had pre-fading and a couple of rips, but they didn't look "designer." They were right in line with Tabitha's current style.

Janice was pretty sure that Tabitha would like them, but she was worried about how their relationship would be affected by giving Tabitha the jeans. It was a little outside of the "warm clothes for cold weather" mandate that the Youth had adopted. However, Janice had recently asked Tabitha about her mom and dad – an awkward question – because she learned about the divorce and the change in financial status. She really should have known better than to ask such a specific question about relationships in Tabitha's life-space, but

she had made some assumptions about a two-parent family.

Janice managed to turn things around and she occasionally gave Tabitha thrift store shopping tips. But clothing might be beyond the expectation, and how would she raise it without drawing attention to Tabitha as a "special" young person?

Janice thought to herself, "I should have brought her with me. More shopping tips and the jeans would be a thank you for helping. Maybe I can get her to volunteer for a couple of nights at homework club, and the jeans can be a thank you." However she managed it, Janice knew that she would need to be conscious of the impact on their relationship and on other relationships in the centre.

Tabitha was a natural leader in the youth centre. She was friendly and very athletic. The skateboard park was cheap and she could practise using their equipment. While she didn't hang out with them much at school, most of the kids there went to her high school. There was an older crowd who hung out in the halls and, Tabitha learned later, they

(Continued)

were the ones to go to for party drugs. There was an older girl (Tabitha thought she was in college) who worked the front desk most nights. She chatted Tabitha up and complimented her on her outfits. Lisa usually had a funny story about school, but tonight when Tabitha arrived she was reading the celebrity gossip columns out loud.

As soon as Lisa saw Tabitha, she launched into a story about someone famous. Tabitha really only listened when there was "grunge" or skateboards involved, and tonight it was something about Justin Bieber and his skateboard antics. Tabitha rolled her eyes.

"Come on, Lisa, he wouldn't hold up here. You know that!"

Tabitha usually came to the Youth on Saturday night and occasionally during the week. She had finished her homework early tonight because it was getting close to the holiday break, and there wasn't much happening. She was hoping to see Janice.

Janice had inquired once why she didn't come right after school (thinking about homework club), and Tabitha explained that her mom wouldn't have allowed her to go out without doing her homework. Most of the other kids came right after school. There was a homework club for help, but they didn't use it because they weren't really into that and their parents never checked anyway. Tonight, Tabitha thought it might be fun to hang out with Janice and Lisa and watch the crowd. There was usually some drama and hysterics, and Tabitha thought Lisa's commentary was hilarious. More importantly, she always learned something when Janice commented or intervened to put the problem to rest.

"Hey Tabitha," said Janice, who was genuinely glad to see her, "I've got a bit of a problem with Grade 8 math in the homework club room. Can you give me a hand? Didn't you say math was your favourite subject?"

Building Relationships: Entering the Life-Space

Building relationship is not a passive activity. Every opportunity must be sought to actively create relationships of trust and caring. If the practitioner works within relationship and within the relational aspects of the young person's life-space, then learning about the life-space of that young person is essential. We might explore questions such as the following:

- Who are the people in the social contexts?
- Where do the relationships occur in place, space and time?
- How do those relationships overlap?
- What meaning does the young person make of those relationships?
- How and where can we join the web of existing and future relationships?
- Where are key points of learning in the social context of the life-space?

Using a relational approach to life-space intervention means that the practitioner co-constructs the relationship with the young person (Garfat, 2008). Self-awareness is essential, and we should be prepared to take note of and bring to the relationship with the young person the following elements:

- The people within our social context

- Where our relationships occur in place, space and time

- How our relationships overlap

- What meaning we make of those relationships and of our relationship with the young person

- Opportunities to extend our web of existing and future relationships

- Openness to what we can learn from that young person

Developing a relationship and entering the life-space of the young person as a significant influence is planned, not happenstance, which means we must actively seek information and go beyond our own social and cultural assumptions about that young person's life-space. In some contexts, the nature of relationships and the norms for social interaction the young person follows are straightforward and self-evident, because both young person and practitioner are familiar with the prevailing culture. When practitioners meet a young person in a high school, they might anticipate that he or she knows how schools work and is familiar with the requirement to study in order to pass, the importance of raising your hand to leave the classroom, and the vice-principal's role in handing out detentions for not following the rules. Practitioners might also anticipate that a representative of the school phones home when one of the rules is broken, and even assume that parents are informed of the meeting between the young person and the child and youth care practitioner.

However, a practitioner working in a large urban school may encounter a young person who has recently immigrated to Canada from Sudan. Immediately, the assumptions about relationships in that young person's life might change. The practitioner might assume that the young person has no parents, or that they do not speak English and do not know about our role. The assumption could be made that the young person does not know the rules for school, and the prerequisite knowledge to learn in class might be missing. There may also be an assumption that the young person has direct experience with war.

In both scenarios, the practitioner isn't using a life-space approach to intervention, or focusing on relational practice. Instead, the focus is on the assumptions. In both cases, these assumptions could be false.

To become more relational and to focus on relationship, we want to enter into and inquire about the life-spaces of young people. We want to find out what makes up their life-space and how they interpret the various aspects of their life-space, who they have relationships with, and what the character of those relationships is. Throughout our learning about those aspects of life-space, we want to offer respect for young people and their life experiences. We also want to develop relationships that they can carry forward and learn from as they manage their life-space(s).

Communication is vital to building a relationship and entering the young person's life-space. Communication is so much more than talking or even conversing. It requires observing, listening actively, and extending an open invitation for the other person to associate with you physically, mentally and virtually. Communication is embedded in language and in culture because words and phrases can carry multiple meanings. Nonverbal communication through voice tone, gestures, facial expressions, and even emoticons in textual messages may vary by cultural, social, and family contexts. In part, developing a relationship and entering the young person's life-space gives you the understanding of these aspects of communication. However, at the same time we must enter into the relationship with sensitivity to difference and to the adult/youth or racial and ethnic power imbalances in the social context.

Dialogical Conversation and Use of Activities

Where does the practitioner begin and how does the co-construction of relationship occur? Dialogical conversation (Peavy, 1998) is an approach to conversation between two people that acknowledges and ideally removes the power dynamic between them. The goal of the conversation is to understand each other, find a common ground, and share the experience of learning something about each other. In this case, understanding the young person's life-space is the goal. Listening, empathy, curiosity and learning about each other are the key ingredients. This requires putting aside the assumptions that we have about the person; we must be prepared to be changed by what we hear. We listen to both what is said and what is not said. Dialogical conversation is about entering the life-space of the other person to explore and understand it. Young people don't always believe that there is a "problem," that they are "at risk," or that there is anything that needs to be "managed more effectively." Therefore, we must put aside these assumptions in conversation and listen to learn how they construct their life-space and how they might weave the practitioner into it.

The conversation could start with "Hi, how are you?" which would elicit the usual response, "Fine." Alternatively, we could start with "What brings you to the centre today?" which requires a more personal and thoughtful response. Even the resistant and rebellious adolescent sarcasm of "the bus" or "my parents" gives us something to converse about and an opening to explore the life-space. "I take the bus to work too. I like the back – the people are more interesting. What about you?" or "Your parents? Did they come in with you?" While we might be interested in the "problem" that brings the young person to us, it is critical to first develop the relationship and explore the life-space of the young person though his or her eyes.

Young people are active, vibrant, and engaged in play and recreation in a way that provides opportunity to develop and expand relationships. Much of their life-space will be active and changing, leaving us scrambling to catch up. A constant complaint of young people is that there's nothing to do, and failure to be constructively engaged is often blamed for the problems of youth. Therefore, involving youth in activities that they find interesting or involving ourselves in their activities are natural strategies for building and deepening relationships. As noted in Chapter 4, the key is mutuality, meaning that we share our interests, talk about them, and invite young people to join in our professional work sphere. As young people grow to be adults, work and recreational activities become increasingly separated, but in professional work with young people we want to consciously decrease this separation. A school-based practitioner may take the youth in an alternative classroom to the gym for training in martial arts as part of their daily schedule. A practitioner may bring in the new release of a favourite video game to share with a fellow enthusiast in the group home. A street outreach worker may carry a portable chess game in a pocket to teach street youth the basics of the game.

Entering the life-space, developing a relationship, and being present as part of the fabric that supports a young person are all fundamental to life-space intervention. In fact, for some young people it is all they need. The added strength and support helps them to be resilient in the face of difficult social contexts. The practitioner knows the life-space, listens, and helps a young person to manage the challenges through relationship. Sometimes, however, more than simply being associated with a young person and present in the life-space is necessary. In these circumstances, the practitioner must make effective use of relationship to prevent challenges that could arise in the life-space and be unmanageable.

Presence

As discussed in Chapter 4, the process of entering and engaging relationally with young people in their life-space requires presence. Like the life-space, presence has a number of dimensions: Physicality, mental attention, and even a virtual background of images, sounds, and emotions that play in the mind. Presence requires a constant shifting between your own life-space and a focus on the relational engagement with the life-space of another person.

Thinking about presence from the perspective of the life-space dimensions defines some strategies for conveying our presence and building relationships. Being physically present and available simply means showing up and being there when you say you will be. This can go a long way toward building trust and understanding when we engage with young people. We also need to develop an understanding of the relationships that young people have with the physical dimensions of life-space. Presence is communicated when we are attentive to and inquire about the young person's experience of the physical surroundings. Immediacy is the skill of communicating our own reflections and experiences of the environment of the moment, and it helps to communicate our presence. More than just "being there," Krueger (2010) describes presence as that sense of being enmeshed with the moment, whether that moment is fun and joyful or a struggle with sadness, fear, or anxiety. It is the idea of being lost in what we are doing – focusing our physicality and mental attention on the young person in the life-space, and thereby enhancing the relationship. Fewster (1990a) describes presence as being in the moment but self-aware, thus limiting our reactiveness. Self-awareness, as described by Fewster, corresponds to the virtual component of our own life-space as it interacts with that of the young person. It is the awareness of our own youthful experiences, in contrast to those of the young person in front of us. Our ability to watch our own memories play out, restrict our own mental and emotional reactions, and remain present and focused on the young person's life-space communicates presence.

Life-Space Mapping

Entering the life-space and developing a relationship and an understanding of the young person's life-space means we actively use open questioning to elicit a description of the young person's life experience and its meaning. Peavy (1998, p. 90) describes the process of life-space mapping as an active strategy that can help young people to "explicate their life-space, describe their concerns and [search] for solutions." Life-space mapping is a method of diagramming the life-space (often informally as a "doodle") and representing the physical, mental, relational and virtual dimensions in a picture. (Examples and additional directions for creating life-space maps can be found at the end of this chapter.)

Life-space mapping can be done several times through the course of the relationship as a concrete depiction of changes in the young person's life-space. According to Peavy, there are several advantages to this visual representation:

- It makes the Self visible and therefore concrete.

- In the co-operative process, power dynamics and the meaning of the exercise are shared, which enhances relationship and mutual understanding.

- It creates a tangible product showing the key features, patterns of interaction, obstacles, and strengths and needs.

- It creates a dynamic picture of the life-space that encourages the young person and the practitioner to view the whole context of the concerns for the young person.

Life-space mapping is not about being factual or about diagramming a family system or the young person's ecological systems, though it may have some features of these processes of diagramming the lives of people we work with. Life-space mapping captures both facts and meaning, as well as relationships and the character of relationships. It is typically experienced as very open and freeing because it allows young people to focus on what is important to them rather than on a predetermined set of criteria (Rodgers, 2006). The dialogue that goes with the exercise is critical because the young person is free to picture the map in any way he or she would like to. Life-space mapping is most effective if a formal helping relationship has been established and the young person acknowledges that there is a reason he or she is meeting with you and that something needs to change.

Since the nature of your relationship with the young person in the life-space is in constant change, many of the strategies for entering the life-space and developing a relationship can also be effective tools in prevention and intervention. If we think of the relationship as constituting the intervention, the impetus for change comes from the youth but the responsibility for creating change is mutual. From this perspective, life-space intervention becomes very freeing for the practitioner because it relieves the pressure to "do something" and means that the change process is jointly owned.

Relationships and Social Control: Prevention in the Life-Space

Social control theory (Hirschi & Gottfredson, 2005) and social learning theory (Bandura, 1977) propose that relationships with other people and with systems and institutions in our lives teach young people not to break the law, and teach them about the social conventions and norms that guide their choices about right and wrong. Both these theories highlight power and control, punishment, and reinforcement as mechanisms of social control. Working relationally in the life-space of the young person requires an understanding of the importance of relationships and their role in power and social control. As discussed in Chapter 3, there are times when we must express caring by exerting our authority and control to prevent young people from engaging in behaviour that is detrimental to their safety or following a path that could lead to danger. Sometimes the practitioner's passive presence as a mental or virtual representation in the young person's life-space is sufficient to prevent danger.

Story: Reducing Risk and Enhancing Competence

Tabitha was "grounded" and at home during the Winter Olympics in Vancouver. She didn't really mind being grounded, but she couldn't understand why she couldn't go to the youth centre. Her mom seemed to like the workers there, and Tabitha had made sure not to tell her mom the whole story about the drug stash Sarah found in the closet at home. Besides, she'd forgotten about the stash by the time her mom found it.

When one of the older kids at the centre gave it to her, Tabitha had never intended to use it. She thought it was nice that they recognized her and wanted to be her friend. They got to know Tabitha hoping to get her to help them out with their dealing. They sometimes gave her stuff, saying that she could use it or sell it. She never did – she usually tossed it. But this time she left it in her pocket and forgot about it. Sarah found it when she was looking in Tabitha's closet for a sweater to wear to work. When she confronted Tabitha, she got mad and blamed her mom, refusing to talk about it. All she would say was, "I wouldn't have it if you weren't working as a stupid waitress."

Tabitha was young enough that she still didn't dare try to ignore or defy her mom, even when Sarah was away at work. Sarah would call home on her break or randomly in between serving tables to make sure that Tabitha was still at home and doing her homework. She had also called the youth worker at the centre and explained the situation. It all seemed kind of punitive and over

the top, but Sarah knew that it also meant that Tabitha was cared about. So Tabitha sat around watching the Winter Olympics speed-skating, skiing, and snowboarding. It all looked like a lot of fun, but the snowboarding looked a lot like what she was doing at the skate park. Tabitha wondered if the skills were transferable. She wondered whether she could do the same thing on snow, and she wished they weren't so poor, so she could take lessons. She decided that, one day, she was going to go to the Olympics. She was going to be one of those snowboarders.

When the school-based youth worker saw Tabitha at school the next day, he had been tipped off by Janice at the youth centre about the grounding, so he asked what Tabitha had watched the previous night and how the Olympics were. Tabitha told him she had been watching the snowboarding.

"Sure looks easy, just like skateboarding," she said. "I think I might go to the Olympics one day."

He agreed. "I'm really glad to hear that you're staying at home and following your mom's rules too. You've done such a great job of resisting the pressure from those guys at the centre, and it would be easy to give up. Can I call your mom? I have an idea about the snowboarding."

He had talked to Janice about offering Tabitha a job teaching skateboarding, and he knew a few people with used snowboarding equipment. But he didn't want to undermine Sarah's authority with Tabitha, so he thought he better call first.

(Continued)

"Yeah," Tabitha said. "Maybe you can convince her that the Youth isn't a problem. She doesn't trust me."

Tabitha's mom knew that snowboarding was expensive. There were all those costs for downhill passes, and for having the right board, good boots, and all that stuff. But the incident of finding the drugs had scared her. If she didn't get Tabitha away from the relationships that she was developing at the youth centre (the not-so-good relationships, because there were good ones there too), she thought that she might lose her completely. If that happened, Sarah wouldn't be able to spend that RESP that she'd been putting money away for.

So Sarah decided to take some of the money from the savings and spend it on equipment. She talked with the youth worker to see if he knew any good instructors or coaches, or even older kids who were into snowboarding and could help Tabitha work toward her dream. She agreed to the skateboarding instruction reluctantly because Janice assured her that Tabitha had the strength to resist the negative peer pressure. The youth worker had a friend with used snowboarding gear that was a good fit for Tabitha, and teaching skateboarding would help pay for the snowboarding lessons.

Passing By

Source: Laine Robertson

Once we begin developing a relationship, the process does not finish, nor does it follow a predictable pattern or timeline. When and how to influence young people relationally to help them make good choices and manage the life-space effectively are not always clear. Nevertheless, there are points during professional relationships with young people when we realize that the relationship gives us the power to stop a young person from losing control, committing a crime, or lashing out in anger at someone in their life-space, even though we are not present at the time.

The relationships that we develop with young people have many aspects that naturally help to prevent young people from making unsafe choices, problem-solving poorly, or getting caught up in particularly risky environments. At the same time, we must balance our influence with enabling them to learn how to manage their life-space and find their own path. The characteristics of a relationship that we have with a young person, such as mutual caring and respect, can give different meaning to the decisions that a young person makes in managing his or her life-space, thereby preventing poor decisions. Fear of losing a relationship, whether real or imagined, can stop young people and lead to re-evaluating a decision or a choice that is presented. The attachment that young children feel to their parents is a known factor controlling how far they wander out of parental sight. Similarly, our consistent modelling of socially appropriate problem-solving and respect for others in the context of our relationship with a young person can prevent them from bullying, insulting, slandering, or intentionally hurting the feelings of a peer.

If the relationship is a professional one, as compared to a relationship with a long-time friend or parent, it can be difficult to know when the natural characteristics of relationship might be helpful to prevent poor choices. Therefore, it is important to consciously develop some of the relational characteristics that will facilitate young people making wise and thoughtful decisions when faced with difficult choices in the life-space.

Anticipating difficult or dangerous situations and communicating what you see to young people helps them to anticipate and know how to respond. It is important to communicate without judgment and to identify choices and potential consequences without imposing control and power. Young people are faced regularly with choices such as whether to experiment with drugs, whether to join a gang, whether to study or go to a party, whether to respond to adult power and control in a respectful or disrespectful manner, and so on. No matter what we think about these scenarios, we want to help them explore what the choices are, the consequences of the decisions that they make, and how their various relationships – including those with us – might be affected. These are difficult conversations, but they are essential to our work in the life-space. Equally essential is accepting the choices young people make (even poor ones) and framing these from the perspective of learning within the life-space so that in another social context the decision might be different.

Evidence suggests that young people adopt the values, morals, and ethics of adults who are important to them. They might do this through simple observation and over a lifetime of exposure to their culture and familial values and morals. In a professional relationship this process needs to be accelerated, and we must recognize that other adults in their lives may not hold the same values and morals as we do. Young people will encounter value conflicts that we need to help them work through. There is something to be said in the relational examination of values and morals for the simplistic strategy of nagging and for in-depth exploration of moral questions. Repeatedly telling a young person who has difficulty sharing toys with others in an after-school program that "We share here" and "Sharing with others is the right thing" may be all that is necessary. However, a young person in his late teens may want to engage in an in-depth discussion about the value of human (or animal) life in the context of ritualistic or even wartime killing, and as a result may decide to disengage from a white supremacy group that has been recruiting in the community. The difficult negotiation for the practitioner in these circumstances is to respect young people's social context, morals and values, and to help young people navigate the laws of the country and the social norms and conventions of family and community.

When we recognize that relationships are extremely powerful to young people, we can use our influence wisely to support them in growing and developing, learning, and managing the challenges of the life-space without imposing intervention to change the trajectory of their development. However, sometimes our use of relationship needs to be more active, more therapeutic, and more explicitly meant to support young people to change and better manage the challenges of their life-space because they are not coping with those challenges. Since relationships play such a significant role in the life-space, they are also an effective approach to reaching beyond prevention to intervention in the life-space.

Relational Work: Intervention

The role of relationship in professional practice has been an ongoing focus of theorizing and applying to practice in child and youth care. The active engagement of relationship in the therapeutic change process is fundamental to therapeutic approaches in most disciplines. When the life-space was conceived of as the residence where children spent the other 23 hours beyond "therapy," established relationships were thought to be critical to influencing behaviour change and facilitating social learning through communication, social reinforcement, and modelling (Trieschman, Whittaker & Brendtro, 1969). The belief that a relationship is a prerequisite for change implies that the practitioner is in control and uses the power of the relationship to create change. The recognition that interpersonal relationships are the supportive fabric for learning and development led to discussion about the importance of being present – of being "in" relationship and attuned to immediate experience (Fewster, 1990b). However, the physical context is the focus of being present in this conceptualization of relationship. The focus may also include other aspects of the life-space as they are experienced in the current physical context. Anglin (2002) found that the building of rapport and relationship by group care workers was an interactional dynamic that led to a sense of belonging and commitment among young people in group care. Therapeutic relationships are formed by professionals for the express purpose of creating change in a young person's life.

Most helping professionals engage in interpersonal relationships as a core feature of their practice, which suggests that the act of engaging in the relationship is critical to the therapy. Reparative relational experiences (Teyber & McClure, 2002) are those in which the young person experiences a relationship in a way that is new and different from previous relationships. Thereafter, the young person is able to enter new relationships with different expectations, and therefore there may be less damage to those future relationships. In a therapeutic relationship, the therapist or practitioner focuses on problematic aspects of a young person's experience and creates projects, interprets actions, and applies the concepts of a specific change theory to lead the young person on a journey of change within that relationship. Therapeutic relationships are purposeful and focused. In contrast, while the relational aspects of the life-space are clearly affected by a therapeutic relationship, these relational dimensions are also shaped by many other factors, including all past and present, real, virtual, and imagined relationships that the young person has experienced.

The concept of relational practice has gradually replaced the ideas of relationship-based practice and therapeutic relationships in child and youth care by recognizing that mutual caring and mutual engagement are also foundational to our work in the life-space. In life-space intervention, the relational characteristics of the life-space make relationship both a requisite for and the medium of active change. Change occurs internally in young people, in their experience of the world – the life-space – and externally in their behaviour and interpersonal interaction in the social contexts that they engage in. Change may occur without any visible indicators, to be externalized at a later point in the young person's life (Ungar, 2006). Change also occurs simultaneously in the practitioner, through openness to relational work; but our focus here is on strategies for relational work that supports change for young people and/or influences the social contexts of their life-space. Our focus is on what the practitioner can do to influence young people's relationships and to influence the social context that young people exist in.

Following a brief look at some of Garfat's suggestions for attending to the relationship, we will extend the concept of relational work into the life-space (beyond place and immediate experience) to consider how relational work attends to the other life-space dimensions.

Attending to the Relationship

Relational work involves "attending to the relationship itself" and "a balance between my experiencing and that of the other; a balance between my actions and those of the other" (Garfat, 2008, p. 21). When the relationship is the intervention, we are interested in how both of us "are" within that relationship. We share our own experience of the moment and we focus on how we (the young person and I) feel *in* the relationship, not on how we feel *about* the relationship. An incident of troubling behaviour or our knowledge of an emotionally difficult event in the young person's life-space might prompt the inquiry "How are you?" The focus of conversation is not on what happened, but rather on how *we* are and on deconstructing the beliefs and assumptions that are interfering with the young person's learning and decision-making in the life-space. Questions that are more challenging than the usual open-ended questions about the event will help the young person explore how the event affects the space within in the relationship.

- What meaning does the young person make of the event or behaviour?
- What is he or she feeling?
- How has it changed the young person?

Sharing our own view in a dialogic approach to the conversation explores the effect of the incident on our relationship. These are important questions that explore life-space but don't actively engage with it. More challenging questions examine and deconstruct beliefs, look at relationships between aspects of the life-space, construct multiple realities (for choice), and create future possible selves. For example,

- What is your belief about families? What makes it so important to *not* be placed in a foster family?
- How does your work affect your schooling?
- What does life look like when you are out with your friends? What does it look like when you are visiting with your mom and sister?
- What do you envision for your Self? What are the possibilities when you think about work, play, family, and religion in the future?

Communication that focuses on relationships is vital. The practitioner may start with a simple observation or an open question, such as

- Today is the big dance.
- Yesterday was the anniversary of your mom's death.
- How are you? How are we?
- I'm concerned.

The direction of the conversation from there is not toward the details of the event, or even the initial response, which may or may not be true of the moment ("I'm fine" is simply a socially acceptable response that may or may not be true in that moment). The intent in relational work in life-space intervention is to genuinely care for others, engage with them in the process of caring and being relational, and therefore help them manage their life-space and be comfortably part of your own life-space. Examples and direction around life-space intervention and the role of relationships in the life-space are very hard to capture because every circumstance is so different from the previous one.

Attending to Physical and Mental Dimensions of Life-Space

Relational work also attends to other characteristics of life-space, such as the physical and mental, through relationship. Our relationships with the material aspects of the life-space can disturb or enhance relational work and therefore need attention. If we are working relationally in the life-space, then we will recognize and address the need for privacy or quiet during a serious conversation. "How are we feeling about having this conversation about your mom here in the school hallway?" Alternatively, we might be aware of the young person's relationship to certain characteristics of the physical dimension and address those. "I know you enjoy the warmth and the sunshine, since your apartment is so cold and dreary. Let's go outside." We might decide together about our relationship to the physical space and negotiate something that works for everyone. "What colour scheme should we use for the main floor area, kitchen and living room?"

Young people may have little to no control over the various physical spaces that make up their life-space, but through relational work we can help them establish their own agency in exploring the effect those physical characteristics have on them and how they might change their relationship to the physical dimensions of their life-space. Sometimes this involves our relationship with the young person, as in the previous examples, and at other times in might involve an exploration of the young person's relationship to the places and spaces in his or her life. When a street worker explores with a homeless young person the relative safety of an alley, a couch, a shelter, or a cockroach infested apartment shared with three other people, she is exploring the relationship of that young person to the physical aspects of those spaces. She might also express her own concern and fear for the young person's safety, or horror at the nature of those conditions.

Helping young people manage the physical and relational components of their life-space occurs in the mental dimension of life-space. Awareness of the thoughts and feelings – the meaning – associated with components of life-space requires skill and mindfulness. Based on their personal history in the life-space, young people quickly form judgments and opinions about the present life-space, reacting emotionally to the environment.

Meaning-making is part of relational work in the life-space. It is crucial to help young people make sense of their relationships and make meaning out of our relationship with them and how it is different from their other relationships. The challenge in meaning-making is sorting through the various relationships in the life-space and the various roles that people play. Questions about how young people's relationships with their friends are affected by their relationship with me, or questions about the character of their relationship with social workers or probation officers and what that means to how they manage their life-space, are fundamental to exploring how they make meaning out of the relationships that are part of their life-space. From this perspective, strategies such as role-taking and perspective-taking become relational interventions.

Role-taking is a strategy that asks young people to situate themselves in a different role as a way of exploring the implications of a choice or decision that they need to make. What would your teacher suggest that you try in order to solve this math problem? What would your doctor say about saving money or time by reusing needles (or having unprotected sex)? What would your mother say if she were here? Questions such as these necessitate that we have explored the young person's life-space and have some knowledge of the other important relationships, both those that might pose risks and those that are protective. We do not always have to send the young person to someone else physically to have that person exert some positive influence in the life-space.

Perspective-taking encourages young people to understand the relational nature of the life-space by placing themselves in someone else's position and exploring the meaning of behaviour from that position. Perspective-taking interventions can happen before, during, or following a difficult incident, and they are often basic to conflict resolution and life-space crisis intervention (LSCI) (Long, Wood & Fecser 2001). When you ask a young person, "How do you think Giacamo felt when you raced on ahead and left him sitting in the hot sun without anyone to push his wheelchair?" you help him or her develop empathy, think about consequences, and move into the life-space of a peer, all of which are vital skills in learning about your own life-space and how to manage it.

Attending to the Virtual Dimensions of Life-Space

Intervention in the virtual dimension of life-space through relational work can extend from simple communications, such as emails or text messages that express concern or remind the young person of our relationship and the need to pay attention to it, to complex exploration, such as carefully entering and understanding the world of madness that a young person finds him- or herself in, without getting lost in that world ourselves. Relational work in these aspects of life-space implies ensuring safety, expressing concern, and attempting to define the difference between the real and the unreal. It is in the juxtaposition of real and unreal that relational work becomes tricky. The socio-cultural context of a young person, the family, and the worker can lead to very different interpretations, and these must be sorted out in the relational work that we do. When a young person dreams at night, has conversations with ghosts, talks out loud to unseen people, or tells them to "Go away and let me sleep," is this real or unreal? A spiritual leader or shaman will tell you one thing, a psychic will tell you something different, and a psychiatrist will tell you something else again. In relational work we want to be concerned about how the young person and the family view these interruptions to sleep and about the extent to which they disrupt the management of day-to-day life in the spaces and places where the young person is located.

Relational intervention requires careful attention to Self and to boundaries (the subject of the next chapter). How else will the practitioner ensure that the focus is on young people and supporting change and management of their life-space, rather than on the practitioner?

Relationship and Systemic Intervention

Most of this book is devoted to working directly with young people and families by entering their life-spaces; forming relationships; caring; and engaging them in managing the physical, mental, virtual, and relational dimensions, learning about Self, and caring about others. Sometimes life-space work requires less direct involvement with young people in their lives and more work with people and systems that influence their lives. We still need to bring relationship to this work. This section briefly considers the practitioner's life-space – the nature of our relationship to team members and other professionals as well as the nature of our relationships with the "system" and how these might become different.

Working with colleagues brings together our life-space with theirs, but rarely do we approach an understanding of the overlap and integration of collegial life-spaces with the same curiosity and understanding that we use when working with young people. The team that works together to manage a residential treatment centre shift is focused on the young people, ensuring their needs are met and actively sharing a relationship with each of them. Relationships with colleagues are given little thought, even though we share a physical space for a large portion of the work day and are in each other's minds as the day ends and people return home. Similarly, in a child protection office, where child and youth care practitioners share job functions with social workers and/or nurses and those trained in psychology or sociology, little thought is given to the shared relational space. In an office setting, there may be some attention to the physical context: "Please be sure to wash your dishes after you use them." There may also be some attention to the mental dimension of the office relationships through team development, but attention is generally limited to the physical confines of the office and rarely given to relationships in other locations. Attending to relationship and entering the life-space of co-workers

Story: Relational Intervention

Tabitha showed up at the Youth one day with dirt and stains on her clothes and a cut over her eye that looked like it was going to develop into a nice shiner. Janice noticed and commented right away.

"Uh, I was just helping out this new kid at school," said Tabitha.

"What kind of help involves getting beat up?" asked Janice. "What's your mom going to think?"

"She won't see my clothes 'cause I'll get the wash done before she comes home, and I'm going to tell her I took a header off my skateboard here. You won't say anything, right?" asked Tabitha.

Janice decided she'd better get some idea of what was going on, but she knew that Tabitha would be less than forthcoming if she thought Janice might share the information with her mother.

"I'm not sure what I'll say to your mom, if anything .... So what's going on at school? I thought you had some kind of agreement with the bullies that was working pretty well."

"Oh, I'm okay with them," acknowledged Tabitha, "but there's this new kid, Kenji, and they've been picking on him. I told them to back off – they were holding him down on the ground, trying to get him to use his karate stuff. They told me to mind my own business, and you guys always say that it *is* my business to make sure we treat other people right. Three of them threw me."

"Well, I didn't mean you should get yourself hurt. There are other people to help, don't you think?" asked Janice.

"Nope."

"Come on – the vice-principal, the new youth worker, a teacher? Who else has some influence over these kids, and what would they think about you taking it on yourself?" asked Janice.

They continued to sort through the various people in the school and how they might respond to the bullies; who could support Kenji and who he might trust; how Tabitha could help get a relationship going for him with the appropriate person; and what she might do the next time she was confronted with the bullies. Janice was worried that the bullying would extend to Tabitha and that the school would have difficulty stopping it. Janice managed to get a promise from Tabitha that she would tell her mother, and an agreement that Janice could initiate some conversations with the school to start to resolve the problem on a bigger scale.

Relationships between the Youth and the school had deteriorated since the old youth worker had left, and they needed to be rebuilt. Some of these kids attended the Youth, so this was a natural place to join together to do some intervention and rebuild both youth and worker relationships. Janice also made a mental note to talk with the young people who had participated in the incident the next time she saw them at the centre. They had discussed things like bullying before, and she was disappointed in their behaviour.

ultimately benefits young people, and it enriches our own life-space. In co-constructing our relationship with co-workers, we attend to questions that are similar to those that frame our work with young people:

- Who are the people in our social contexts?
- Where do our relationships occur in place, space, and time?
- How do our relationships overlap?
- What meaning do we make of those relationships?
- How and where can we join our webs of existing and future relationships?
- Where are key points of learning?

Effective attention to life-space within our teamwork is not just about playing soccer together or going out for a drink after work, although we might do those things. All the strategies for entering the life-spaces of young people apply to our co-workers. Attention to relationships with co-workers means that we know when a colleague is ill, distracted by issues at home, or struggling with a relationship with one of the youth. As a result of our understanding of the life-space of co-workers, we might decide collaboratively to adjust the work that needs to be done, or we may simply be aware and express caring for the other person.

Attention to the relationship aspects of virtual team work is critical since much of today's communication comes through electronic means. Electronic modes of communication such as email, texting, blogs and social media sites absorb and influence relationships. Therefore, attention must be paid to the emotional messages conveyed in such communications. We need "real" conversation to explore the life-space of the receiver and the sender, and to understand how our co-workers' life-spaces influence the intent of the message. Similarly, virtual worlds such as Second Life and networking tools such as Facebook can enhance or detract from the relationships that team members construct and the work that they do together.

Working on the perfect team is the ideal vision of most practitioners, but since we each construct mental images of the ideal team from within our own life-space, we all have different ideals. Ideals and the expectations that accompany them can be a source of conflict, disagreement, gossip, and critique among co-workers. Understanding the team ideal in the life-space of co-workers can help us to construct a common ideal. Teams that have worked together for a long time develop a common language and a common set of norms that they have all agreed to over time. They may speak as a unit: "We use relationships with residents" or "We do a high school clinic." Members of the team have co-constructed the team space through conversation, curiosity, working through disagreement, and coming to understand where each person ends and the next begins and where the common relational aspects of their joined team space are. Achieving collegial teamwork takes time and attention, through real (and usually) face-to-face communication and interaction with people.

Teams are nested in organizations and broader systems that demand increasingly complex webs of relationships, both with people and with the rules and policies created to structure our work. Relationships form the group culture of organizations and exert social control, sometimes through formal policies and procedures and at other times informally through norms and habits.

Senge's (1990) concept of the learning organization takes the concept of life-space as a learning environment to a systemic level. He proposed that learning organizations are places where people expand their capacity to learn, to grow and develop, and to create a collective vision and a collective learning about managing the problems of the organization. It is unlikely that as a practitioner you will work in a learning organization with the values and beliefs that Senge describes. However, try to consider how the various dimensions of life-space manifest themselves in teams, organizations, and systems and to use some relational strategies to understand and perhaps influence the nature of the organization you are located in. If you succeed, you will have exerted some personal agency toward enhancing the life-space of not only yourself, but also the young people and co-workers that you relate to.

The next section describes a more systematic approach to intervention using relational strategies in the extended life-space of organizations and systems.

Relational Systemic Change: Advocacy

When decision-making that affects the lives of the young people, families, and our co-workers occurs at higher levels of the organization, or in the policy setting of governments that fund our work, we often refer to "the system," forgetting that the system is composed of people. Our work with young people and families sometimes leads to advocacy for systemic change to better meet their needs and help them manage their life-space in a fair and just world. Relationship plays a major role in these efforts for change.

In almost every major effort for systemic change, there is a young person in the minds and hearts of the change makers. Direct (and co-constructed) relationships with individual young people occur when advocates are created for them. A lawyer appointed to act for the child during a court case is doing the same job that a child advocate working in a safe house or a shelter for women does. Their role is to ensure that the interests of the child in any decision are considered separately from the interests of the adults. Individual advocacy for young people ensures that power imbalances are corrected.

In systemic advocacy efforts, we may not have a direct relationship with the young person, but the image and the life-space struggles of young people have been incorporated into our life-space as an advocate. Jordon's Principle is an example that honours the memory of an Aboriginal child who was caught in a jurisdictional dispute between federal and provincial governments in Canada (First Nations Child and Family Caring Society, n.d.). The dispute prevented him from going home from the hospital to live in a family home. Jordan has become a rallying point for discussions to resolve such systemic disagreements. Jordan's Principle received unanimous parliamentary support for a child-first principle in such disputes. Even though Jordan died, his image and his relationship with family and professionals lives on as a symbol for change.

Systemic change requires thinking about points of influence and how our relationship(s) can influence other people and other relationships within the system. When we acknowledge to ourselves that power and hierarchy are structures in any social context, we also need to recognize that people hold these positions of power and are subject to influence through relationships. This is quite different from relational work in the life-space with young people. To identify points of influence in your own life-space, take note of people and relationships between people, particularly in the professional and work-based aspects of your life-space. Identify who may hold similar values and beliefs about the need for change, and who either has some power to create and implement a change in practice, policy or law, or knows someone else who does. These are people with whom you want to actively create a relationship, drawing them into conversations about the young people who best represent the need for change. Those in positions of power can assist with advocacy for change in the system and advise what can be done to create change.

Social justice, the work that we do to ensure that young people are not denied opportunities based on social conditions beyond their control, requires advocacy and interpersonal relationships with many people. It becomes critical to identify values, find common spaces of safety and understanding, and help young people develop strategies for becoming powerful in their own right. The energy and effort required to create such change demands that practitioners who take on systemic change must be prepared to draw on the relationships they have with family, co-workers, and friends as they attempt this type of influence. In our vision of a caring, engaging, and relational life-space, co-construction of relationship and mutual care and concern are strongly held values and beliefs about interpersonal interaction. In advocacy work, we often represent groups of young people and families who are oppressed by the strength and power of relationships between members of dominate groups. Working against a dominant and powerful belief system necessitates that we draw on the care and concern of people in our own life-space to support our efforts and renew our energy.

Summary

This chapter described the role of relationships in life-space intervention. *Relationship* was described as an association between two or more things, often characterized with an adjective that describes the nature of the relationship (such as therapeutic, friendly, difficult, honest). Interpersonal relationships are of interest in child and youth care practice and are developed with young people, families, and colleagues. We also have relationships to and with systems that represent a larger collection of people with some common decision-making power. Engaging and entering the young person's life-space is largely a function of relationship and can be done through dialogical conversation, activities, and sensitivity to language and cultural norms. The power of relationships to influence social behaviour was described, and social control theories were used to explain the way behavioural norms and a civil society are maintained through the use of relationship. We recognized that relationships have a power element and yet, at the same time, our goal in life-space intervention is to equalize power and co-construct relationships with young people. The power of relationships can also be applied to good effect in the advocacy work for systemic change and in relational work in conflicted societies.

Discussion and Exercises

Reflection in Practice

Choose a situation in which you can observe and perhaps meet large numbers of young people. Go for a walk, enter a corner store beside a high school during lunch break, or catch the subway or a city bus just as school gets out. Observe the young people and their relationships. Notice the young people and who draws your attention.

1. What draws your attention and what assumptions do you make about them?
2. What emotions do you notice in yourself?
3. What meaning are you making out of their behaviour?
4. Take a deep breath, exhale, and let all these thoughts and observations go.
    What did you learn about yourself?

Reflection on Practice

In the opening story about Tabitha, identify examples of the following:

1. Professional relationships that were being developed consciously for specific purposes
2. Family relationships and how they followed Tabitha into the challenges of her life-space
3. The changing nature of peer relationships and how those challenged Tabitha's construction of her life-space

Reflection for Practice

If you were to begin a dialogical conversation with one of the young people you observed in the Reflection in Practice exercise above, or with Tabitha as a youth worker in the recreation centre, what would be your opening? Give an example of each type of opening.

1. A question
2. An observation statement
3. An action you might take

Theory in Action

Relational practice is an approach to practice that seeks to understand the kinship between people, and how they relate to and make meaning of the various people and objects in their life-space. It attends to the relationship itself as a component of change.

Consider the concepts that are part of relational practice and identify examples of them in your day-to-day life-space.

1. Relationships with objects and symbols
2. Dialogic conversation

3. Role-taking
4. Perspective-taking
5. Relational influence

Theory in Action: Life-Space Mapping Directions

Begin by introducing to the young person the idea that sometimes understanding life and how it influences us cannot be expressed in words. Drawing or doodling life can help both practitioner and young person understand more clearly what life is like and what the influences are. Ask if the young person is willing to give this a try and explain that this "mapping" might occur several times to see how things change, because there are always changes. Also explain that there is no right way to create the picture – words, lines, squiggles, circles, or detailed drawings are all part of it.

Ensure that the young person has a selection of different papers (background to life-space can be important). Something like an old wallpaper sample book might provide a selection of different backgrounds, but a simple white sheet of paper, large or small, will also do. Have a selection of coloured pens and markers available as well. Remember that questioning, being curious, reflecting, and inquiring about meaning to the young person are all important parts of the process.

Life-space mapping can be repeated as a regular activity in the work that practitioners do with a young person, thus representing the changing life-space and the outcomes that happen as a result of our involvement. Keep the construction of each map focused in the present to get a good representation, but remember that life-space includes memories of the past and dreams of the future, so these may appear in the map.

You will want to expand the following sequence through reflective questioning, but these questions (Peavy, 1998; Rodgers, 2006) provide a starting point:

1. Think of this whole sheet of paper as your life-space (or the "space of your life").
2. Put yourself on the paper. Label it or make it distinctive so we know it's you.
3. Let's represent the reason you are here. What is the best way to draw "the problem"?
4. What else is difficult for you right now? Let's represent that on the paper.
5. Everyone also has strengths, activities, memories, relationships, important places and things that are part of their lives. What seems to be important to you right now? Let's draw that.
6. Practitioners also have a view of the young person's life and can add their perspective to the map if the young person provides permission. Representing different aspects of the life-space from another perspective adds depth of understanding and multiple points for engagement (now and in the future).
7. Continue adding and discussing the map. Inquire about sources of tension, conflict, joy, and pleasure.
8. Ask about goals for the short-term and long-term future.
9. It is helpful (for later review and reflection on the map) to add names and labels. Use questioning to inquire about labels. This might be your job as the helper. If the

young person is intent on a visual product and finds labels intrusive, then small, clear sticky notes can be used to label the map being developed.

Remember that the goal for the practitioner and the young person is to understand this moment of the life-space and the mapping activity or tool that can facilitate that understanding.

The life-space maps below were done by a young woman recalling her life-space in two of the three decades of her life. She described herself as having a life in three parts, each very different from the others. She agreed to create these maps by reflecting on those parts to help herself explain and integrate these different life-spaces into one, and to reflect on the values and supports she carried with her into the future

In the first decade, at age 8 (below on the left), she represented herself as a tree, laying down growth rings, surrounded by relationships with family, school, and recreational activities that brought together key adult figures in her life. Each relationship made an important contribution to her core beliefs and values. They taught her about love, discipline, structure, achievement, security, and guidance. These important values continued into her life during the third decade (below on the right), as did some of the relationships. New relationships were also present, and these relationships made similar contributions to her ability to manage her life-space and added new supports such as wisdom, strength, and the ability to listen. She evolved in the third decade into a triangle (representing the three phases of her life that gave her strength) and she had incorporated some of the characteristics that she valued in others (love, structure, and discipline) into her Self.

First Decade at Age 8   Third Decade

In her vision for the (immediate) future (below), the triangle had evolved into a square, representing balance, and had incorporated additional characteristics (in the centre). The relationships with people and places had evolved somewhat, but many of the same relationships were still present in different forms, such as long-distance relationships and those via the Internet.

The Future Vision

CHAPTER 6

Negotiating and Constructing Boundaries: Creating a Safe Life-Space

Callie

Source: Kyle Stewart

Life-space work requires a deep understanding of personal, professional, and system boundaries as well as boundary shaping and boundary management. In life-space intervention, practitioners work within the young person's milieu, where young people experience very little separation from daily life while engaged in professional relationships. Therefore, practitioners must understand the fluidity of boundaries and be comfortable with discussing and negotiating boundaries with young people, families, and the organizations and systems they work in. Young people may have experienced dysfunctional relationships and be uncertain about boundaries. A portion of our work in the life-space is to help young people shape their boundaries and learn how to negotiate and reshape those boundaries as the need arises. Much of what we do on a daily basis is to prevent and address boundary violations.

The concept of a boundary or border between two entities is common to many fields of study. Boundaries exist at multiple levels. For example, at the level of the individual, boundaries are thought to surround and contain personal identity and separate consciousness from the unconsciousness. This ensures that as individuals we have a good sense of reality as distinct from the imagination or insanity (Gabbard & Lester, 2003). Boundaries are also conceived of by psychotherapists as the border between Self and Other, and at times as a border surrounding the therapeutic event. If the therapist crosses or violates a boundary, therapy is compromised (Zur, 2007). The idea that there is a boundary around a therapeutic event has led to a proliferation of specific ethical guidelines that speak to "boundary issues," such as dual relationships, appropriate physical touch, giving or receiving gifts and food, personal space, and lending/borrowing personal objects. Researchers and therapists are interested in the nature of boundaries within and around systems comprised of groups or families and how these boundaries affect group membership as people enter and/or leave the system. Groups of friends, interdisciplinary teams, school classes, and neighbourhood sports teams all have boundaries around them that define inclusion, exclusion, roles and relationships in the group. On a macro level, boundaries exist around large systems, such as the child welfare system and the education system, that make it difficult for young people who need intensive assistance from both systems to receive help. Finally, boundaries exist geographically to define country, homeland, and rules for entry and exit. These boundaries may also be associated with disputes based in religion or culture.

Najwah's Story: The Importance of Boundaries

Najwah was thrilled to be starting her first full-time job after graduating with a degree in child and youth care. Her position as a youth and family support worker with a rural Children's Aid Society in the northern part of the province was to start next week. Her responsibilities included a mixed case load of young people who were living independently with the support of the Society and young families who were struggling with parenting their children. She would be travelling among five small towns and occasionally into the local farming communities to meet clients and address the issues that had brought them to the attention of the Society.

Najwah was pleased to be moving back to the small community where she had grown up; her parents would be available to babysit her 2-year-old daughter. Her hours were irregular and her husband trusted her parents to help the baby learn their Muslin traditions even though, as a modern family, he and Najwah both needed to work. His career in the bank was just beginning, and his employer anticipated that he would be able to attract more members of the Muslim community to their services, since Najwah's parents were respected local leaders.

Najwah fully anticipated the need to address interpersonal boundaries with her clients. Indeed, her interviewers had made a significant issue of boundaries when they learned that she had grown up in the area. The interviewer asked how she would manage if she was assigned a client with whom she went to high school.

Najwah had already thought about this question, since she had encountered the situation while in high school years ago. She told the interview panel about her experience as a peer counsellor in high school.

Najwah had been approached by a girl new to the community whom she had met the previous week at the mosque. Nashida had said that she really needed someone to talk to about her family. She had insisted that Najwah was the only person she could talk to because no one else would understand; they were the only two Muslim girls in the school (at that time). Najwah had hoped that they would become good friends, and she had been excited to have someone who would understand her religion and the customs that she followed. But her peer counselling supervisor had made it very clear that certain boundaries were not negotiable, and that difficult issues

were to be referred to the guidance counsellor.

As they got to know each other, Nashida shared some stories about her father's abusive behaviour. He would beat her for talking with other girls in school and insisted that Nashida had to come straight home after school and not go out with friends, even Najwah. Najwah knew that sometimes traditional families still followed old customs and traditional beliefs about "the property of woman," even though her family was not as traditional.

Najwah had become worried when Nashida didn't come to school one day, so she had gone to her peer counselling supervisor and told her some of the stories. A report was made to the child protection authorities, and the next day in school Nashida refused to talk to Najwah. Later that week, Nashida passed a note through a mutual friend saying that she was deeply offended that Najwah had broken her commitment not to tell, and that her father was only trying to teach her the traditions of their culture. Now Nashida had no one to talk to.

Najwah had done a lot of reflecting on this incident and others throughout her education. She now saw many opportunities for talking about boundaries, creating them together, and determining how she might have helped Nashida learn about setting her own boundaries for safety and still fit within the traditions of her family.

Defining Boundaries in Life-Space Work

Relational boundaries maintain the distinct identities and roles of people who are involved in a relationship, and the nature of the relationship has implications for the boundaries that are developed. Since life-space work is based on relationship, we will consider the different definition of boundaries required in life-space work in contrast to other professional roles. We will also distinguish how limits and ethics are related to boundaries.

Boundaries represent implicit and explicit group norms, organizational rules and cultural expectations about group membership, power and authority, and social interaction. Boundaries may define and protect membership in the group, and they nest groups within larger communities and social contexts with common approaches to communication, privacy and the nature of relationships.

We define boundaries and discuss their role and function in life-space work within the overlap among individual, group, system, and culture. Boundaries are the interface of communication between people nested within multiple social contexts, where each context contributes to defining the boundaries of the others. This means that any type of boundary construction, boundary disturbance, or boundary ambiguity has multiple effects, just like the ripples of a stone thrown in a pond. Our focus here is primarily on the construct of boundaries as it applies to practitioner relationships with young people when we encounter them in a professional context and enter their life-space.

Ideas about boundaries develop from family, social, cultural, and individual norms and considerations. They evolve as we grow, develop and learn from our social context. They are pliable, with some variation from relationship to relationship. The nature of acceptable interpersonal behaviour that determines when you are "taking advantage of," "causing harm to," "hurting the feelings of," or "disclosing more than you should" is individually defined, both for you and for the other person, and it differs according to your social group and current context. Boundaries are set in the social context and the nature of the relationships that exist in that social context. Therapeutic relationships often imply a safe connection between client and therapist based on the client's needs (Peterson, 1992). Parent–child relationships imply a duty to unconditionally love, protect, and guide the child on a developmental path toward adulthood in today's challenging society. Teaching or mentoring relationships focus on learning and conveying knowledge to a young person. A helping relationship includes problem-solving and guidance toward the "right choice" under a particular circumstance. The expectations we have of others and our understanding of what are "proper" actions within their roles are guided by our own ideas about relational boundaries.

The distinction between personal and professional boundaries in the life-space of young people and their families is an arbitrary and simplistic one. In most professional therapeutic work, boundaries are defined by specific times and places for "therapy." Indeed, professional boundaries are often codified in professional cthical codes and in many psychotherapeutic encounters a written informed consent procedure defines the nature of the therapeutic boundaries and addresses potential boundary issues. Statements such as "[the practitioner] ensures that the boundaries between professional and personal relationships with clients is [sic] explicitly understood and respected, and that the practitioner's behavior is appropriate to this difference" (Association of Child and Youth Care Practice, 1995) are common to ethical codes developed by child and youth care professional associations. We would like to suggest that the distinction between personal and professional boundaries is less clear in practice and is particularly unclear in life-space work.

Child and youth care practice is often defined by its *lack* of restricted times and places because it occurs in the natural milieu of the young person rather than in an office space. When a street worker encounters a young person and begins to build the relationship, written informed consent will likely be counterproductive to the ultimate goal of safety, and there is no "office" to contain the therapy. Young people expect and thrive on the more intimate "knowing" of the other person that occurs in life-space interaction. The practitioner must carefully consider what the professional boundaries are or should be under the circumstances, and how to communicate them. Understanding the difference between limits, ethics, and boundaries is a beginning point for a deeper understanding of the boundary work required in life-space intervention.

Limits

Boundaries sometimes require setting limits. When you tell a friend, "Don't do that" or "If you do that I'll never speak to you again," you are conveying a limit. When a parent yells "STOP" at a young child as he nears a busy street, a limit has been set that ensures the child's safety. Limits involve safety—not just physical safety but also protection from emotional or psychological harm. Limit setting is a component of intervention that is critical to helping children develop a sense of self and communicating to others who we are and what we believe is acceptable behaviour. Research indicates that children understand the reasons for their parents' limit setting; that rural and urban children have different limits and boundaries set for them by parents; and that rural families are more open to negotiating boundaries than urban parents, who are uncertain how to negotiate in this context given their safety concerns (MacDougall, Schiller & Darbyshire, 2009).

Limit setting is also essential to a practitioner's safety and well-being. Practitioners must consider the circumstances, the means of communicating their limits about personal information, and their tolerance for certain behaviours such as swearing or personal posturing. Limits are the external expression of our internal boundaries and represent the "bottom line" of what behaviours we will accept in an interpersonal relationship.

Ethics

Ethics are the codified moral rules that we adhere to and that govern our behaviour and our interpretation of the "rightness" of the behaviour of others (Ricks & Charlesworth, 2003). Ethics are based on morals and values formed during childhood and fairly well established by the end of adolescence. Developmental research has shown that universal ethics do not exist, and that while expressed morals and values may be relatively stable, ethics tend to be situational (Santrock, MacKenzie-Rivers, Leung & Malcomson, 2008). When you get angry at a friend for sharing a secret or telling you a lie, it's because the friend has broken one of your personal moral and ethical codes. However, under certain circumstances, you might do the same. Ethics can also be an expression of our boundaries. Professional ethical codes are developed as the collective professional community's "group" rules for behaviour. Professional ethics have a legalistic basis since they codify what is collectively defined as "wrong" behaviour, and they often provide ethical guidelines for boundary issues. For example, virtually all ethical codes prohibit sexual relationships between professionals and clients.

While ethical codes may distinguish between personal and professional boundaries, they do not address all boundary issues because the social context, the organizational context, and the nature of your relationship with a young person or family can have a strong influence on boundaries. Therefore, practitioners must be prepared to give careful attention to boundary issues in a professional context and understand how to help young people manage their personal boundaries.

Having defined boundaries in life-space work and considered the differences between boundaries, limits and ethics, we will now turn our attention to how life-space work affects our understanding of boundaries.

Story: The Personal/Professional Conversation with the Self

In her job interview Najwah described how, during her last visit to the community, she had attended Nashida's wedding and talked with her about how they could re-establish a relationship and what the interpersonal boundaries might be in the future. It would take a while to re-build trust, but they both realized that the issues they dealt with in high school were big issues for 15-year-olds to manage and they had done what they needed to do at the time.

In her work with clients, Najwah intended to discuss boundaries in the first visit and in most visits afterward. She knew she would need to discuss what to do if she met a client in the community and how to acknowledge each other. She might have to discuss how she would handle safety concerns that were visible or reported to her (given her obligation under the child protection legislation) and how people felt about her visiting in their home. If they offered her drinks or food, she would have to deal with her religious obligations and still manage to be caring and respectful of their offer. People might know her husband through their banking activities, and she would need to keep that relationship separate.

However, she anticipated that, when the Muslim community (which had grown significantly since her youth) learned of her presence with the Society, young people might be contacting her asking for help and support with independent living arrangements, because there were young girls still living in circumstances similar to those experienced by Nashida. She anticipated being approached by older sisters at the mosque with information about girls who were still living at home, because she was a visible and trusted member of the community. These situations could pose safety issues for her own family, and Najwah needed to be conscious of this and talk with her parents and her husband.

There were many boundary issues to address, and Najwah knew that her colleagues also experienced them, given that there were several small and close-knit communities in the jurisdiction of the Society. Moreover, the Society had a preference for hiring people who were local in order to reduce staff turnover.

What Najwah did not anticipate was that her struggle with boundaries would start before her first day on the job. Many issues arose simply through her move, and she was grateful for the emphasis that her education had placed on self-reflection and considerations about negotiating boundaries. During the move from the city to the small town, Najwah went ahead with her daughter in the car; her husband and his cousins drove the rental truck with their furniture. She took her daughter to her parents' home while they unloaded the truck. She was surprised and a little anxious to find several other grandparents with toddlers there, and all the children out in the backyard unsupervised except by an occasional glance out the window. They were wandering in and out of the woods that bordered the unfenced backyard, picking up pine cones and sticks to play with. Najwah told her mother that she didn't want her daughter out there unsupervised because it was dangerous. Her mother said, "No, no, it's perfectly safe. You just aren't used to the country. Everyone does this."

While driving over to the apartment to meet the truck, Najwah found herself reflecting on her professional training, trying to recall the developmental capacities of a 2-year-old and assessing her daughter's capacity to keep herself safe in this new environment. Finally, she phoned her mother and asked where the baby was.

"Outside."

"Who's with her?"

"No one. I can see her from here."

Najwah explained, "She's not used to being by herself in such an open space. You have to remember that we come from the city and she's lived her life in an apartment, not like those other kids. She won't know what's safe and what's not. She might eat something and she's probably scared because she doesn't know anyone."

Her mother agreed to go and check in on the baby and play with her for a while. Najwah felt good about setting a limit in her own relationship with her mother, and realized that these were things she would have to explore with her professional colleagues because she didn't have a good sense of appropriate limits for children in the rural context. Given her role in supporting new parents and at the same time assessing child protection concerns, she would need to get a better sense of the community norms to meet her ethical and legal responsibilities to keep children safe. She also realized that at times she might use her own daughter, or her own concerns as a parent, as an example, but that she would have to carefully assess this self-disclosure and when it might be appropriate.

As Najwah walked down the apartment hallway and observed the scruffy children playing in the halls and on the sidewalk out front, she wondered again about the wisdom of renting a separate space instead of using the basement suite that her parents had offered to them. She just really wanted to keep the boundary between her little family and her extended family more physically separate. She knew that relationally there was very little separation. She made a note in her mind to explore this again with her husband, if she could ever get him away from his cousins.

Understanding Boundaries in the Life-Space Context

The physical dimensions of life-space provide a number of natural forums for setting boundaries. By virtue of our work in the milieu, the discussion of physical boundaries in the workplace is essential. Most physical environments have natural boundaries between safe and unsafe places, and professional settings often designate specific places for professionals that are separate from the places for young people. Schools and community centres, for example, are fenced, perhaps to keep young people in a safe zone where strangers cannot reach them. Family homes have doors (inside and outside) that lock, schools have staff rooms, residential centres have staff offices, and youth centres have programmer offices and reception desks where staff do paperwork, have confidential conversations, and plan meetings. These physical locations communicate boundaries and define professional relationships for young people. These boundaries may be related to safety or they may be related to adult perceptions of power or the privacy required for setting professional boundaries. Regardless of how we explain the intent of these separations in the physical dimension of the life-space, a message is communicated to young people through the creation of physical boundaries and separated places for "professionals."

Young people also define physical boundaries by placing "Keep Out" signs on their bedroom doors or by finding and creating private places for themselves, such as a grove of trees in a park where they can sit and converse or participate in a variety of activities away from adult eyes. Both professional and youth "places" and the boundaries of those places can be violated. Young people may create physical boundaries that exclude practitioners and give themselves privacy just as practitioners have created the office or the staff room, and the appropriateness of these boundaries is an opportunity for discussion.

The mental dimensions of the life-space bring a different understanding of boundaries. As professionals, our work in the life-space includes love and caring, and it engages young people on a personal level. We must pay attention to issues related to power and the language that represents our thoughts and feelings. Such an approach may be very different from a young person's experience of other professionals, and even different from his or her experience of other adults.

Young people who have experienced abuse or neglect as part of their social context may have very open and inclusive boundaries, seeking love and affection from any adult. Alternatively, they may have very closed boundaries and seek to reject adults in order to keep themselves safe. Groups of young people collectively define a boundary to their group that can be intentionally difficult for adults to engage. Thus, we are faced with negotiating boundaries that communicate love and caring, and that minimize our own emotional reactions to the behaviour of young people as a result of their initial assumptions about boundaries. Similarly we are faced with determining the extent of emotional involvement that we will have in the work we do with each young person, and it will be different with each young person because the social context is different. Helping professionals are easily accused of being too emotionally involved when they advocate strongly or express caring and love for young people. Yet life-space work may demand an expression of love and caring about young people that is genuine and supported by a careful consideration of boundaries and the meaning of this type of involvement, both to the practitioner and to the young person.

It is the relational aspects of "working" in the young person's life-space that make boundaries both challenging to negotiate and effective as a component of life-space intervention. The co-creation of relationships and boundaries must involve mutuality. As practitioners co-create a sense of love and caring, they are responsible for identifying the young person's emotional responses as well as their own, reflecting some of those responses back to the young person, and encouraging learning about the mutuality of the relationship and how to adjust boundaries as emotions emerge. Practitioners and young people are mutually responsible for boundary shaping, but professional responsibility means that practitioners are *accountable* for the nature and safety of the relational boundary work in the life-space. "Setting" boundaries in life-space work could work against the relational aspects of the work described in the Chapter 5, and it places the power in the relationship with the practitioner. Instead, boundaries should be co-constructed in light of the social context and with an awareness and understanding of cultural norms and the complexity of multiple relationships.

Young people have a web of relationships in their life-space, and the practitioner is only one component of that web. Work in the life-space of the young person means that the traditional definition of dual relationships takes on new meaning. The traditional definition of a dual relationship is one in which the professional is engaged in two or more relational roles with the young person, such as friend, practitioner, foster parent, and neighbour (Reamer, 2003). To the young person, the "non-professional" relationship is of fundamental importance in life-space work. Young people describe their relationships with child and youth practitioners as friendships, motherly or fatherly, and various other terms that indicate the multiplicity of interpretations that they apply to these relationships (McMillan, Stuart & Vincent, 2011). At the same time, they refer to the same people as their key worker, primary worker, or street worker, representing the language of the professional relationship. The dual relationship is increasingly recognized as having some therapeutic benefit (Zur, 2007), and for life-space work it may be an essential component of intervention.

The virtual dimension of life-space brings forward many considerations in understanding boundaries. Changing social norms, the role of technology in social networking, and the increasing diversity and globalization of the life-space bring new issues and considerations to how boundaries are negotiated and how interpersonal boundaries in all social contexts are interpreted.

Young people have a strong online presence today and tend to be more open, independent, accepting of difference and aware of social inequity (Bibby, 2009). Prior to the advent of social networking sites, youth presence on the Internet required a reasonable command of technology, and interpersonal relationships in this virtual dimension of the life-space tended to be anonymous and text based. Today, youth have adopted social networking sites as a way to stay in touch with others and express themselves to the world. With this practice comes the danger of expanded boundaries and privacy concerns. The Internet is also a place with the potential for abuse or boundary violations through child luring and sexual solicitation, cyber-bullying, and unwanted or unexpected exposure to sexual material.

Decisions about boundaries on social networking sites are made in isolation of the interpersonal relationship and of communication available in face-to-face meetings. Young people may be unaware of who is interacting with their site and accessing their personal information. Relationships that are mediated through technology may limit the opportunity for a discussion about boundaries if young people "meet" each other online without "greeting" each other by acknowledging that they have already been viewing the site. Technology allows those who are capable and willing to follow the directions to set boundaries on the personal information that they share on these sites. However, depending on how public a social network page is, knowing the other person and developing a sense of relationship can be very one-sided. The virtual nature of social networking sites and their role in a young person's life-space raise many questions. How flexible are the boundaries on a social networking site? Can they be adjusted according to the nature of the person you are interacting with? How open will we become as a society? What are the privacy ethics involved when parents (or professionals) review a young person's social networking site (Ledbetter et al., 2010)?

Cyberspace as an intervention medium has developed significantly over the last ten to fifteen years, and it provides an adjunct for life-space intervention (Martin & Stuart, 2011). Internet-based sites for counselling provide clear guidelines about boundaries to maintain anonymity and confidentiality. Considerations related to privacy and confidentiality on these sites have been developed to conform to ethical codes, but as young people interact with essentially anonymous helpers they need assistance to consider how to manage information and boundaries. Today's "reality TV" shows and video and online games also increasingly blur the boundaries between fantasy and reality and have implications for the construction of boundaries.

The virtual dimensions of the life-space go beyond the influence of technology to include the imagination and the transformation of the mental aspects of life-space into something that others simply cannot understand—the virtual space of "madness." The imagination plays a significant role in the development of boundaries. Very young children have active imaginations and incorporate fantasy play into their day-to-day activities, gradually internalizing the imagination and separating fantasy from reality as they grow older. Young adolescents do not always share their fantasies and dreams with peers, and may be even more limited in sharing with adults. However, we need to be aware of the imagination in our work and consider its role in boundary development. In the early stages of a career in youth work, the age difference between practitioner and youth may be minimal, opening the way for fantasies regarding friendship or romance. Different (but just as possible) are the activities of the imagination that place the child or young person into the practitioner's family, finding safety in that home. Life-space intervention requires discussion with young people about what they can learn through the interface between imagination/fantasy and the more tangible aspects of their life-space.

Madness has implications for how relational boundaries are defined between practitioner and young person. When young people break from reality into the cognitive space that is madness, any boundaries that have been previously constructed with a helping practitioner may be forgotten or changed. Rational capacity to negotiate boundaries will change, and then change again as madness dissipates. There are cultural definitions of madness (and sanity) that are beyond the scope of this discussion, and as a person enters the realm of madness there may be multiple organizational boundaries that begin to influence the life-space. Incarceration or secure confinement that does not require the permission of the young person may be viewed as a boundary violation by the young person and most certainly involves the boundaries of multiple systems, which may facilitate or hinder the interventions we undertake. These are issues that practitioners should take into consideration as they work with young people affected by mental illness.

Having explored the concept of boundaries and some of the implications of life-space dimensions for how boundaries are defined, we now turn to how to shape and manage boundaries and how boundaries can be violated in life-space work with young people.

Story: The Social Boundaries of Care and Concern

Najwah met her first client at the new shelter/youth drop-in support centre. Youth homelessness and housing for youth were invisible issues in the community that were just beginning to be addressed, and there were no programs specific to housing for youth. Some local social justice advocates and volunteers were coordinating an "Inn from the Cold" program that operated out of local religious centres from November 1 to April 1. People without housing were able to come to one of the locations that provided sleeping pads, sleeping bags, and overnight accommodation in the basement of the centre. The locations rotated through five local centres, including the mosque.

One of these centres, the "Youth Christian Ministry," also ran an employment support program that encouraged youth to drop in to use the computers for job searches and talk with volunteers or the minister about employment goals. The minister had phoned the Society when Callie confessed that she was 15, not 16 as required by the "Inn" rules. The minister knew her family and recognized the last name. When he called the Society, he recommended that it provide support because the situation at Callie's home was unsafe, even for a 15-year-old.

Najwah was meeting Callie to assess whether the Society could or should provide housing support and support for her to complete her education. When she got to the drop-in centre, Callie wasn't there; the minister said she had gone to get coffee and doughnuts for the group. He told

Najwah that he was very concerned about Callie, and now that he knew her age he would have to tell the other centre coordinators. Callie would not be able to sleep in any of the centres again.

The minister offered to let Callie stay at his home and implied that he might be willing to provide ongoing housing. Najwah asked if he had ever done that for any other young people. He hadn't, but he was very concerned about her safety.

Callie returned, and after handing the minister a coffee she asked if Najwah would mind if they went for a walk to talk about the situation. She said she needed a smoke. Najwah inquired whether there would be enough privacy on the walk and Callie said, "More than here for sure." So they headed for Main Street, where Najwah knew there were a few quiet family restaurants that wouldn't have anyone in them yet.

In addition to the standard assessment questions about money, safety, educational goals, family situation, and so on, Najwah also had in her head a set of boundary issues to address:

(1) The nature of their relationship and potential dual relationships
(2) Self-disclosure
(3) Privacy for both of them, including Najwah's knowledge of community members
(4) Confidentiality of information to and from other professionals

Najwah planned to make social conversation until she saw a suitable

(Continued)

restaurant or other quiet spot to sit, but Callie jumped right in and Najwah was forced to add another boundary issue to her list.

"That guy gives me the creeps," said Callie. "It's like he thinks I'm a homeless, abandoned puppy and he can just take me home. He doesn't get that staying with him would be worse, and my friends would all think I was sleeping with him. I don't do that stuff. He creeps me out!"

Najwah nodded and added another item to the list in her head.

(5) Dealing with the boundaries of another colleague

"He's really concerned about your safety, and he says he knows your family. He called me hoping that I can help because the Society has a program to help with housing and educational support for people under 18. My role is to see if you qualify, help get you set up, and then stick around and support you and make sure everything is okay." (Najwah thought, partial check on #1.)

"What did he say, or do, that gives you the creeps?" she asked.

"Wellllll. . . It's just the opposite of what you said. You told me what you can do for me. He knows my family and that's how he knows I'm only 15. I've stayed in a couple of those other Inn nights and some of them know my family too. *They* didn't blow the whistle. It's like an unwritten rule. This is a small town—you gotta ignore some stuff. But noooo. . ., he calls you. That's okay, I can use the help, I guess. I was already looking up on the Internet the rules about welfare if you're under 18, but he offers to take me home because I don't meet the rules for the Inn. That's just creepy—like he doesn't get that maybe I'm doing an okay job taking care of myself and maybe he should just ignore the age rules, like he's ignoring the rule about no personal relationships with the client."

Whew, thought Najwah. I think she's pretty clear about small-town boundaries and the formal boundaries that the Inn set up. It should be pretty easy to figure out and talk about the rest of the boundary stuff. I hope the service assessment is just as easy.

Shaping: Co-constructing Boundaries

The focus in this section is on the boundaries between practitioner and young person, and the boundaries around their relationship. These boundaries both contain the relationship and provide a forum for young people to learn about their own boundaries and the boundaries of systems and social contexts that influence their life-space. Relational boundaries foster safety for self-disclosure; determine the context for authority, trust, and dependence; and make it possible for the young person to express fears, worries, and frustrations without judgment on the part of the practitioner. Boundaries in life-space practice are flexible and co-constructed within the day-to-day milieu of the young person, which increases the potential for boundary ambiguity.

Daily events and the emotional reactions associated with those events provide the substance for co-creating boundaries with intention and purpose in a manner that is guided by the practitioner and considers the young person's needs and social context. Clinical professional relationships are very different from youth work, social justice work, child protection work, community development work, and other types of family work that require forming personal relationships, "working" side by side, and doing home visits (Freud & Krug, 2002) or working in the life-space of young people and families. Therefore, the usual professional ethical guidelines about boundaries do not necessarily apply. This provides limited direction and leaves the life-space practitioner reliant on self-knowledge and reflective discussion with peers and supervisors when co-constructing boundaries. The following discussion highlights several strategies for approaching and discussing the boundary ambiguity created in life-space intervention.

Perception Sharing

Perception sharing (Berge & Holm, 2007) involves discussing with young people how they see the role of the practitioner (or their own roles) and what this means for membership in groups and chance encounters in the settings in which they are both present. Simple things like how to acknowledge each other if you live in the same community and use the same gym or grocery store are essential. How a young person feels and thinks about stopping a school-based practitioner in the hallway and asking for information on drugs, sexual health, bullying, or date rape are best discussed beforehand. A simple acknowledgment such as "I've seen you at the gym over on Bloor Street before. How do you feel about working with me on this anti-racism project?" are just as essential as "How would you feel about me visiting you at home and talking with your mom about the concerns you have about her depression?" Sharing thoughts and feelings about the parameters of the role of the practitioner in the young person's life-space begins to define the nature of the work that they will do together.

Multiple Roles and Relationships

Labelling the multiplicity of relationships (Berge & Holm, 2007) is essential to the negotiation of boundaries. Young people easily recognize the variety of possibilities and the similarity of their relationship with the practitioner to other relationships in their life. Making these explicit will help to keep the practitioner's role clear and can facilitate addressing the nature of the relationship and the boundaries in those other relationships. Comments like "That's what my Dad says" provide an opportunity to discuss not only how the practitioner is different from Dad but also how the nature of the young person's relationship with Dad might change. Practitioners also play multiple roles within their role as helper in the young person's life-space. They are members of a team in a pick-up game and therapists during the crisis that occurs following a friend's death. The middle of a basketball game is not necessarily a good time to talk about a young person's anger or hurt, but aggressive play might indicate its presence. This can be labelled with a commitment to discuss the details later, thus differentiating the role of team player from therapist/problem solver. Similarly, practitioners can help create a boundary around the pain of a crisis event, supporting the young person to manage pain and anxiety without avoiding it.

Dialectical Thinking

Holding two opposing views at one time regarding a particular situation requires dialectical thinking and is an important strategy for knowing what boundaries to set in which social context (Berge & Holm, 2007). In contrast, absolute thinking holds that there is only one "truth" about a situation. Young people whom we work with and new practitioners may need assistance with dialectical thinking about boundaries.

Learning to care for and work with a young person who has committed a sexual offence requires dialectical thinking. Appreciating the need the young person has to be cared about, identifying and acting on appropriate types of touch, and helping the young person construct acceptable boundaries related to sexual behaviour with peers are all part of shaping and co-constructing boundaries. The practitioner may be in the role of both enforcer (on a probation order, for example) and counsellor, teaching the young person about adolescent sexuality. Helping young people understand these dual roles and their own internal boundaries related to sexual identity requires dialectical thinking and is part of the work of shaping the boundaries for the relationship.

Being Personal

Personal self-disclosure is sometimes frowned upon in professional training. However, "being personal" (Krueger, 2007) can shape the boundaries of a relationship in life-space intervention by equalizing the power differential between practitioner and young person that is created when young people are expected to share personal information and practitioners are not. With caution and consideration, practitioners may disclose feelings and reactions to the social contexts they share with young people. They might disclose some personal history and solutions to their own problems, their current issues and concerns, unresolved dilemmas and conflicts, and stories about others and their reactions. Self-disclosure is a method of establishing mutuality in a relationship and reduces the power imbalance inherent in a practitioner–client relationship. For Aboriginal people (and for some other groups), self-disclosure and storytelling help to establish authenticity in the helping relationship.

The approach to being personal that the practitioner chooses depends on multiple factors, such as personal ethics and rules for behaviour, the practitioner's internal boundary around self-disclosure, and the nature of the young person's boundaries and needs at a given time. This is part of the co-creation of the boundary between practitioner and young person.

Reconstructing Boundaries

In traditional helping approaches, boundaries recognize the separateness of the young person and service provider and validate their distinctness. In life-space work, while we act to co-construct boundaries, sometimes altering boundaries to reconstruct them in a manner that is different from previous relational boundaries may become a therapeutic strategy. Shifting or crossing boundaries to alter those already established in the helping relationship may be a strategy to help the young person manage his or her own life-space. In this way, our relationship with the young person is itself a therapeutic process (Fewster, 2005; Garfat & Charles, 2007; Stuart, 2009).

There are three ways to alter or reconstruct the boundaries established in a helping relationship: Boundary violations (discussed in the next section and *not* therapeutic), boundary crossings, and boundary shifts. Boundary crossings involve a departure from commonly accepted clinical practice and may be purposefully undertaken to benefit the young person, or they may be unintentional or of no benefit (Smith & Fitzpatrick, 1995). Boundary shifts are purposeful changes that encourage the young person to take more responsibility and power in the relationship (Harper & Steadman, 2003).

Boundary crossing involves a sudden departure from a previously negotiated boundary with the young person. An obvious example is when young people who have participated in community programs are hired to assist in the program or operate a component of it. This is a strategy employed in community youth work that recognizes the value and importance of the work that young people can do for their own community. A more controversial boundary crossing would involve, for example, a practitioner agreeing with a young person that their conversations are confidential and then reporting a disclosure of abuse or knowledge of illegal activity. While the young person may benefit and be safe from future abuse as a result, the initial discussion about confidentiality should have included those circumstances under which crossing that boundary would be necessary. There may be some damage to the relationship, and some additional discussion and re-shaping of boundaries will no doubt be necessary.

The fluidity of life-space work means that the practitioner could instead create a boundary shift by helping the young person report abuse or criminal activity and going along for support and encouragement. The boundary between worker and young person shifts slightly to increase self-responsibility while at the same time making it clear that full confidentiality is no longer possible. Boundary shifts may also occur as young people grow and mature, either in age or in the depth of relationships that they have with practitioners. In community settings, where young people start attending neighbourhood drop-ins as early as 8 years of age and continue coming well into their teens, the initial role of the young person as a participant may shift at a later age to include volunteer leadership or coaching of the basketball or soccer team. This shift, which provides an opportunity to develop leadership skills, to explore sports or working with children, and to build a history of volunteer work on a resumé, should include some discussion of new roles and responsibilities. The practitioner who is present in the life-space and the young person work through these relational boundary shifts together.

In the context of life-space work, boundaries are often defined by the organization(s) that practitioners work for. Boundaries surrounding physical contact and ongoing relationships post-discharge are good examples of organizational boundary setting. Boundaries are not only governed by organizational and systemic rules and regulations; they are also affected by the cultural norms we have been raised in and the cultural norms of the young person. Being personal with young people requires an initial examination of how we construct boundaries around personal information. We all grow up learning boundaries and norms that pertain to personal disclosure. The stiff upper lip associated with the British, the Latin lover, and the reserved and unfailingly polite Japanese are stereotyped exaggerations of the boundaries we learn in our families, communities, and cultures. As practitioners we must assess, examine, and reassess these ideas about relational boundaries. We must also identify our own comfort level and the comfort level of each young person with his or her boundaries and self-identity in relationship with the practitioner and in relationships with others in the young person's own social contexts.

Boundary Management

Boundary management in life-space intervention involves ongoing renegotiation of the boundaries of the practice relationship as well as a focus on helping young people learn about and manage their own boundaries in a variety of social contexts. Key areas of boundary management that address safety, trust, and attachment include touch of various forms (greetings, affection, horseplay/hitting), personal and professional disclosure (confidentiality), personal space, and privacy.

We cannot discuss boundaries in child and youth care practice without considering boundaries related to touch. The potential implications of touch are of significant concern to many practitioners. At the same time, touch is also one of the greatest developmental needs that children have. Organizations fearful of accusations made by young people about abuse and regulators who believe that legal controls are the best way to ensure children's safety have created structures that discourage touch and focus on the right of young people for safety. These structures are critical for the protection of both practitioners and young people, but they neither support developmental needs for affection nor acknowledge the importance of human touch in the healing process. Arguments against overly rigid organizational structures advocate for respectful physical contact to convey a sense of connectedness that cannot be accomplished verbally (Maidment, 2006) and for properly managed horseplay so that young people learn where the boundaries lie and how to play by the rules, as well as experience essential physical contact in culturally acceptable ways (Smith, 2006). When a young teen leaps on a practitioner's back, an opportunity is presented for identifying limits and discussing or renegotiating a more developmentally appropriate boundary on touch. The key to resolving these issues lies in discussing and negotiating boundaries and managing them through renegotiation as necessary and appropriate.

The rituals and routines associated with greeting people and saying goodbye are important times for learning about boundaries, for both practitioner and young person (Mann-Feder, 1999). Building rituals that are representative of the unique relationship with each child is a strategy that communicates boundaries and links the child to the social context. Ritual statements such as "Drive safely," "Love you," or a kiss on the cheek may represent the norm for longer absences, and a simple "Have a good day" may work for short absences. Parents teach their children these rituals and the cultural boundaries that accompany them—consciously, by way of instructions, and unconsciously, through modelling. The boundaries of social interaction, flexibility, and the appropriate circumstances for various boundaries are set at an early age. For children with social and emotional problems who are cared for by strangers, these rituals need to be created or modified specifically for each young person. The practitioner observes and negotiates shifting boundaries and creates opportunities to establish boundary rituals as they interact. The practitioner should also take a life-span perspective and look ahead to teach other rituals and routines that the young person may find useful in future social circumstance and networks.

Similarly, boundaries on personal space need to be considered and managed. Personal space involves physical and mental or perceived aspects that are often dictated by family and culture. For young people struggling to manage their life-space, saying "You are standing too close to me" might be a new skill. Alternatively, the reminders to a young child about giving adults some time to think or to finish reading or relaxing are important learning moments about personal space. Practitioners have an obligation to be sensitive to the individual nuances of personal space and to discuss these as appropriate, making sure that young people are comfortable with the space (physical and mental) provided to them by the practitioner. "How may I best help you?" is an inquiry that respects the personal space of a young person with a disability much more than simply giving him or her assistance up a hill or opening a door without asking.

Boundary management surrounding privacy and a young person's right to privacy takes on a new perspective in the life-space. Keeping a professional relationship as private knowledge between the young person and the practitioner is rarely possible in life-space intervention because the practitioner meets with young people in their milieu. Practitioners must balance privacy with strategies for engagement of other characters in the young person's life-space.

At the same time, practitioners must often take measures to protect their own privacy in order to mitigate risks. The nature of the job and the young people that one works with will govern some of these decisions. Working as a gang interventionist in a community centre may involve some personal risk, and determining how to protect one's own safety and privacy is a consideration. These issues may be of less concern when one is working as an early interventionist with developmentally delayed infants and their families in their own homes in a rural community. The reality of life-space work is that the milieus where practitioners engage with young people vary widely and may overlap with their own communities.

The boundaries surrounding disclosure of information to others can be considered from two different perspectives. The first is the management of self-disclosure by the practitioner or young person, and the second is the management of disclosure of information about the young person to others (confidentiality). Self-disclosure or sharing personal information with someone else is an essential component of relationship development, and we all develop our own boundaries surrounding disclosure to others as we grow up. Issues of trust are at the core of boundaries on self-disclosure. What will the other person do with the information? Will it be shared with someone else without our knowledge, or used to hurt our feelings or damage our reputation? Young people need to learn their own boundaries on self-disclosure and the circumstances under which it is safe to discuss increasingly personal layers of information, thoughts, and feelings. Explicitly addressing how to make these decisions is a natural part of life-space intervention.

At the same time, practitioner self-disclosure can be useful to the young person. The general guideline on boundary setting in this area, advocated by most professional writing on self-disclosure, is that disclosure by the practitioner must be of benefit to the client. These guidelines are drawn primarily from office-based work and do not consider the more subtle forms of self-disclosure present in life-space intervention and work directly in the milieu. (See Zur [2007] for a detailed and thoughtful discussion of the parameters of self-disclosure for psychotherapists who see clients in a home-based office.) Casual conversations about things like recreational interests (sports, outdoor living), family members, weekend activities, religious beliefs, food preferences, and vacations are all components of self-disclosure that are readily part of life-space intervention and indeed provide opportunities for learning for young people that can be applied to their own life-space. They are also examples of areas in which the practitioner needs to consider how much to disclose and perhaps how to communicate personal boundaries about not disclosing, because young people will ask.

Confidentiality and the sharing of information about the young person's personal troubles, family circumstances, or life issues are almost always directly addressed in professional codes of ethics. When young people formally approach a service provider for assistance with a specific issue, the boundaries of confidentiality are discussed and the circumstances under which confidentiality will be broken are also typically discussed. It is important to recognize that such discussions cannot be a one-time activity. Instead, the explication of confidentiality arrangements needs to be present on a daily basis and attended to through careful attention to a balance of risk (that the young person will leave and not return) and ethical responsibility (to ensure that young people know who else might potentially receive information about them). At a minimum, practitioners need to consider a variety of circumstances—and define those to both themselves and young people—under which they will break the trust that young people have given them and share personal information with others. These circumstances will vary according to professional role and community, organizational, and systemic norms. If managed effectively, the learning about boundaries will stay with the young person for life, particularly when the current practitioner moves on and a new professional engages in a relationship and begins shaping the boundaries.

Story: Shaping and Managing Boundaries

The second client that Najwah was assigned in her new role was a young mother, Ruby, who was 17 years old. Ruby was Aboriginal and held treaty status, so she already had educational support and she was receiving housing support. She refused to live on-reserve but wanted to be close to her friends and family who all lived on-reserve.

Ruby's daughter was born with mild cerebral palsy, and Ruby needed access to the services at the local hospital and public health clinic. The Aboriginal child welfare services had an agreement that the Society would provide intensive in-home support to their off-reserve clients, when necessary, on a fee-for-service basis.

Najwah didn't know much about Chippewayan cultural traditions, but she was curious about them. Given her own commitment to religion and culture, she believed that her clients should also have the opportunity to explore these aspects of their lives.

Najwah and Ruby had worked out some initial boundary parameters that involved careful protection of privacy—they only acknowledged each other in the comfort of Ruby's apartment. The Aboriginal welfare agency required monthly status reports from the Society, so Najwah and Ruby set their confidentiality boundaries within that agreement. They agreed that Ruby would review the reports before Najwah submitted them, but that Najwah still had the right to say something that Ruby disagreed with, though it would be discussed and there would be a rationale.

Najwah decided to let Ruby know that her daughter was about the same age as Ruby's, but said that her religion and culture were so different that she couldn't imagine that Ruby would find this useful information. She did this partly because she knew that chances were high that she would see Ruby around town, and partly as a therapeutic strategy designed to join them relationally in a common life event and open the door to discussion about how cultural traditions can influence parenting. Najwah knew that her religion and culture were somewhat obvious from her wearing of the niqab, but that Ruby would likely not know a lot about her background.

Najwah noticed in her first few visits that Ruby interacted little with her daughter. She left the baby in the crib or stroller for long periods of time and didn't hold her much. There was no swing or cradleboard like the ones discussed at Najwah's Aboriginal cross-cultural training, and Ruby didn't seem to know how to relate to the baby except by providing for basic physical needs such as food and hygiene. Najwah just wanted to pick up the baby and cuddle her—she was so tiny and sweet, and she always smiled and giggled at Najwah as soon as she came in the door. Najwah disclosed this to Ruby, who just said, "Go ahead, I don't mind." Najwah decided to discuss the boundary this crossed for her and her lack of comfort.

"I know you don't mind, but I'm not sure that it's best for the baby if I pick her up. She might think I'm her mother. But I never see you cuddle with her.

How does she know that you are her mother?"

"She'll find out when she grows up, like I did. My mother never picked me up either. All the other ladies did all around. I got lots of hugs from my aunties," said Ruby.

"So would I be Auntie Najwah then?"

"You already are. She gets really excited when I tell her Auntie Najwah is coming to visit us. In my tradition, any older woman is an auntie, and they all hug and cuddle the kids."

"Okay, I can be her auntie and your support worker. But I'm still worried. You're off-reserve and there aren't a lot of aunties. You've decided to raise her differently, but you're hanging onto old traditions about relationships with children that might not work in town. We should think about what you want for new traditions, what old traditions still make sense, and how to teach those to yourself and to the baby."

"Maybe."

"I don't usually get into specifics with my colleagues about clients, but would you mind if I talked to a couple of them about your situation? There are other young moms who are off-reserve and they must be experiencing similar issues. Maybe they have some ideas."

"Really? There's other people who don't want to live in that gossip hole? Maybe we could be mini-aunties for each other?"

"That's a possibility, but you wouldn't be so private any longer. It's just something to think about. Will you let me talk to my colleagues first? I won't use your name, but they might know anyway."

Moonscape

Source: Talia Jackson-King

Boundary Violations

Boundary violations are evident when the safety experienced by a young person in the relationship is compromised, often through a misuse of practitioner power or a departure from accepted practice that increases the risk of harm to the young person. In life-space work, identifying the nature of accepted practice may be more difficult since the work is more personalized. Therefore, increased attention to power, safety, and trust is essential. Even if a practitioner has shaped and managed boundaries in a collaborative and engaged way, it is still possible to either knowingly or naively violate the boundaries of a young person or family. It is therefore important to contemplate not only the prevention of boundary violations, but also the healing process following a boundary violation that might enable the practitioner to continue working with the young person.

Preventing a boundary violation is accomplished through open and honest communication and discussion of what the boundaries, limits, and rules of behaviour are within a variety of social contexts, starting with the one in which practitioner and young person encounter each other. The practitioner makes conscious and informed decisions about how best to work with the youth to shape the boundaries of disclosure and emotional involvement using the unique circumstances of each child.

Prevention is facilitated by awareness of the effects of boundary violations experienced by the young person in the past. Sexual abuse, for example, is both illegal and a boundary violation that may affect the capacity of young people to set their own boundaries or to trust others. It may also raise areas of boundary sensitivity related to touch and personal self-disclosure for the young person. While awareness of and sensitivity to previous relationships and boundary violations are helpful, practitioners can also prevent boundary violations by creating a partnership of accountability (Stacey et al., 2002). In such a partnership, power imbalances between youth and workers are explicitly identified and discussed, and appropriate decision-making processes are implemented when power issues arise. Nevertheless, no matter how carefully a practitioner attends to boundaries in life-space work, the risk of violating a young person's boundaries is high, and therefore the need for healing such violations may well present itself.

Boundary violations are difficult to heal. If the practitioner and young person want to continue working together, rebuilding the safety of the relational connection is vital. In spite of the responsibility and accountability often given to the practitioner to construct, maintain, and manage boundaries, once a violation occurs both parties have a role in the process of healing. Young people will work to heal the core Self, be angry about the violation, and release the hurt while moving toward being able to trust again. Confronting the practitioner may be an important part of that healing. The practitioner may face feelings of shame and embarrassment as well as the potential loss of both reputation and income. Honesty with the Self becomes essential when the practitioner considers how the boundary violation occurred and works to establish safeguards to prevent future occurrences.

The first step in healing a boundary violation is to acknowledge that it occurred. When practitioners take responsibility for a boundary violation they acknowledge the power that is implied in the helping role. Describing the violation, why it was inappropriate, and exploring the feelings of the young person are essential steps to re-establishing both the process of co-creating boundaries and the actual boundary. The expression of anger, shame, and hurt on the part of the young person will help to cleanse the hurt and re-establish the ability to feel safe in a relationship. Apologizing for the hurt caused lays a foundation for re-establishing a caring relationship. Since boundary violations are often unintentional and may take place gradually, with both practitioner and young person not noticing the slippage from clarity to boundary crossing to boundary violation, it may be important to review what the catalyst was and what the ongoing risks are. Depending on the nature of the boundary violation, it may be necessary to involve another practitioner to facilitate the discussion and provide a more neutral perspective.

Attending to the issues related to power, caring, structure, and the agency of the young person and the practitioner will take some time and effort. To facilitate healing, the young person who experienced the violation should both be safe and feel safe. The interpersonal boundary between young person and practitioner needs to be reconstructed and maintained via enhanced vigilance and discussions about mutual accountability and boundary setting.

Boundary violations are difficult, and the practitioner needs to draw on self-awareness, caring, integrity, and courage to decide whether rebuilding the relationship and reconstructing the boundary is possible. Alternatively, it may be that a different practitioner is available to work with the young person within the organizational structure. When boundary violations are ignored, the young person may stop attending the program or may not be able to find the help he or she needs. The practitioner's obligation to care for and about young people and ensure their continued growth, development and participation in our society is at stake.

Story: Boundary Violations and Healing

Najwah had been working with Callie for about three months and had helped her find an apartment with a roommate, a Society ward attending the local community college. Callie was doing well in high school and was attempting to re-establish contact with her siblings. She was not interested in having her parents know where she was, and was rigidly protective of her privacy and very respectful of Najwah's personal privacy. It was an odd contrast to their first meeting, when Callie had just let everything go in the middle of Main Street. Najwah had emphasized personal safety concerns and taught Callie how to communicate her own boundaries to the minister as well as to friends. They had begun to talk about the boundaries around family roles and systems.

Callie was taking a family studies course in high school and her roommate was in the social service worker program. They talked about things like enmeshed families, closed and open family systems, and socially appropriate boundaries for friends, family, professionals, and adult acquaintances.

Overall, things were going really smoothly, and Najwah was surprised to see Callie's cellphone number pop up on her emergency-only work cellphone. She routinely gave the number to her clients with the instruction that she might not answer if it wasn't her work shift, but they could leave a message and she would call them back as soon as she could. She also talked with them about the different options, like the crisis line or her standard office phone line, and the different circumstances that might prompt them to need to contact her between visits. It was part of her process of helping them understand boundaries in their own lives and appreciate the fluidity of boundaries in the lives of others.

Callie was clear enough on boundaries, and when Najwah gave her the cell number she said, "Oh, I'll never use that, nothing is serious enough to disturb you at home." So even though Najwah had just finished work, she had not yet left the office, and she decided to answer.

"Hi," whispered Callie.

"Hi. What's up?" said Najwah.

"That creepy minister just showed up at my door," Callie whispered. "Did you tell him where I live? My roommate is here, and she's talking to him. I made really big eyes at her and told him I just had to go get something. So I think she knows who he is."

After a moment of reflection, Najwah realized that the previous week she had been at a meeting about the "Inn from the Cold," advocating for the need for a separate youth program. All the program coordinators were there. She had referred to the "several" youth that the Society was supporting and the importance of locating a separate Inn program for youth on one of the two bus routes to the local college and close to the high school. The high school guidance counsellor had also been there, the same person who had supervised Najwah as a peer counsellor during her high school years and with whom Callie had a good relationship. Najwah had been feeling tired and overworked. She was also stressed about a colleague who had been asking what Najwah considered to be overly personal questions. Rather than returning to her office and calling the guidance counsellor for an update on Callie at school (something Callie knew Najwah did), she had just stopped the guidance counsellor after the meeting. She realized now that the minister had hung around after as well.

While there was no indication that Callie was unsafe with the minister, this visit to her apartment certainly was an invasion of privacy on his part and a lapse in boundary judgment on hers. Najwah figured that he had been able to determine Callie's approximate address from information at the meeting and had also overheard her conversation with the counsellor, in which she had lamented the limited apartment building options she had for independent wards in high school.

"I'll be right there," she said to Callie and headed for the car.

On the way over she considered a number of things.

- How to approach the minister about his intentions in visiting Callie, unannounced, and how to convey to him again the inappropriateness and his lack of professional boundaries. Callie was well taken care of, but he still didn't seem to understand that she was fine. Was there something else going on, or did he just not "get it"?

- She would need to address her own indiscretion and boundary violation with Callie, and then with the guidance counsellor, and begin a healing process so that they could all continue to work together. She was very worried that Callie would never trust her again.

- She tried to reflect on what had increased the potential for this boundary violation. The risks of small town work were always high. Callie was a vulnerable client because of her family and her age. Najwah tried to counter that by being accountable to a number of her own peers: The guidance counsellor and her colleagues at work. They talked about the volunteers at the Inn and discussed client privilege boundaries with the coordinators on a regular basis. She had felt so rushed last week that the combination of the pressure and Callie's mature and responsible performance at school seemed to be the catalyst that led her to break with her usual procedure of doing check-ins in the safety of her office. She had thought there was so little to talk about, but it turned out that Callie had expressed some worry to the guidance counsellor about the location of the apartment and her nighttime safety on Main Street. The minister must have overheard that.

(Continued)

Najwah pulled the car into a parking spot, called her mother to say she would be late, and took a few minutes to breathe and prioritize her initial plan.

1. Ask the minister to leave and set an appointment with him for another day. Tell him clearly that she appreciated his concern, but Callie did not want him involved in helping her and he was *not* to come here again.

2. Take whatever time she needed with Callie to make sure she felt safe and to explain and apologize for her indiscretion the previous week. They would need to talk

again about small-town boundaries and about how to ensure Callie both was safe and *felt* safe.

3. Call and leave a message on the secure line for the guidance counsellor about the incident and ask for some time for a discussion. They might need to involve Callie in that discussion. Najwah trusted the guidance counsellor and thought that, if necessary, she could facilitate a repair to the relationship she had with Callie.

Najwah knew this could all change as soon as she walked in the door, but at least it was a start.

Beyond the Young Person

Although we have focused in this chapter on boundaries between practitioners and young people, we want to briefly acknowledge that boundaries do not occur solely within the practitioner–young person relationship. Boundaries are found in the inter-professional, organizational, and systemic contexts of human services as well. Most of the concepts previously discussed can be applied to co-worker relationships and boundaries within those relationships. In that context, too, we must attend to shaping, constructing and managing boundaries and be wary of boundary violations. Recent research into the role of group-home treatment workers in controlling access to young people placed in the treatment centre revealed that child and youth care workers exercised control over physical access to young people as well as access to information about those young people (Salhani & Grant, 2007). Such rigid boundary construction by one person for another is problematic and can be guarded against by applying self-awareness and caring to the relationship boundaries developed with other members of the team. Individual and group negotiation of boundaries should occur and issues specific to team dynamics can be addressed while negotiating team boundaries.

As teams and groups come together, boundaries are created within and between organizations that define the mandate of a professional group, and their aims and objectives in the work they do with young people. Thus, systems with specific jurisdictional mandates are created and barriers spring up within a young person's life-space. Jurisdictional boundaries and mandates can be a great frustration in life-space work with young people. When young people are in crisis (for example, without housing or needing essential access to a first-incident mental health assessment) or require immediate action and that action is blocked by jurisdictional mandates, the boundaries surrounding the system have become too rigid and the professionals involved are too reliant on structure. Considering these issues from a boundary perspective in life-space work suggests that a boundary spanner could be useful.

Story: The Boundaries of Work Relationships

Given the incident with Callie, Najwah decided to schedule a meeting with her supervisor. She specifically asked to talk about boundaries and how best to address them in the context of the work that they did together as a team.

Najwah had a number of things on her mind. The incident with Callie was one, but she also wanted to discuss her concern about another worker, who seemed to be rigidly refusing to work with young people who he felt posed safety risks because of criminal charges. The same worker had been asking her a lot of questions about her religion and her relationship with her husband. While she didn't mind the questions about her religious beliefs, some of the questions felt overly personal and she was becoming increasingly uncomfortable with answering them. Her husband's suggestion was "Just tell him to mind his own business," but Najwah wanted a more carefully thought out answer in the context of the relationship she had with him. Exploring the issues and how to approach them with her supervisor seemed like a good option.

According to Miller (2009, p. 622), boundary spanning is an emergent area of leadership that can be filled by "leaders who move freely and flexibly within and between organizations and communities." It is unlikely that front-line practitioners who work for specific services and are embedded within teams can perform the role of a boundary spanner. Effective spanning of boundaries between systems and organizations requires someone who is not limited physically, organizationally, or politically. He or she must be able to move between the different physical and organizational geographies of young people's life-space, building coalitions, bringing people together formally and informally, and facilitating problem-solving and decision-making to enhance the lives of the young people who are affected by these jurisdictional boundaries. This work is essential in the lives of young people who can be simultaneously involved with child welfare, the justice system and mental health services, since these services are funded by different government programs and often don't talk with each other.

Summary

In this chapter we have considered the nature of boundaries in the life-spaces of young people and of practitioners. Boundaries are complicated when practitioners adopt a life-space approach to intervention, in which the work is not contained by physical walls in an office setting. Boundary setting is also a life skill, and as such the relational work that we do with young people and their families provides a forum for discussing boundaries and for learning about how to set appropriate personal, family, and system boundaries in their own lives. We explored the implications of boundary violations, prevention strategies, and approaches to healing such violations when necessary. The structure created by formal organizations and systems results in boundaries between jurisdictions and organizations that can form rigid barriers to effective work with young people and families. The concept of boundary spanning was introduced as an essential component of working toward integrating service delivery and personalizing services in the life-space. Finally, the concepts of boundary negotiation were extended to working with colleagues and teams.

Discussion and Exercises

Reflection in Practice

In this exercise in self-awareness and self-observation, you will consciously attend to boundaries in your day-to-day interactions. Choose three very different social contexts in which you regularly interact with people, such as your work in a retail outlet, the Saturday night social event, your family dinner, coffee with a friend, and an interaction via a social networking site. Observe yourself during the event and try to determine your personal boundaries.

1. Observe your personal space in each circumstance. Is it different? How close are you to the person? What type of emotional responsiveness do you feel?

2. How would you describe your role in this interaction?

Reflection on Practice

Choose a colleague and engage in a discussion about boundaries. Begin by talking about what boundaries are, and discuss what each of you think are the most difficult boundary issues in your practice with young people. Describe any boundary violations that you are aware of or have observed. Move the discussion to talking about boundaries with colleagues and the most difficult boundary issues that you have encountered in working with colleagues. You may also want to specifically discuss the boundaries of your relationship with your colleague.

After the discussion with your colleague, reflect on the following questions:

1. How did it feel to have this discussion?

2. What were your thoughts during the discussion? What are your thoughts now?

3. What was the most important thing you learned from the discussion?

4. How would you frame your language differently if you were talking to a different colleague? To a young person?

Reflection for Practice

Brainstorm five boundary issues that you anticipate will be difficult to deal with and that you might meet in the early stages of your practice. For each issue identify and describe the following:

1. What is your current belief about how people should act related to this issue?

2. Identify the cultural, religious, familial and community influences on the behaviour.

3. Identify the practice setting that you hope to work in and research what the organizational rules might be.

4. Determine how you think it would be appropriate to act or deal with the issue at work and how your approach might be different from the approaches of others in the work or social context.

5. Discuss and compare with two friends, one in human services and another who works in a very different field (such as business or science).

Theory in Action

Boundary Management

This series of exercises helps young people assess and consider their boundaries, and those of others, in multiple relationships and varied social contexts. Young people who have moved a lot, who live in chaotic families, and who have immigrated and are integrating into a very different cultural environment may all benefit from some or all of these exercises. Be sure to discuss the importance of voluntary participation in the exercises and identify any potentially sensitive boundary issues as you work with the young person (such as touch and personal disclosure).

Physical

Introduce the concept of personal space, including your own comfort zone. With the young person, demonstrate standing very close and talking, and standing far away and talking. Inquire about

- Feelings
- Language and "signs" that they use to mark their personal space at home
- The parental space or sibling space and how it is "marked"

Mental

Ask about how the young person protects his or her private thoughts. Where do they begin and another person end? Ask him or her to develop a metaphor for the relationship that you have with them. Explore the metaphor and expand it.

Relational

Ask the young person who is in his or her family? Point out that identifying some people as being within the family and other people being outside the family is a kind of boundary around family. Would the young person extend that boundary to include other people? Under what circumstances?

The same questions can be applied to friends, acquaintances and enemies.

Draw the web of relationships—the social network that the young person exists in.

Virtual

Inquire about social networking on the Web and how the young person establishes privacy.

CHAPTER 7

Right Here, Right Now: The Learning Journey

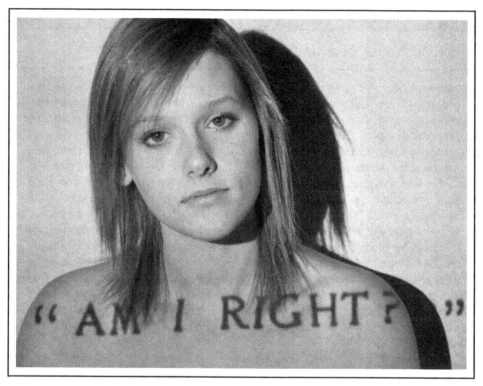

Agents of Change
Source: Laine Robertson

"Tell me and I forget. Show me and I remember. Involve me and I understand."
– Chinese proverb

The Conference

Change, Intervention, Learning

The tag line for the conference leaped off the poster in the window of Storefront as Najwah was walking up Main Street. She liked the brevity and simple meaningfulness of a tag line. It captured all the key values and actions at the same time. The tag line from her undergraduate education came back to her often in her work – *Connecting, Transforming, Caring*. It described the process she tried to undertake as a practitioner so that she could help the young people she worked with move from isolation to a transformed life-space in which they cared about themselves and other people. There were so many subtle nuances to a tag line.

Callie waved at her from behind the poster as she put the final bit of tape on to secure it in the window. Najwah decided to take the extra time she had allotted for getting coffee on the way to her next client and drop in and see how Callie was doing and what the conference was all about. Callie was happy to see her and launched right into an advert for the youth conference.

Life Is About Learning I

Learning goes on throughout our lives and makes an important contribution to the growth and development of young people and adults. The contribution of learning to adult development is often forgotten when adults interact with young people who may be creating or facing significant challenges coping in the parameters of their life-space. Too often, the goal of adults is social control and conformity for young people. Young people do learn something when adult goals focus on control. But they don't necessarily learn how to conform and follow society's expectations, even though this is the hope of the adults imposing social control.

In previous chapters we discussed six concepts related to life-space intervention:

- A new way of thinking about life-space
- Structure and agency in the life-space
- Caring
- Engagement
- Relationships
- Boundaries

We illustrated the discussion with stories about young people and photos and drawings done by young people. In

this chapter, we continue those stories. We describe the agency that the characters we created have and the learning that they undertook as they interacted with the practitioners who joined their life-space(s) for the briefest of times. We've chosen to make their stories the main text in this final chapter about *learning* – the core function of the life-space. We will articulate the connections between intervention, change and learning, and construct a framework for life-space intervention based on the six concepts. This framework is theoretically clear and it provides a clear path to its application in the everyday work of engaging with young people.

We will demonstrate life-space intervention through the perspectives of the young people depicted in the stories as well as their workers. Interspersed throughout the chapter and between stories are short theoretical arguments and historical explanations to help the reader connect theory and practice.

In child and youth care practice, we often start with a desire for *change* – a desire to make things different. We have learned, however, that when we focus on our own desire for things to be different, we quickly begin to focus on social control. The encounter with young people who struggle because of the experience of abuse or neglect, mental health issues or poverty, leads to a temptation to impart change quickly.

Depending on our own experiences, we may also assume that if we show a struggling young person enough love and provide enough nurture, the young person will regain confidence and trust in others, awaken to a more optimistic view of the future, and ultimately get things together and move forward.

Alternatively, we may believe that change and growth for a young person, no matter what the issues might be, will ultimately require discipline and a clear understanding of social limits. As a result, we might provide firm direction and high expectations, mixed with clear incentives to perform and consequences for non-performance.

It is also possible to frame intervention in the language of evidence-based practice, which refers to using intervention methods and approaches that have been shown to work elsewhere. This language marginalizes the subjective, experiential and personal perspective of young people and practitioners and replaces these perspectives with quasi-scientific evidence of what works. Change and intervention in the broader framework of evidence-based practice are simply a function of reproduction – we reproduce programs, services and specific ways of responding to young people based on outcomes achieved under similar circumstances elsewhere.

Each of these approaches to change has merit and produces some result. However, while the motivation behind these approaches is almost always virtuous, the approaches themselves are not entirely democratic, at least not

in the sense that they afford agency to the young people involved. As a result, none of these approaches is consistent with life-space intervention, at least not as we have articulated this concept in the previous chapters.

In the context of life-space intervention, change is measured not by specific behavioural outcomes or enhanced performance. Instead, change is assessed by the extent of learning that has taken place for the young person. In life-space intervention, the goal of intervention is to promote the young person's learning with respect to navigating the multiple dimensions of the life-space. Such navigation requires the young person to learn the subtleties of agency and structure and how these interact and become entangled in the everyday context of the life-space.

When we let go of our own ideas about what needs to be different for young people, our practice becomes more *intervention* oriented. We give up, or at least put aside, our own ideas in the interests of listening to young people and what they identify as their needs. We work together with the young person, side by side, to create the change. We want to create a sustainable opportunity for change by having the young person engage in *learning*.

Learning develops competency that carries forward into other realms in life once we, the practitioners, have left the material life-space of the young person. While *change* makes things better for the young person, and *intervention* involves the young person in decision-making, *learning* develops young people's capacity for the future and their resourcefulness so that they continue changing as new challenges present themselves.

"This conference is going to be amazing," she said. "Remember that child and youth care conference you went to a couple of years ago in Winnipeg? Just before you started working with me? I think you were a student. You told me about how exciting it was to go and learn from people you had been reading about in school. You also said that you went to some workshops that were youth-led and they had such great ideas, and that you couldn't imagine how they had ever been in trouble with any kind of challenges."

Najwah smiled at her enthusiasm; she was really proud of Callie and her role at Storefront as the youth education coordinator. The half-time position allowed Callie to take university courses and supplement the tuition support that Najwah had worked so hard to get for her from the child welfare agency. More importantly, Callie was really good at the work. She found all manner of ways to involve other young people in the community who came in to Storefront for help with health concerns, educational crises, housing needs, or protection needs. Callie's belief that giving back was the best way to help yourself was infectious for the adults who supported the centre and for the youth that came in when they were in need. Najwah just knew that Callie was going to be a fine young entrepreneur with a great social justice consciousness when she finished her business degree. Putting those thoughts aside, she said, "Tell me about it. Maybe I'll go."

"Maybe I'll take you," retorted Callie. "The idea of the conference is that young people who are interested in social issues and have experience with receiving government services will get together, invite their workers, and discuss how to change things. The conference is supposed to end with some specific projects that we can do and get some funding from the government. I've got this great group of people across Canada and around the world to work with, and Ruby's working on the Aboriginal perspective. Isn't it a great idea? We bring the workers this time!"

Andre spotted the poster in the youth centre on Denis's door. *Change, Intervention, Learning.* It reminded him of the three professionals in his life and their approach to working with him. Sahim had been focused on the hallucinations during Andre's time in the hospital. She worked really hard with the doctors to adjust his medication and eliminate the drug-induced psychosis. She was convinced that the hallucinations were bad for him and that he really needed to be thinking clearly. He needed to go to physio and push himself to do the exercises, and then he would get better faster. Andre found the resultant pain excruciating, and he would beg Monique to talk to Sahim and convince her that he needed something to control the pain. He figured the best answer was the morphine, but they were reducing the dosage to prevent the hallucinations. Monique had made some very forceful points for him with the inter-professional team. The team backed off the reductions a little bit because Monique said they needed time to implement the mindfulness strategies and the deep breathing that she was teaching him as alternatives for pain management. Andre still remembered really clearly the day Denis showed up for one of his semi-regular visits and brought a couple of the guys from the youth centre. Andre was complaining about the hallucinations, about the "dumb" mindfulness and breathing exercises and about how the pain wouldn't go away. Denis said, "Doesn't talking about it make it worse sometimes? I brought these guys to take your mind off it. How 'bout a game of team checkers?"

While they were playing, Denis started talking about yoga, one of the new programs at the youth centre. Pete and Kyle jumped right in.

"Yeah – hot girls in yoga pants! That'll take your mind off this pain stuff," said Pete.

Life Is About Learning II

Intervention is a complex concept, particularly when it is positioned between the concepts of change and learning. Most interventions are unintentional or unexpected and go unnoticed by the intervener. Most of the time, the response to an intervention by the receiver is unspoken, reflective and silent. Interventions are usually thought of as active measures designed to initiate change, adjust behaviour, or impose consequences. This concept of intervention, as it is used in practice with young people, reflects a view that the purpose of working with young people facing challenges is to change their circumstances so that they perform in a manner that meets the (minimum) standards of societal expectations: Housing, a job, and abstinence from crime and substance use.

In practice, traditional intervention often targets three distinct aspects of life-space. The first and most common entry point for professionals in the lives of young people are interventions designed to stop the young person from doing certain things, such as using drugs, committing crimes, joining a gang, or displaying violent outbursts. These are control-focused interventions that use aversion to punishment as the core ingredient for achieving change.

A second possible focus for intervention is to use reinforcement as an incentive for change. Here, practitioners try to get the young person to initiate behaviours, such as attending school, being polite, taking responsibility, managing health or symptoms of illness, or developing healthy relationships. These interventions are often manipulative and the incentive is their primary tool for change.

A third focus of intervention is directed at the social or ecological context of the young person. This kind of intervention, which is based on Bronfenbrenner's (1979) ecological systems, is a false pretense at life-space intervention. The focus of intervention is the physical or social places and spaces where the young person is experiencing adversity. Strategies such as advocacy at school to get a suspension overturned, therapy with family members to create a more inviting and workable situation at home, and speaking at court to minimize the legal consequences of the young person's latest mischief negate agency of the young person. This form of intervention is a false pretense at life-space intervention because the ecological issues are challenged through interventions that are still focused on how the case is being managed and moved forward by the professionals. Such interventions are not related to how the young person constructs the life-space. Instead, they represent the **social construction** of where life ought to unfold, and therefore almost never consider the mental and virtual dimensions of life-space that exist for young people.

In the context of life-space intervention, we recognize that any interventions we suggest will impact in ways that we intend and in unintended and

(Continued)

less predictable ways. Enforcing conse-quences, for example, may have the intended effect of stopping the inappro-priate behaviour, but it may also have the unintended effect of affecting how young people mentally construct our roles in their lives. Conversely, non-action on the part of the practitioner may result in the young person experiencing a significant intervention. For example, when a practi-tioner decides to overlook an infraction in a residential program, the experience of the young person may be one that shakes his or her confidence in the practi-tioner's expression of caring, integrity or sense of boundaries. Although the practi-tioner did not intend to intervene, the act of overlooking the infraction was experi-enced as a significant intervention on the part of the young person.

In reality, the very presence of the practitioner in a young person's life-space constitutes an intervention. When we expand our presence in physical places to include the mental and virtual dimensions of the life-space, we dem-onstrate a commitment to "making our presence count." From the perspective of the young person, this is a consider-able intervention in the life-space, which is otherwise the subject of continuous efforts at structuration by the young per-son who is always attempting to balance agency with the imposed structures. Our presence provides opportunities for the young person to redirect the strug-gle against structure by focusing on the relational dimensions of the life-space and our presence in this dimension.

Young people can use their agency to allow themselves to be vulnerable in relation to structure by trusting that the relationship evolving between them-selves and the practitioner will mitigate against any unreasonable or oppressive impositions of structure. Rather than acting toward anything in particular (stopping or starting a behaviour, or changing the ecology), life-space inter-vention is about creating possibilities to navigate and manage the young per-son's life-space challenges together. Life-space intervention is about helping young people engage with the structures around them in ways that make sense to them, while at the same time remaining present and ready to engage young people about the outcomes of their unrestrained use of agency. The out-comes that we hope for with life-space intervention are not changes (specific to the intervention itself) but rather learn-ing. In the short and medium terms, life-space intervention privileges learning over change since, in the long term, it is learning that leads to sustained change.

"And where else can you take a nap before you exercise?" added Kyle.

Denis shook his head. "Aren't you guys learning anything? Come on . . . you must see some pay-off in the rest of your life. You can watch girls and take naps in school, or anywhere else for that matter."

"Well, the focusing during Shavasana is pretty cool," said Pete. "The music really helps to try to keep a blank mind. Sometimes I come into class all focused on how badly I'm doing in school or how angry I am at somebody, and I have to keep sending those ideas away. I even caught myself doing it just now. I was thinking about something else when I made that last move and you jumped my man. I have to push that sh— out of my mind."

"The stretching is great," said Kyle. "I got tossed the other day in karate." He grinned at Andre. "Just wait 'til you get back. I'm going to kick your butt. . . . It hurt a lot – I think my hip and my knee were all messed up. And it hurt so much to do those sun salutations. But you know what? At the end, after Shavasana, I didn't hurt anymore. It's true what the teacher says – your body absorbs the benefits afterward."

It was after that visit that Andre asked Denis if they could have a few yoga classes in the recreation room at the hospital with some of the guys, and he did find it helpful. The inter-professional team was amazed at his progress after that. Now Andre brought mindfulness and breathing into lots of aspects of his life, including school and karate.

Andre brought his mind back to the present and stuck his head in the door to ask Denis about the conference poster, thinking he might want to go.

Balance

Jennifer was nervous. She paced back and forth in the hotel room, trying to calm the anxiety she was feeling about the upcoming session, "Personalizing the Adolescent Psychiatric Ward." When she caught herself scratching at her wrists, she stopped and sat on her hands, a little trick that Jerome had taught her when she was in the hospital. She wondered where Jerome was – he had vanished so suddenly just before she was discharged from the hospital. She remembered his last words, accompanied by a chocolate bar, when he stuck his head in her room after the last case conference, which had established her discharge plan.

"Remember, it's not about who wins, it's about who you meet, how you play the game, and what you learn for next time."

Her response at the time was "I know, I know. That's what my soccer coach says: It's not about who wins, it's about how you play the game."

"That's not what I said," snapped Jerome. "Think about it – you're going to need it."

He was still smarting from the conversation with Jennifer's psychiatrists. They had informed him that his services were no longer needed and that he was not to say goodbye to her because they wanted to see how she managed unplanned separation. In the past it had triggered her cutting. Jerome felt confined by the directive. If he didn't follow it they would keep her longer than planned because the "evidence" of her improvement would not be tested. If he did follow it, Jennifer would have one more reason not to trust professionals, and it might prevent her from seeking someone out on her own in the future. He felt that the comment and the chocolate bar were within the parameters of the directive but might leave her with something useful to think about for her future encounters with the many structures that would surround her journey in the mental health system.

In spite of her reluctance to connect and engage with Jerome, Jennifer had indeed felt abandoned when Jerome did not appear the next day, or the next. She began to obsessively review that last conversation with him to see what she did that drove him away. In doing, she so kept repeating what he said: "Remember, it's not about who wins, it's about who you meet, how you play the game, and what you learn for next time."

It had (unintentionally) become a mantra through her last week in the hospital. During that time, and without realizing it, she had begun to connect with some of the other young people there, her nurses, and the child and youth care counsellor who worked there. None of them would answer her questions about Jerome; they would only say that he wouldn't be back. The child and youth care counsellor asked her one day, "What have you learned while you were here about expressing your feelings more appropriately?"

Jennifer had been tempted to growl, "Nothing," but the word *learned* reverberated in her head and she re-thought her response.

"Well, you taught me about how the thoughts and feelings in my head repeat and repeat and build up a huge pain centre that has to be discharged. If I notice the thoughts and talk about the feelings, then I don't cut," said Jennifer. But inside, she thought "That's what you taught me, but what I learned was that the rules to be followed aren't always clear and I need to take a little time to figure out the unwritten rules before I charge ahead with my own plan."

"What did you learn from me?" Jennifer couldn't resist throwing back.

"A lot," said the child and youth counsellor. "You didn't respond at all to cognitive behaviour therapy or the mindfulness techniques. You followed the rewards and punishments schedule precisely, but it felt fake and we didn't know why. We're looking at the structure now to see how we can better meet the needs of adolescents who are smart enough to follow the rules but still don't release their pain. We're going to do a focus group."

"Can I run it?" asked Jennifer sarcastically.

That had been the start of things. She had never expected them to take her up on it, and now she was at this conference to talk about what they had done at the hospital to involve the patients in changing things on the adolescent ward. Her audience was young people her own age or younger and maybe a few practitioners. "Just there to keep an eye on the young people," Jennifer thought to herself.

She stopped sitting on her hands to get a pencil and write out her main points again:

- Change what you're doing in order to understand yourself, and then try to change the system.
- Worker interventions aren't always obvious.
- Share what you've learned with others – surprise them and yourself.

Tabitha and Sarah (her mom) were preparing for the keynote address at the conference. Tabitha had been invited because she was the Canadian Junior Women's Halfpipe Champion. After doing a few of the women-only snowboard camps in Alberta, she had been encouraged to compete on the national circuit and had enough points to go to the

Life Is About Learning III

When learning is viewed as an independent outcome of intervention rather than a process that is required during intervention, practitioners are released from the need to evidence immediate effectiveness because learning is not always linear or measureable.

Change and learning are easily confused with each other. When a young person demonstrates desirable behaviour in response to repeated interventions designed to promote such desirable behaviour, practitioners are easily misled to believing that the young person has learned the benefits of the desirable behaviour. The changed behaviour is considered evidence that the young person has not only chosen to do things differently, but has accepted and learned the wisdom of doing so. In other words, the "successful" intervention that generates a change in behaviour is thought to have pedagogic content. It is thought that the intervention has taught something, and the young person has learned from this teaching.

Equating change and learning is problematic. This difficulty may explain why so many seemingly successful interventions that generate changes for young people work in the moment and in a specific setting or context but are not sustained over time and do not transfer to other contexts. There is no evidence, for example, that the changes in young people's conduct generated by point and level systems in residential or classroom settings last beyond discharge or produce performance and conduct changes in young people within their families, peer groups or other social contexts.

The purpose of life-space intervention is to create learning even if that learning is not always accompanied by changes in performance or conduct in the here and now. Life-space intervention is inherently pedagogic in its orientation, and as such the interventions attempted should challenge the uncritical and unreflective use of agency that often causes young people to rebel against structure without any specific cause.

One of the core challenges of life-space intervention as an approach is the challenge of measuring outcomes. When change is defined as an observable difference in performance or conduct, it can easily be quantified and measured. But learning is not always accompanied by visible change, and therefore it cannot be measured using standard variables and measurement tools. This presents a challenging dilemma with respect to everyday service provision: While we know that when we impose changes this does not create sustainable futures for young people, we also know that learning as an independent outcome of life-space intervention cannot be verified immediately and may not be evident until after our direct involvement with the young person has ended. In scientific terminology, we are unable to "control" for outside influences, including our own influence, because it is the accumulation of these influences and learning over time that leads to the changes in young people's approach to managing the life-space.

How can we resolve this dilemma, or at least be confident that our relationship with a young person has an impact beyond this moment? The task of life-space intervention is right here, right now, but we hope for outcomes that transcend the present. To address this dilemma we will consider the pedagogic content of life-space intervention. We recognize that the term *pedagogy* has limited currency in North America, and when it is used at all, it typically refers simply to the process of teaching. In other jurisdictions around the world, however, **pedagogy** has been the basis of child- and youth-focused work. In Europe, this term refers not to teaching per se, but rather to the "upbringing" of children. Incorporating this concept of upbringing or pedagogy into the thinking about life-space intervention helps us to better understand learning as a core process *and* outcome of life-space intervention.

Nationals in her first year. It helped that Nationals were in Alberta, which kept the costs down, but she still had to fundraise so she could afford the entry fees and the travel. Janice and Lisa at the Youth had helped her with fundraising strategies. They even offered the centre for an evening of skateboarding, when local boarders competed against Tabitha in an event titled: "Be Inspired: Hear about how to be a champion and try to beat the champ." The idea was that Tabitha would do a short class similar to her previous work for the youth centre (30 minutes of teaching on the skateboard), then give a presentation about her experiences in life and with snowboarding to inspire the young kids, and then compete head-to-head with the older kids. Each competitor paid $20 to compete against her. If the other competitors won, their entry fee was returned. Everything was judged by a panel of kids and adults.

That first speech had been really hard for Tabitha, and she relied on her mom and Janice for lots of help and practice. She wanted to make three points:

- You can be whoever you want to be.

- Respect yourself and everyone else.

- Commitment takes you forward.

She used her personal story well to illustrate how hard it was to stay on track when her dad left and her mom needed to work a second job to make ends meet. She kept going back to how often she had been angry and disrespectful to her mother, and Sarah had responded kindly or firmly and with respect, repeating over and over, "I trust you, but there is a lot of pressure on you right now, just as there is on me. I don't think you should put yourself in that situation. Please tell me that I'm wrong and it won't be unsafe."

The Youth

Source: Laine Robertson

Life Is About Learning IV: Social Pedagogy as a Framework for Life-Space Intervention

Throughout this book, we have developed the concept of life-space as a unitary construct, meaning that for every young person there is a single life-space that is ever-present and that travels along with the movements of the young person.

This unitary life-space has multiple dimensions that are constantly and perpetually interacting, interdependent, and mutually reconstructive – nothing stays the same in the life-space of a young person for very long. For example, a new relationship results in shifts in all of the other dimensions: The young person hangs out in different places relevant to the new relationship, representing a shift in the physical dimension of life-space; self-esteem and self-confidence may be temporarily increased, a shift in the mental dimension of the life-space; and an update to the relationship status, the appearance of new photo albums, and perhaps even the accumulation of new "friends" on a social networking site represent a shift in the virtual dimension of the life-space. It becomes apparent that any change, even a trivial one, to a young person's life-space results in a series of unpredictable, sometimes complex scenarios that have consequences and create circumstances that the young person must respond to and somehow manage.

Trying to change a young person does not provide much of a foundation for him or her to take responsibility, and whatever change might be achieved is not likely to be relevant to the ongoing adjustments in life-space dynamics. Learning as an evolving outcome of life-space intervention provides the foundation for young people to extend their understanding of what is good and what is bad, what will benefit them and what won't, and what works and what doesn't to the specific circumstances or scenarios in the dynamics of their life-space right here, right now. What young people learn informs their agency and moderates how they use agency in reaction to structural impositions. In other words, what young people learn they own, and what they own they can make use of over and over again, making slight adjustments and adaptations to fit the evolving circumstances.

A Brief History of Pedagogy

The concept of pedagogy has been around for a very long time. In Western philosophy, what constitutes pedagogy and what role pedagogy plays in the development of social and political systems has been at the centre of debate for over two millennia (Böhm, 2010; Cordasco, 1970). Some 2500 years ago, the Greek sophists saw pedagogy as a system of reproduction. The goal of pedagogic activity was to ensure that generations would follow the examples of social and political conduct set by previous generations. The elders in society were role models for the young, and so long as the young understood that their developmental journey entailed emulating their elders, all was well in the Greek city-states.

Socrates complicated matters by introducing the pedagogy of justice. In

(Continued)

Socrates' writings the goal of pedagogy is reflection and critical discourse. The creation of a just society and the implementation of justice depended on young people being capable of understanding the fundamental nature of justice and therefore making adjustments and changes to social and political structures.

Plato's *Republic* has often been described as the most holistic and comprehensive pedagogic model ever produced, and it was the beginning of a trend that considered pedagogy in terms of ideals. In Plato's case, the ideal was polity (Hobson, 1993).

Aristotle contributed two major elements to modern pedagogy. First, he helped to manifest pedagogy as an applied science (giving it the status of an academic, if not professional, discipline). Secondly, he introduced the teleological principle, which holds that everyone ultimately becomes what they should; our future is embedded deeply within us.

These early reflections on pedagogy represent the core of what life-space intervention is all about, even if the context and the language of the Greek sophists and philosophers is quite different than what we might encounter today. Socrates and Aristotle were concerned with understanding how knowledge about life and living was transmitted from one generation to the next. Both were also concerned about issues of conformity versus disobedience, compliance versus rebellious activity, and loyalty versus treachery. Inasmuch as life-space intervention connects the concepts of intervention, change and learning, it mirrors the goals of the Greek philosophers. The philosophers were simply trying to understand the multiple dimensions in which we live our lives, how those dimensions influence our agency, and the structures that affect that agency. The practical question facing us is "How do we learn about managing the multi-dimensional complexity of our life-space?"

Tabitha was going to make some of the same points in the keynote for the conference. She was used to speaking now and telling her story, but she had asked the organizers if Sarah could join her in the keynote to describe the parent perspective. Sarah would focus on these points:

- Young people are in the moment. It's a parent's job to connect the moment to the past and the future, and help them learn socially acceptable values and morals.
- Respect the agency of young people but don't let that agency be disrespectful.
- Change and the chaos that results are imposed from outside, but they can be an opportunity for learning.

Sarah was thinking about how carefully she picked her battles with Tabitha, even today. She had just chosen not to pursue an argument about Tabitha's decision to talk about their struggles with poverty (Sarah didn't like to think of them as poor) in favour of a discussion about the importance of acknowledging and praising the adults at the conference who were interested in the learning aspect of change. Tabitha wanted to berate them to listen and be sure to help these kids because there was so much wrong with the system. Sarah suggested that they were already on-side, but they needed some specific helpful actions and to know that the young people would be co-operative.

From Practice to History: Caring Actions That Create Moral Structure

The Greek philosophers did not produce answers that would help us learn how to manage our life-space today. Indeed, following Aristotle's thinking about pedagogy, the concept entered a long period of religious evolution with an overarching focus on the moral development of young people, largely due to the centrality (and politics) of the Christian faith. Much of pedagogy for the first 1200 years of the Common Era was really geared toward containing passion and desire in favour of duty and the will to serve (God, the family, the church, the state, and the feudal lords).

Modern articulations of pedagogy began with the onset of the Enlightenment period in the late seventeenth century (Böhm, 2010; Outram, 2005). Two of the greatest influences on contemporary thought about pedagogy in the Western world (particularly in Europe)

were John Locke and Jean-Jacques Rousseau. Following in the traditions of the Greek philosophers, Locke provided a sketch of the ideal man in modern society, and argued that the goal of pedagogy is to emulate this ideal man as much as possible.

Locke also argued that it is the privileged and the middle classes that must be given education and guidance, while the children of the poorer classes should be sent to work schools so that they might be kept busy and not become a burden on society. In other words, according to Locke, pedagogy (unlike the modern concept of universal access to education) was strongly associated with maintaining the intellectual momentum toward revising the structure of society (represented by government), and in particular the aristocratic version of democracy.

Caring

Medhi was remembering the day he moved into the group home again, as he worked on the social networking site that he had created. It wasn't just the cookies that Mike had offered him, it was that the cookies were *akhrot ka halwa* (his favourite), almond, and chocolate chip, and they were hot – just like his mom usually served them. It had almost made him cry.

In that moment he had learned that he really loved his family and he wanted them to be back in his life. Up until then he had only been angry.

How did Mike know that those were his favourite cookies?

When Medhi asked him later, Mike just smiled that secret smile and offered him a cookie from the plate that was always on the kitchen table. The cookies were a symbol that Medhi eventually thought he had figured out – the recipes changed constantly because there were people with so many different backgrounds coming through the group home, but they were always warm and always delicious. Medhi even learned how to cook them and took them on his first home visit as a peace offering to his family. Mike had suggested that he needed a hostess gift, one of those traditions that seemed to cross many cultures. He remembered his mom worrying about what to take when she went to visit his auntie. He resisted Mike at first, but then he realized that taking a gift was a way that he could apologize for all the hurt he caused them and it was one of those "structures" that Mike sometimes referred to. It might allow him to have some control over in the whole process of getting back together with his family. It became a habit for him to bake some cookies before he went for a home visit, but he tried all kinds of different recipes, trying to get the message across to his parents that he was his own person.

The social networking site that Mehdi created was premised on this idea of cookies representing the ideas of connecting and collaborating between young people and workers. He wanted to attract young people like himself who had been in care but didn't necessarily agree with the decisions about why they were there, or who were in a group home that wasn't so great. He was hoping to create a network that focused on caring about each other and connecting people – when they were ready – to the additional help they needed. He called it Have a Cookie? He was inviting care workers and youth, and linking them to the other networks out there.

Engagement

Jerome was looking forward to meeting Safid in person at the conference. They were presenting together on a panel to debate the merits of residential care versus foster care as the best milieu placement for young people. Medhi had recruited them through Have a Cookie? Both of them had signed up early in the social networking group's history. They jointly started a debate with the young people about the best approaches to the engagement and interaction that practitioners should have with young people when they first encountered each other. Jerome favoured chocolate bars over cookies and so he initially began the discussion with Medhi as a way of engaging Medhi in the virtual network space. The discussion expanded when Safid jumped in with his example of the Germany soccer shirt and suggested that there was a "youth uniform" that was a better place for connection and engagement than food. He linked a picture from Johannes' Facebook page that showed him wearing a Canada hockey jersey at the airport in Germany. Young people from all over Canada and ultimately in Germany, Holland, England, Scotland and the United States had joined in, sharing stories about what they remembered from the first meeting they had with their workers in residential care and in foster care, and the symbols that indicated to them whether this was a person worth getting to know. This discussion was quickly followed with some debate about the "rules" in residential care and foster care that the practitioners felt limited by, particularly during the intake process. Medhi wanted to have some influence on the impersonal intake policies that made young people so uncomfortable, scared and dehumanized when they arrived at what would be their home for the next few months (or more), so he organized a session and was actively promoting the conference on his site.

Johannes was still debating whether he wanted to reconnect with Safid. In two years of work with Safid, Johannes had learned a lot about something that Safid called "the pedagogy of oppression," particularly the oppression of young people by society. The foster parents that Johannes lived with during that time had been very focused on changing his attitude – as they called it – and making sure that he got good grades, studied hard, played sports (soccer *and* hockey, specifically), had good manners, and was polite and respectful with adults. They gave him some specific tips for how to interact with people that he found helpful.

From Practice to History: Engagement in Life and Social Structures

Rousseau's approach to pedagogy also accounted for the interdependency and mutual reinforcement of agency and structure (Sahakian & Sahakian, 1974). Rousseau argued that Man in a state of nature (uncorrupted by **social conventions**) was basically good, and that the purpose and goal of education was to integrate Man from the state of nature into society without negating his identity. At the same time, a perpetual goal of human development was to guide Man's identity to become something that was sought after.

In this way, Rousseau provided an important foundation for thinking about the connections between pedagogy and life-space intervention. His work suggested that what young people are taught and what they might learn from others and their social context must transcend knowledge and performance to include issues of identity and everyday lived experiences (Böhm, 2010). These are core elements of the dimension of the life-space that we identified throughout this book.

Indeed, Rousseau's work on pedagogy is the basis of some core principles established later by a range of thinkers and educators. Kant, for example, argued passionately that the idea of raising children in a manner that simply reflects the current social dynamics and priorities is shortsighted. Instead, a more systematic approach is needed through which children can be raised in relation to the whole context of being human and of

humanity. Pestalozzi, who is often considered the father of pedagogy in Europe, emphasized the importance of using pedagogy as a preparation for life and living life, in ways that complement existing social conventions and that might generate new social conventions of universal benefit (Downs, 1975).

During the nineteenth and twentieth centuries, another major element was added to pedagogy. In the works of Marx, Gramsci and later Freire, we encounter the concept of the pedagogy of emancipation. The emphasis was on an upbringing for children and youth that ensured their consciousness of and learning about their own oppression. Sources of oppression included capitalist exploitation and corrupt postcolonial leadership.

By the mid-twentieth century, the whole project of pedagogy was questioned based on the critiques of critical and post-modernist theorists, who argued that the upbringing of young people necessarily reflected an agenda-driven society that was preoccupied with the reproduction of power dynamics and language conventions that sustained such dynamics. Proponents of this perspective argued that we must move beyond the resistance elements presented in the emancipating pedagogy of Marx and Freire to move toward a radical youth work in which pedagogy focuses on identity and the creative spaces of culture and subculture (Skott-Myhre, 2008).

They had been pretty clear with him that they were committed until he turned 18. It didn't matter what he did, they weren't going to kick him out, and if he followed the rules he got rewarded for doing well. They praised him when he got good grades, but they also helped him set some academic goals and sat with him every night to help with his homework when Safid wasn't around to help. They praised his sports accomplishments and they insisted that he get a part-time job and bank his money for college tuition. They had helped him figure out how to interact with his employer, who was very difficult. They would occasionally ground him for a day or two as punishment, but it was always for something he had screwed up at school, like the time he got into a huge fight. They had had to convince the principal not to have the police charge him with assault, explaining that Safid had just left and Johannes was missing him. The punishment and reward system was very similar to what Johannes remembered of his parents before they were killed, so it was a little reassuring for him, even though he often complained to Safid.

These complaints had elicited the long and interesting discussions about the pedagogy of oppression imposed on young people. So Johannes wasn't sure if he wanted to reconnect yet. He knew that Safid had left and moved out west because he was becoming increasingly dissatisfied with the foster care agency's treatment philosophy. That intake meeting where he first met Safid really stood out in Johannes' mind as one of the worst experiences of his life. If Safid hadn't worn that shirt and given him the thumbs up, he probably would have walked out and ended up in a shelter somewhere. Johannes had been that angry about the rules that were forcing him to move.

Relationship

Johannes was contemplating whether to "Facebook" Safid after he noticed that he had been tagged in a photo on a new site called Have a Cookie? He went in right away and removed the tag, thinking it was his own fault for tagging that picture and making another mental note about the privacy issues with Facebook. But when he discovered it was Safid who had posted it, he followed the discussion on the wall for a bit and then went and lurked around in Safid's page for a while. He could tell there would be more to see if he made a friend request, but he wasn't sure he wanted to.

So much had changed in two years. He had met his girlfriend, Beatriz, in Grade 11, just after Safid's departure for the west. She had come along at just the right time. Johannes remembered how wonderful it was to be "adopted" and accepted by all her friends and later her family, and how it had opened up so many new doors for him. Beatriz didn't seem to care that he was a foster kid, and neither did her parents. He remembered how nervous he was before he met her parents. He had a reputation in the community (he thought) for being a bad-ass, and he didn't think they would want him hanging around. He really wished then that Safid was around to help him figure this one out, but he finally said something to his foster parents because he didn't want to blow it and he had no idea how to act. They were so helpful; they role-played the meeting with him in lots of different ways and reminded him about all the social manners they had taught him for dealing with teachers and how to use those with the parents.

He wondered if Safid would be angry with him for "joining the oppressors," because Beatriz came from such a well-off, traditional family. But they were German, and Johannes felt very comfortable with that. Since he had returned from visiting his relatives, he wanted to know more about German culture and how immigrants managed here in Canada. He knew from his visit with his relatives that if he had been in Germany over the past five years and behaved in the same way he had in Canada, he likely would have been sent to a residential care program and would be doing an educational program that trained him in a specific vocation. Here in Canada he had been able to live with foster families instead and he had stayed in the regular education stream and was planning to go to college. What would Safid think of how traditional he had become?

From Practice to Theory: Pedagogy as a Framework for Life-Space Intervention

Life-space intervention is different from behavioural interventions, crisis intervention and physical interventions because it tries to influence how young people manage their relationships and boundaries wherever their lives unfold.

Behavioural interventions focus on adjusting how a young person interacts in a particular context, and they are usually intentionally directive. Behavioural interventions not only try to stop young people from certain conduct, but also offer a limited menu of options for appropriate conduct within a particular context.

Crisis intervention is specifically focused on stopping young people from conduct that puts them or others at risk. Here, the focus is on a particular space and a particular time in the life of the young person in need of a crisis intervention.

Physical interventions are the most directive, in that the multiplicity and diversity of the life-space come crashing down. All agency on the part of a young person is eliminated, and the young person is forced to comply.

Other approaches to intervention, such as psychotherapeutic counseling, solution-focused therapies and family work, add many layers of complexity and nuance to the everyday approaches to intervention. But these examples are all outcome-based interventions that are increasingly governed by evidence-based methods and language.

A fundamental premise of life-space intervention is that change in the lives of young people is first and foremost self-directed. If we are particularly concerned about growth and change that will be sustained beyond the everyday interventions of professional helpers, supporting the strength and sophistication of self-directed change is a core element of meaningful intervention. Young people's life-spaces are continuous entities that transcend the timelines and preprogrammed intervention strategies of service systems and exist even after the relationship with a professional ends. Concepts such as *aging out* of care at a specific age, *eligibility* for children's services, and referral to adult services set an expectation that capacity to manage and accomplish the milestones of adolescence and early adulthood can be continuously increased in a linear and sequential process of change. These concepts and the linear approach to change are incompatible with the unitary

(Continued)

nature of the life-space in which young people grow up. Ultimately, it is the lessons young people learn and the knowledge they gain over the course of their involvement in professional relationships that support them and guide them beyond the points where they transition in and out of services and systems.

Not all of the lessons and knowledge gained through professional intervention are pedagogically useful. Much of what young people learn from behavioural interventions, physical interventions and crisis interventions is limited to the particular context in which the intervention occurred, and these lessons do not transfer to other experiences in the life-space. The knowledge obtained does little to enhance young people's ability to manage their relationships and boundaries in the multiple dimensions of their life-space.

From the perspective of pedagogy, young people benefit from learning and knowledge that is organically tied into their everyday life-space experience. These lessons about Self transcend the immediate context of place and interpersonal relationships – they are deeply connected to the narrative of Self that the young person owns. In this context, young people maintain their agency over Self while they explore and learn about the complex relationship between structure (including the social conventions and imperatives faced every day) and the freedom and power of their own agency – their capacity to make choices, accept or reject what is offered, and to find their own path.

Pedagogy provides an entirely different framework for life-space intervention. As contemplated by the philosophers over more than two thousand years, pedagogy demands attention

not to the performance of the individual but to the quality of lives as they are lived every day. From the perspective of pedagogy, the goal of intervention with young people facing a wide range of challenges in life is to enhance their capacity, and their confidence, in their everyday preoccupation with and management of all the dimensions of life-space. Life-space intervention, therefore, focuses on the physical, mental, virtual and relational dimensions and pedagogical interventions in each of these dimensions that generate integrated knowledge for the young person about Self in relation to the unitary life-space.

From the practitioner's perspective, the goal of life-space intervention is reshaped and redefined when the framework is articulated in terms of pedagogy. Instead of the goal being one that focuses on changing young people's behaviour or aspects of their environment, the goal of the practitioner is to ensure that the everyday experiences of young people, especially those with relationships and boundaries, are integrated into an ever-expanding but always reflective basket of knowledge about Self. Young people own this reflective knowledge and can use it to protect their never-ending involvement in the dynamics of structuration.

Pedagogy provides a framework for understanding intervention that has previously been sidelined by the more traditional focus on behavioural outcomes with young people. As evidenced in the history of the development of pedagogy, pedagogically informed interventions inquire about how to integrate young people into current societal dynamics and processes, thereby ensuring that they adopt societal values and expectations. These interventions also inquire about how young people can be agents of change and contribute to the development of societies at large.

While earlier articulations of pedagogy, such as those of the sophists, the Greek philosophers and the Stoics, focused on how pedagogy could ensure that young people conformed, there has more recently been an entrenched recognition that our interventions with young people should also generate new ideas, new societal direction and ultimately new life. The emancipatory pedagogy of Marx and, more recently, Freire (2010 [1970]) further promotes the concept of critical disobedience, defiance and revolution, in contrast to the conformist paradigms of early pedagogy and treatment-based intervention with young people.

With this we come full circle. On the one hand, life-space intervention is an approach to being with young people who face challenges in their lives. On the other hand, it is also the political context within which young people can begin to recognize and own their agency to influence and eventually change societal structures, values and processes. The purpose of focusing our intervention on the singular and unified life-space that is operationalized through multiple dimensions is to connect with and influence the very personal context of young people as well as their ecological context.

Since Bronfenbrenner (1979) articulated his **ecological perspective**, the way in which young people connect with and are connected to each other, their institutions and broader societal structures has changed. Aside from having a physical presence within each

of the ecological systems, we now recognize the influences of virtual, mental and relational dimensions of life-space that transcend the physical differentiation of life-spaces in time and place. Thus, the idea of having school-focused intervention as distinct and separate from counselling interventions, and having family interventions as distinct and separate from community or group-care interventions, is being replaced with the idea that practitioners and young people develop mutually meaningful interventions aimed squarely at the life-space, including all of its dimensions. Clearly, then, the story or narrative of intervention now becomes significantly more complex. The setting is multilayered rather that made up of multiple physical locations, the timeframe is both forward-moving and regressive, and the characters must be adaptable and of relevance through time, place and space.

Throughout this book, we have developed the concept of life-space as a unitary construct – for every young person, there is a single life-space that is ever-present and that moves along with the movements of the young person. Such unitary life-space does, however, have multiple dimensions that are constantly and perpetually interacting. These dimensions are interdependent, and they reconstruct each other in the constant process of internalized structuration. This means that nothing stays the same in the life-space of a young person for very long. A new relationship results in shifts within all of the other dimensions. As a result, the young person hangs out in different places relevant to the new relationship, thereby shifting the physical dimension of life-space; self-esteem and self-confidence may be

(Continued)

temporarily increased, thereby shifting the mental dimension of the life-space; and updating the relationship status, posting new photo albums and perhaps even making new "friends" on the social networking site represent a shift in the virtual dimension of the life-space.

It becomes apparent that any change, even seemingly trivial change, to a young person's life-space results in a series of unpredictable, sometimes very complex and always consequential scenarios and circumstances that the young person must respond to and manage on a day-to-day basis. When practitioners try to change a young person, they do not provide a foundation for young people to take responsibility for their life-space, and whatever change might be achieved is not likely to be relevant to the next permutation of the life-space dynamic. However, when learning is the goal of an evolving outcome of life-space intervention, this goal provides the foundation for young people to extend their understanding of what is good and what is bad, what will benefit them and what won't, and what works and what doesn't to the circumstances and scenarios embedded in their life-space dynamics right here, right now. What young people learn will inform their agency and moderate their use of agency in reaction to structural impositions. In other words, what young people learn, they can own, and what they own they can use over and over again, making slight adjustments and adaptations to fit the circumstances as they see them.

Johannes noticed that Have a Cookie? was advertising a youth conference that was inviting young people to give feedback and work toward changing child welfare policies. He had no interest in participating in the conference; he didn't like to talk about his background. He was worried that if he sent a friend request to Safid that he would be expected to go. It might be taken as an indication that he wanted to "change the system," but he didn't.

Boundaries

Safid sat down in the workers' row for the closing session of the conference. He was smiling to himself at his reaction to being restricted to sitting in a specific area. He really wanted to rebel and take the front row, but his compliance with the general norm that you shouldn't sit in the front row and his curiosity about what these young people had learned about setting limits and boundaries led him to follow the handwritten directions. Besides, he had just noticed his new friend Jerome halfway down the row, and they had not yet had a chance to talk about how the debate had gone the previous day.

"Excuse me," he said, standing and stepping over the traditional sari of a woman with beautiful eyes sitting two seats over from Jerome.

"Certainly," Najwah said, standing quickly for him to pass. "It feels odd to be relegated to the back row, doesn't it? One of my former clients is moderating this session. I'm very proud of her."

Jerome heard her and leaned over as Safid sat down. "Isn't it incredible?" he said. "Jennifer – that's her up on the stage – is someone that I worked with two years ago. I didn't even know that she would be here. I was ordered to leave and not say goodbye to her, and I haven't seen her since. It's so wonderful to know that she survived the hospital mental health system."

Safid sighed. "I keep hoping to see Johannes. I taught him so much about the oppression of the system with young people. I thought for sure he would be here. But he's not. I know that he got the information, because it was on the Cookie site and he was there sometime to remove his tagged photo."

They settled in to listen.

Callie was checking in with the other presenters on stage, reminding each of them to take a couple of deep breaths before they spoke and asking how they wanted to be introduced – how much personal information, how much about the "system" they were going to be addressing in their presentations, and so on.

Andre was going to speak about the school policies that directed young people with learning disabilities into applied streams rather than academic streams, thereby restricting their access to university education and – more importantly – making them feel stupid for learning differently. He had been very articulate in a session on educational policies and was advocating for policies that viewed young people as experts on their learning styles and courses that approached teaching from many different perspectives, such as experiential, social-relational, memory and language, and so on.

"Just don't mention my hospital stay, Callie," he said. "I don't want to undermine my credibility." Andre had discussed with Denis how much to share about his background, and while Denis suggested that there would be less judgment about mental illness and the "madness" of hallucinations in this crowd, Andre still wanted to wrap a boundary around disclosure on that part of his life when he was talking in a more public context. He was fine with the young people, but uncomfortable when there were strangers in the crowd.

Jennifer, of course, was speaking about hospital policies and how they could become more youth friendly and personal within the evidence-based demands of that system.

"I don't have any personal boundaries. You know that, Callie. You can tell them I've been there, I'm a cutter, and until the people at the hospital learned that the 'interventions' [she made the quote sign in the air] don't work for everyone, I was treated like a crazy person. But," she added, "don't tell them that I know all the lingo now. I want some respect from the kids – they might think I've crossed over. Oh, and maybe you could do a shout-out for me to Jerome. I didn't know he was here, but I see him hiding in the back row there."

Callie laughed. "Oh, I bet they won't be thinking that you crossed over," she said as she went on to Tabitha.

"Well," said Tabitha, "I was pretty open about my story in my speech, so you probably don't need to repeat it. Maybe you could focus on the poverty experience so the bureaucrats get it that recreation programs for free or cheap are part of the 'interventions.'" She did the double quote gesture as Jennifer had done. "Nice work, Jen."

Tabitha was also thinking about how to get across the concept of talking to other professionals in the community and sharing information. She remembered how at first she had felt betrayed that Janice had talked to the youth worker at the school and the school counsellor about the bullies and the fighting at school. Then, when she realized how that might have changed her experience, she started talking with Janice about confidentiality versus caring and how Janice made those decisions. The recreation programmers and the community youth workers had such different norms about sharing information, and Tabitha and Jennifer had engaged in several in-depth discussions over the last few days about the differences.

Callie left her to think and moved on to Medhi. He was hoping to influence the policies on social networking for the kids and the workers in group-care programs. His site was blocked by most agency firewalls, even though he had set up some educational sections on the privacy functions and how to use them, and the privacy policy was constantly evolving with the input of the young people and the workers. Most of the membership and the active discussion was occurring with young people who were no longer in care and with workers on their own time because of the firewalls.

"Just tell them that I lived in a group home and now I'm at home with my parents," said Medhi, "and that Have a Cookie? is the safest and easiest site to use."

Ruby looked like she was ready to run off the stage. Callie knew her nervousness well, since they had worked together on making the access system for homeless youth in their community safer and easier to use. It was the same look Ruby had every time they got into a political meeting and Ruby had to speak about her own experiences.

"I won't say anything about where you're from," Callie reassured her. "Just look out there and talk to Najwah. See her? In the back row." Callie waved and Najwah waved back.

"Naw, it's okay," said Ruby. "Tell them I'm Oji-Cree and I've been on my own for five years and my daughter is three." She thought this would lend some credibility to her messages for change about the Indian Affairs/band council/social services/health care system morass she had been trying to navigate now for five years. "I'm going to focus on that group in the third row. They were all in my session and they're Cree, Ojibwa, Mohawk, Haisla, and Mi'kmaq. They'll support me in this mess." Ruby waved back at Najwah.

Callie checked her watch and stepped up to the microphone.

"Welcome," she said. "Thanks to everyone for coming. All you young people in the front rows here, I want you to turn around and thank those workers for sitting in the back. They really believe in your messages and that's why they're here. I wouldn't be here if I hadn't learned something from my workers, even the ones who didn't believe in me, or wanted to control me. I learned something from every one of them."

"This is our final session," she continued. "I also want to thank the policymakers and the service leaders, who are sitting right behind our youth, for being here today and for supporting this conference. We really think we have some creative and *possible* solutions."

"I've got five people up on stage here who are going to share the recommendations of the conference and tell you about the projects that those policymakers and service leaders have agreed to fund. I want to introduce them, and then I'm going to turn it over to them, because you all have some great ideas for social change and that's what they are going to talk about."

From Practice to Theory: The Entanglement of the Four Dimensions of Life-Space

At the beginning of this book, we suggested that if we asked people where they live, the response would be different than if we ask where their life unfolds.

The former question queries a place. The latter seems to transcend the idea of place and encourage the respondent to think more broadly about place, life and space before arriving at this nebulous and ever-shifting metaphorical location we refer to as the life-space.

And yet even there, within the life-space, we cannot come to a singular and recognizable location – one image of where life unfolds – because we are still affected by how life-space manifests itself based on the four dimensions through which it is constituted. Our mental location may or may not correspond to our physical location, and neither may be anywhere near our virtual location. The relational dimension of life-space always lurks in the background. No matter where we might go physically, mentally or even through our virtual agency, the question ultimately arises of whether the relational dimension of life-space will back us up and provide the necessary foundation for sustaining wherever we are or may wish to be at any moment. Will our familial relationships provide us with the security to tame anxieties at school or among peers? Will the physical location of the treatment institution be secure enough to keep out the virtual demons of our imagination?

Sooner or later, it dawns on us that life-space may well be a unitary concept in that it surrounds us regardless of where we go physically. However, life-space is not so singular that its dimensions come together into a consistent and predictable form with clear guidance and guaranteed personal safety. The four dimensions of life-space are entangled within their unification; they complement and clash with one another at different moments in time, usually without giving notice of impending conflicts or dialectical movement. Yet these four dimensions also achieve harmony among themselves. Some dimensions are more clear and stable than others, but all rely on their entanglement for overall stability.

Figure 7.1 illustrates how the four dimensions of life-space are entangled and how these dimensions relate to the pedagogical interventions embedded in caring, engagement, boundaries and relationships. While each dimension has unlimited potential for exploration and getting lost, it also provides a connection to the life-space as a whole, and in this way, all four dimensions intersect. The space around this intersection is the learning zone. It is here that young people develop their unique approaches to life in all its dimensions. It is within this learning zone that the practitioner tries to influence young people so that they can learn to manage the complexities of their life-space.

There is no expectation that young people can consistently manage themselves in their life-space in such a way that they are always in the learning zone. To the contrary, for most young people, expeditions into the great unknown of any one of the life-space dimensions are the norm. These expeditions may manifest themselves as a preoccupation with gaming (the virtual dimension) or falling in love (the relationship dimension). The pedagogy of life-space intervention is not about abruptly putting an end to these expeditions. Instead, it is about ensuring that young people can find their way back to the learning zone, to that space where all the dimensions of life-space intersect.

The four core concepts that we have presented in this book, caring, engagement, boundaries and relationships, are

(Continued)

life-space interventions that complement young people's safety, growth, and well-being. Practitioners cannot always be present to contribute to young people's decisions and experiences, but they can ensure that they have a presence with young people even while those young people are far away on an expedition into the mental dimension of their life-space.

Through caring (as we articulated it in Chapter 3), the practitioner's presence is reflected in the ongoing dialogue and sharing of experiences between the practitioner and the young person related to the young person's expeditions into the unknown spaces of the four dimensions.

Through engagement (as we articulated it in Chapter 4), the practitioner and the young person share agency and their responses to structure in a way that always invites the young person back into the learning zone, and toward the centre of the entangled four dimensions.

Through boundaries (as we articulated them in Chapter 6), the practitioner maintains with the young person an ongoing watchful eye for danger. Sometimes treading into such danger is meaningful, so long as the escape route is clear. Other times, turning away from such danger is necessary to avoid too great an injury.

Finally, through relationships (as we articulated them in Chapter 5), the young person's position in relation to the interpersonal dynamics of the life-space is secured as one that is sustainable and meaningful.

Life-space intervention is ultimately about confirming the possibility of learning and growth, even in situations where some of the dimensions of life-space appear to be pulling a young person toward danger. Danger may be of a physical or of a symbolic nature, such as the danger of social alienation and isolation found in the virtual and mental dimensions of the life-space.

FIGURE 7.1	Four Dimensions of Life-Space: Entanglement of Life-Space and Pedagogical Intervention

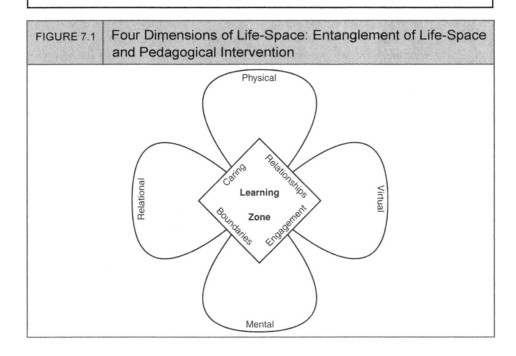

Summary: Right Here, Right Now

During the period of Enlightenment, Rousseau turned his attention to the issue of pedagogy and specifically the question of how to manage the developmental journey of young people. To do this, he created a fictional character named Emile (Rousseau, 1979 [1762]). Rousseau developed a pedagogic experience for Emile from birth to the age of 25, detailing what Emile needed to be taught by adults, what he learned from adults and from his own experiences, and how he interacted pedagogically with society at large. Rousseau argued that the common goal of all humanity is to live life, and pedagogy aims to ensure that humans learn to live life well. Ultimately it is the preparation for living life well that provides the impetus for doing other jobs well. Rousseau articulated the upbringing of Emile in relation to several contradictions (or dialectical movements): Individual versus the community, freedom versus determinism, and reason versus emotion. The success of Emile was then evaluated – not based on his performance at school or even within the context of social life conventions such as marriage (Emile married and divorced before the age of 25), but rather by what was learned. Emile was judged a success because he had learned the fundamental dimensions of the life-space and their connectedness.

In our stories about the young people and practitioners introduced in each chapter of this book, we have tried to illustrate and bring to life the core concepts of life-space intervention. In the process, we discovered that our fictional characters have found their way into our (the authors') life-space. Long after the stories of Johannes and Jennifer, Andre and Callie, and all the others were written, these characters continued to be present in our minds, and sometimes their stories continued in our imaginations beyond what we had written (and we suddenly found them telling the story in this chapter).

We learned from this process that life-space intervention is a very difficult approach to being with young people, and that perhaps this difficulty is one reason why interventions in child and youth care practice and other disciplines so often become control-oriented, solution-focused, and evidence-based. The concreteness of the physical context (right here) and the desire to see young people not only change but demonstrate this change in their everyday decision-making and performance (right now) is strong and often deterministic. To get from the point of dysfunction and social ineptitude to the point of performance and social conformity, our interventions must achieve visible and measurable outcomes within specified timeframes. Within this "evidence-required" frame of reference, *right here, right now* is a way of expressing our desire (or impatience) to see young people succeed.

In the context of life-space intervention, in contrast, we recognize that *right here, right now* is not at all about the changes we want to see based on the performance of the young people in whose lives we have intervened. *Right here* refers to our presence with the young person, defined not in physical terms but in metaphorical language and inclusive of the mental, virtual and relational dimensions of the life-space. Furthermore, *right here* refers to our capacity as practitioners to look beyond the physical context of a person's life and find ways of caring and engaging with a view to embedding our presence wherever the young person's life might be unfolding. *Right now* means that we don't wait to set up our interventions when the program or the service calls for it. Intervention is not limited to particular activities, approaches, interactions, expectations or case management features.

Intervention is not limited to the confines of "treatment." Instead, *right now* means that intervention is happening in the moment, in every moment, and through the connections between moments.

At the End of the Day: Our Future

Source: Kiaras Gharabaghi

"There is no difference between living and learning . . . it is impossible and misleading and harmful to think of them as being separate. Teaching is human communication and like all communication, elusive and difficult . . . we must be wary of the feeling that we know what we are doing. . . ." (Holt, 1970).

Glossary

Agency an individual's inherent capacity to take action, either physically or emotionally, in order to affect or respond to the requirements of structure.

Caring to Control imposing control and limitations to promote safety and well-being when necessary.

Choice the ability to decide on directions and opportunities while facing the consequences of one's decisions, whether these are positive or negative.

Connectivity ways of ensuring that the professional's interactions with young people relate to various places and spaces in their lives.

Dialectical having two interdependent processes that are unfolding at the same time and moving in opposite directions.

Ecological Perspective a perspective that takes into account the social, emotional, institutional and physical environments of young people when working with them.

Engagement a way of being together that focuses on mutuality and "give-and-take" interaction.

Escape Routes ways for young people to avoid issues or situations for which they feel unprepared.

Experiential/Lived Experience how we make sense of things in our everyday lives, and how we integrate these specific experiences into our **life-space**.

Intervention being together with intention and strategic purpose; all of the actions taken by the professional and the young person and their combined meanings.

Life-Space the places and spaces where one's life unfolds.

Life-Space Story a metaphor for how young people organize their thoughts and memories of their experiences in their life-space.

Living Space the physical spaces where we live and in which we become engaged.

Madness in the specific context of this book, the hallucinatory states that accompany various forms of mental illness and usually result in hospital confinement.

Material/Non-material Life-Space Components these terms differentiate between physical dimensions, physical places and relationships with actual people on the one hand, and emotional, mental, virtual and imaginary relationships and places on the other hand.

Mutuality the understanding of each person's need to be reflected in the relationship right here, right now.

Pedagogy a term that represents many different perspectives related to the upbringing of children.

Power Imbalances a range of issues including differential access to knowledge, information, economic resources, and decision-making authority, and even societal perceptions of youth versus educated professionals.

Power to Care using the inherent power imbalances of the practitioner–young person relationship to impose safety at times of acute risk to the young person.

Presence/Being present sharing the experience of someone else's everyday life in physical, mental and virtual contexts.

Relational focusing on the conscious atten-
dance to the relationship on the part of the
individuals finding themselves in relationship

Relationship the process of coming together
in a young person's life-space.

Social Construction (Construction) a critique of any perspective that assumes things
to be true simply because our own criteria for
truth are satisfied.

Social Conventions the ways in which
things have come to unfold over time, and
the ways in which we think about things
uncritically.

Social Learning the idea that young people
benefit from learning about how societies
work and how they might find places of comfort and safety in society, but not necessarily
through the mechanisms of compliance and
conformity that are embedded in the ideology
of social learning theory.

Social Pedagogy the European version of
managing the upbringing of young people.

Structuration Theory a theoretical
approach that resolves the structure/agency

dilemma by suggesting that the two are locked
in interdependency through a perpetual
dynamic of co-creation.

Structure the social and institutional context in which we make choices and decisions,
and take action.

Structure/Agency Dilemma Which comes
first, structure or agency?

Symbiotic the opposite of dialectical;
having two processes that are dependent upon
each other and mutually reinforcing. In life-
space intervention, **presence** and **engagement**
are symbiotic processes.

Transcendental Engagement engaging
young people across the dimensions of life-
space.

Transition Paths opportunities for young
people to move from one part of their life-
space to another in order to re-focus energy
and attention on functioning in another
setting.

Transitional Objects objects that provide
comfort to young people as they transition
from place to place.

References

Adler, P., & Adler, P. (1998). *Peer power: Preadolescent culture and identity.* New Brunswick, NJ: Rutgers University Press.

Ainsworth, F., & Fulcher, L. (2006). Creating and sustaining a culture of group care. *Child & Youth Services, 28*(1/2), 151–176.

Anderson-Butcher, D., Cash, S., Saltzburg, S., Midle, T., & Pace, D. (2004). Institutions of youth development: The significance of staff-youth relationships. *Journal of Human Behavior in the Social Environment, 9*(1/2), 83–99.

Anglin, J. (2002). *Pain, normality, and the struggle for congruence: Reinterpreting residential care for children and youth.* New York, NY: The Haworth Press.

Association of Child and Youth Care Practice. (1995). *Ethics of child and youth care professionals.* Retrieved from www.acycp.org/standards/CYC%20Ethics%20Code%20Rev%209.2009.pdf

Austin, D., & Halpin, W. (1987). Seeing "I" to "I": A phenomenological analysis of the caring relationship. *Journal of Child and Youth Care, 3*(3), 37–42.

Bandura, A. (1977). *Social learning theory.* Englewood Cliffs, NJ: Prentice Hall.

Bath, H. (2008). The three pillars of trauma-informed care. *Reclaiming Children and Youth, 17*(3), 17–21.

Batsleer, J. R. (2006). *Informal learning in youth work.* London: SAGE.

Beker, J., & Maier, H. W. (1988). *Developmental group care of children and youth: Concepts and practice.* London: Routledge.

Berge, J. M., & Holm, K. E. (2007). Boundary ambiguity in parents with chronically ill children: Integrating theory and research. *Family Relations, 56*(2), 123–134.

Berscheid, E. (1999). The greening of relationship science. *American Psychologist, 54*(4), 260–266.

Bibby, R. (2009). *The emerging millennials: How Canada's newest generation is responding to change and choice.* Lethbridge, AB: Project Canada Books.

Block, J. J. (2008). Issues for DSM-V: Internet addiction. *American Journal of Psychiatry, 165,* 306–307.

Böhm, W. (2010). *Geschichte der Pädagogik: Von Platon bis zur Gegenwart.* Munich, Germany: Verlag CH Beck.

Boss, P., & Greenberg, J. (1984). Family boundary ambiguity: A new variable in family stress theory. *Family Process, 23,* 535–546.

Bosworth, K. (1995). Caring for others and being cared for. *Phi Delta Kappan, 76*(9), 686–694.

Brannen, J., Mooney, A., & Statham, J. (2009). Childhood experiences: A commitment to caring and carework with vulnerable children. *Childhood, 16*(3), 377–393.

Brendtro, L., Ness, A., & Mitchell, M. (2005). *No disposable kids.* Bloomington, IN: National Education Service.

Bronfenbrenner, U. (1979). *The ecology of human development: Experiments by nature and design.* Cambridge, MA: Harvard University Press.

Burns, M. (1987). Rapport and relationships as the basis of child care. *Journal of Child and Youth Care, 2*(2), 47–57.

Burns, M. (2006). *Healing spaces: The therapeutic milieu in child care and youth work.* Toronto: Child Care Press.

Burrow, A., O'Dell, A., & Hill, P. (2010). Profiles of a developmental asset: Youth purpose as a context for hope and well-being. *Journal of Youth & Adolescence, 39*(11), 1265–1273.

Charlesworth, J. (2008). Inquiry into issues of voice in relational practice. In G. Bellefeuille & F. Ricks (Eds.), *Standing on the precipice: Inquiry into the creative potential of child and youth care practice* (pp. 231–280). Edmonton: MacEwan Press.

Cho, S. (2010). Politics of critical pedagogy and new social movements. *Educational Philosophy and Theory, 42*(3), 310–325.

Cordasco, F. (1970). *A brief history of education* (2nd ed.). Lanham, MD: Rowman & Littlefield.

Côtèa, J., & Bynnerb, J. M. (2008). Changes in the transition to adulthood in the UK and Canada: The role of structure and agency in emerging adulthood. *Journal of Youth Studies, 11*(3), 251–268.

Crowden, A. (2008). Professional boundaries and the ethics of dual and multiple overlapping relationships in psychotherapy. *Monash Bioethical Review, 27*(4), 10–27.

Crowe, K. M. (2007). Using youth expertise at all levels: The essential resource for effective child welfare practice. *New Directions for Youth Development, 113*, 139–149.

Crowe, N., & Bradford, S. (2006). "Hanging out in Runescape": Identity, work and leisure in the virtual playground. *Children's Geographies, 4*(3), 331–346.

Cunningham, W., Duffee, D., Yufan, H., Steinke, C., & Naccarato, T. (2009). On the meaning and measurement of engagement in youth residential treatment centres. *Research on Social Work Practice, 19*(1), 63–76.

DiTomaso, N. (1982). Sociological reductionism from Parsons to Althusser: Linking action and structure in social theory. *American Sociological Review, 47*, 14–28.

Downs, R. B. (1975). *Heinrich Pestalozzi: Father of modern pedagogy*. New York, NY: Twayne.

Englebrecht, C., Peterson, D., Scherer, A., & Naccarato, T. (2008). "It's not my fault": Acceptance as a component of engagement in juvenile residential treatment. *Children & Youth Services Review, 30*(4), 466–484.

Fewster, G. (1990a). *Being in child care: A journey into self*. Binghampton, NY: Haworth Press.

Fewster, G. (1990b). Growing together: The personal relationship in child and youth care. In J. Anglin, C. Denholm, R. Ferguson, & A. Pence (Eds.), *Perspectives in professional child and youth care* (pp. 25–40). New York, NY: Haworth Press.

Fewster, G. (2001). Growing together: The personal relationship in child and youth care. *Journal of Child and Youth Care, 15*(4), 5–16.

Fewster, G. (2005). Making contact: Personal boundaries in professional practice. *Relational Child and Youth Care Practice, 18*(2), 7–13.

First Nations Child and Family Caring Society of Canada. (n.d.). Jordan's story. Retrieved from www.fncfcs.com/jordans-principle/jordans-story

Fox, L. (1985). Who put the care in child care? *Child Care, 3*(2), 1–5.

Fox, L. (1994). The catastrophe of compliance. *Journal of Child and Youth Care, 9*(1), 3–18.

Freire, P. (2010). *Pedagogy of the oppressed*. New York, NY: Continuum. (Original work published 1970)

Freud, S., & Krug, S. (2002). Beyond the code of ethics, part II: Dual relationships revisited. *Families in Society, 83*(5/6), 483–492.

Fulcher, L., & Ainsworth, F. (2005). The soul, rhythms and blues of responsive child and youth care at home and away from home. *Child & Youth Services, 27*(1/2), 27–50.

Gabbard, G. O. & Lester, E. P. (2003). *Boundaries and boundary violations in psychoanalysis*. Washington, DC: American Psychiatric Association.

Garfat, T. (1998). The effective child and youth care intervention: A phenomenological inquiry. *Journal of Child and Youth Care, 12*(1/2), 1–122.

Garfat, T. (Ed.) (2003). *A child and youth care approach to working with families*. New York, NY: Haworth Press.

Garfat, T. (2004). Working with families. *Child & Youth Services, 25*(1/2), 7–37.

Garfat, T. (2008). The inter-personal in-between: An exploration of relational child and youth care practice. In G. Bellefeuille & F. Ricks (Eds.), *Standing on the precipice: An inquiry in the creative potential of child and youth care practice* (pp. 7–34). Edmonton: MacEwan Press.

Garfat, T. & Charles, G. (2007). How am I who I am? Self in child and youth care practice. *Relational Child and Youth Care Practice, 20*(3), 6–15.

Gentile, D. (2009). Pathological video-game use among youth ages 8–18: A national study. *Psychological Science, 20*(5), 594–602.

Gharabaghi, K. (2010). *Professional issues in child and youth care practice.* London: Routledge.

Giddens, A. (1973). *Class structure of the advanced societies.* New York, NY: Barnes & Noble.

Giddens, A. (1979). *Central problems in social theory: Action, structure and contradiction in social analysis.* Berkeley, CA: University of California Press.

Giddens, A. (1990). *The consequences of modernity.* Stanford, CA: Stanford University Press.

Giddens, A., & Held, D. (Eds.) (1982). *Classes, power and conflict: Classical and contemporary debates.* Berkeley, CA: University of California Press.

Ginwright, S., & James, T. (2002). From assets to agents of change: Social justice, organizing and youth development. *New Directions for Youth Development, 96,* 27–46.

Greenwald, M. (2007). Ethics is hot: So what? *Relational Child and Youth Care Practice 20*(1), 27–33.

Greenwald, M. (2008). The virtuous child and youth care practitioner: Exploring identity and ethical practice. In G. Bellefeuille & F. Ricks (Eds.), *Standing on the precipice: An inquiry into the creative potential of child and youth care practice* (pp. 169–203). Edmonton: MacEwan Press.

Harper, K., & Steadman, J. (2003). Therapeutic boundary issues in working with childhood sexual-abuse survivors. *American Journal of Psychotherapy, 57*(1), 64–79.

Henggeler, S. W. (1993). *Multisystemic treatment of serious juvenile offenders: Implications for the treatment of substance abusing youths* (NIH Publication No. 93-3684). Rockville, MD: National Institute on Drug Abuse Research Monograph 137.

Hirschi, T., & Gottfredson, M. R. (2005). Punishment of children from the perspective of control theory. In M. Donnelly & M. A. Straus (Eds.), *Corporal punishment of children in theoretical perspective* (pp. 214–222). New Haven: Yale University Press.

Hobson, P. (1993). "Is it time for another look at Plato?": A contemporary assessment of his educational theory. *Journal of Thought 3/4,* 77–86.

Holder, K. V., & Schenthal, S. J. (2007). Watch your step: Nursing and professional boundaries. *Nursing Management, 38*(2), 24–29.

Holt, J. (1970). *What Do I Do Monday?* New York: Dutton.

Howard, B. (2008). The three pillars of trauma-informed care. *Reclaiming Children & Youth, 17*(3), 17–21.

Krueger, M. (1991). Coming from your center, being there, meeting them where they're at, interacting together, counseling on the go, creating circles of caring, discovering and using self, and caring for one another: Central themes in professional child and youth care. *Journal of Child and Youth Care, 5*(1), 77–87.

Krueger, M. (2007). *Sketching youth, self, and youth work.* Rotterdam, Netherlands: Sense.

Krueger, M. (2009). Waiting for someone real. *Reclaiming Children & Youth, 18*(1), 49–50.

Krueger, M. (2010). *Images of thought: Presence, place, motion, rhizomes, lunch and noise in child and youth care.* South Africa: Pre-text.

Lawson, L. (1998). Milieu management of traumatized youngsters. *Journal of Child*

& *Adolescent Psychiatric Nursing, 11*(3), 99–107.

Ledbetter, A. M., Heiss, S., Sibal, K., Lev, E., Battle-Fisher, M., & Shubert, N. (2010). Parental invasive and children's defensive behaviors at home and away at college: Mediated communication and privacy boundary management. *Communication Studies, 61*(2), 184–204.

Lewin, K. (1948). *Resolving social conflicts.* New York, NY: Harper and Row.

Long, N., Wood, M. M., & Fecser, F. A. (2001). *Life-space crisis intervention: Talking with students in conflict* (2nd ed.). Austin, TX: Pro-ed.

MacDougall, C., Schiller, W., & Darbyshire, P. (2009). What are our boundaries and where can we play? Perspectives from eight- to ten-year-old Australian metropolitan and rural children. *Early Child Development & Care, 179*(2), 189–204.

Magnuson, D. (2007). The perils, promise and practice of youth work in conflict societies. In D. Magnuson & M. Baizerman (Eds.), *Work with youth in divided and contested societies* (pp. 3–12). Rotterdam, The Netherlands: Sense.

Maidment, J. (2006). The quiet remedy: A dialogue on reshaping professional relationships. *Families in Society, 87*(1), 115–121.

Maier, H. (2003). What to say when first meeting a person each day. *Relational Child and Youth Care Practice, 15*(1), 49–52.

Mandell, D. (2008). Power, care and vulnerability: Considering use of self in child welfare work. *Journal of Social Work Practice, 22*(2), 235–248.

Mann-Feder, V. (1999). You/me/us: Thoughts on boundary management in child and youth care. *Journal of Child and Youth Care, 13*, 93–98.

Manning, S. S. (1997). The social worker as moral citizen: Ethics in action. *Social Work 42*(3), 223–230.

Martin, A. J. (2008). Enhancing student motivation and engagement: The effects of a multidimensional intervention. *Contempo-* *rary Educational Psychology, 33*(2), 239–269.

Martin, J., & Stuart, C. A. (2011). Working with cyber-space in the life-space. *Relational Child and Youth Care Practice, 24*(1/2), 55–66.

McMillan, C., Stuart, C., & Vincent, J. (2011). Tell it like you see it: Youth perceptions of child and youth care practitioner interventions and outcomes in an alternative school setting. *International Journal of Child, Youth and Family Studies.* Manuscript submitted for publication.

Miller, M. (2009). Boundary spanning in homeless children's education: Notes from an emergent faculty role in Pittsburgh. *Educational Administration Quarterly, 45*(4), 616–630. Retrieved from www.ebscohost.com

Outram, D. (2005). *The enlightenment* (2nd ed.). Cambridge, NY: Cambridge University Press.

Parry, P. (1999). Relationships: Thoughts on their origin and their power. *Journal of Child and Youth Care, 13*(2), 9–16.

Parsons, T. (1937). *Structure of social action.* New York, NY: McGraw Hill.

Pazaratz, D. (2009). *Residential treatment of adolescents: Integrative principles and practices.* London: Routledge.

Peavy, V. R. (1998). *Socio-dynamic counselling: A constructivist perspective.* Victoria, BC: Tafford.

Peterson, M. R. (1992). *At personal risk: Boundary violations in professional-client relationships.* New York: W.W. Norton.

Phelan, J. (2008). External controls: A child and youth care framework. *Relational Child and Youth Care Practice, 21*(1), 38–41.

Phelan, J. (2009). Activities of daily living and controls from within. *Relational Child and Youth Care Practice, 22*(4), 46–51.

Prinstein, M. J., & Dodge, K. A. (2008). *Understanding peer influence in children and adolescents.* New York, NY: Guilford.

Raftery, J. N., Steinke, C. M., & Nickerson, A. B. (2010). Engagement, residential treatment staff cognitive and behavioral disputations, and youth problem-solving. *Child & Youth Care Forum, 39*(3), 167–185.

Reamer, F. G. (2003). Boundary issues in social work: Managing dual relationships. *Social Work, 48*(1), 121–133.

Redl, F., & Wineman, D. (1951). *Children who hate: A sensitive analysis of the anti-social behavior of children in their response to the adult world.* New York, NY: Macmillan Canada.

Redl, F., & Wineman, D. (1952). *Controls from within: Techniques for the treatment of the aggressive child.* New York, NY: Macmillan Canada.

Ricks, F., & Charlesworth, J. (2003). *Emergent practice planning.* New York, NY: Kluwer Academic/Plenum.

Rodgers, B. (2006). Life space mapping: Preliminary results from the development of a new method for investigating counselling outcomes. *Counselling and Psychotherapy Research, 6*(4), 227–232.

Rose-Krasnor, L. (2009). Future directions in youth involvement research. *Social Development, 18*(2), 497–509.

Rousseau, Jean-Jacques (1979). *On education.* New York, NY: Basic Books. (Original work published 1762)

Sahakian, M. L., & Sahakian, W. S. (1974). *Rousseau as educator.* New York, NY: Twayne.

Salhani, D., & Grant, C. (2007). The dynamics of an inter-professional team: The interplay of child and youth care with other professions within a residential treatment milieu. *Relational Child and Youth Care Practice, 20*(4), 12–21.

Santrock, J. W., MacKenzie-Rivers, A., Leung, K. H., & Malcomson, T. (2008). *Life-span development* (3rd Canadian ed.). Toronto: McGraw-Hill Ryerson.

Senge, P. (1990). *The fifth discipline: The art and practice of the learning organization.* New York, NY: Doubleday.

Skott-Myhre, H. (2008). *Youth and subculture as creative force: Creating new spaces for radical youth work.* Toronto: Toronto University Press.

Smith, B., Duffee, D., Steinke, C., Yufan, H., & Larkin, H. (2008). Outcomes in residential treatment for youth: The role of early engagement. *Children & Youth Services Review, 30*(12), 1425–1436.

Smith, D., & Fitzpatrick, M. (1995). Patient-therapist boundary issues: An integrative review of theory and research. *Professional Psychology: Research and Practice, 26*(5), 499–506.

Smith, M. (2006). Don't touch. *The International Child and Youth Care Network, 94.* Retrieved from www.cyc-net.org/cyc-online/cycol-0611-smith.html

Smyth, J. (2006). "When students have power": Student engagement, student voice, and the possibilities for school reform around "dropping out" of school. *International Journal of Leadership in Education, 9*(4), 285–298.

Stacey, K., Webb, E., Hills, S., Lagzdins, N., Moulds, D., Phillips, T., et al. (2002). Relationships and power. *Youth Studies Australia, 21*(1), 44-51.

Stuart, C. (2008). Shaping the Rules: Child and youth care boundaries in the context of relationship. Bonsai! In Bellefeuille, G. & Ricks, F. (Eds.) *Standing on the precipice: An Inquiry into the creative potential of child and youth care practice* (pp. 135–168). Edmonton: MacEwan Press.

Stuart, C. (2009). *Foundations of child and youth care practice.* Dubuque, IA: Kendall/Hunt.

Takahashi, T. (2010). MySpace or Mixi? Japanese engagement with SNS (social networking sites) in the global age. *New Media & Society, 12*(3), 453–475.

Teyber, E., & McClure, F. H. (2002). *Casebook in child and adolescent treatment: Cultural and familial contexts.* New York, NY: Wadsworth.

Trieschman, A. E., Whittaker, J. K., & Brendtro, L. K. (1969). *The other 23 hours: Child care work with emotionally disturbed children in a therapeutic milieu.* New York, NY: Aldine.

Ungar, M. (2002). *Playing at being bad: The hidden resilience of troubled teens.* Toronto: University of Toronto Press.

Ungar, M. (2006). *Strengths-based counselling with at-risk youth.* Thousand Oaks, CA: Corwin Press.

Ungar, M. (2008). Overprotective parenting: Helping parents provide children the right amount of risk and responsibility. *American Journal of Family Therapy, 37*(3), 258–271.

Ungar, M. (2009). Too safe schools, too safe families: Denying children the risk taker's advantage. *Education Canada, 48*(1), 6–10.

Vandell, D. L., Shernoff, D. J., Pierce, K. M., Bolt, D. M., Dadisman, K., & Brown, B. B. (2005). Activities, engagement and emotion in after-school programs (and elsewhere). *New Directions for Youth Development, 105,* 121–129.

VanderVen, K. (1995). "Point and level systems": Another way to fail children and youth. *Child and Youth Care Forum, 24*(6), 345–367.

VanderVen, K. (2003). Activity-oriented, family-focused child and youth work in group care: Integrating streams of thought into a river of progress. *Child & Youth Services, 25*(1/2), 131–147.

VanderVen, K. (2004). Beyond fun and games towards a meaningful theory of play: Can a hermeneutic perspective contribute? In J. A. Sutterby (Ed.), *Social contexts of early education and reconceptualizing play* (pp.165–205). Bingley, UK: Emerald Group.

Wood, M. M., & Long, N. (1991). *Life-space intervention: Talking with children and youth in crisis.* Austin, TX: Pro-ed.

Woodman, D. (2009). The mysterious case of the pervasive choice biography: Ulrich Beck, structure/agency and the middling state of theory in the sociology of youth. *Journal of Youth Studies, 12*(3), 243–256.

Zur, O. (2007). *Boundaries in psychotherapy: Ethical and clinical explorations.* Washington, DC: American Psychological Association.

Index